A Gift That Cannot Be Refused

Recent Titles in
Contributions to the Study of World Literature

Becoming True to Ourselves: Cultural Decolonization and National Identity in the Literature of the Portuguese-Speaking World
Maria Luisa Nunes

George Orwell
Courtney T. Wemyss and Alexej Ugrinsky, editors

The Cast of Consciousness: Concepts of the Mind in British and American Romanticism
Beverly Taylor and Robert Bain, editors

Friedrich von Schiller and the Drama of Human Existence
Alexej Ugrinsky, editor

Jules Verne Rediscovered: Didacticism and the Scientific Novel
Arthur B. Evans

Contemporary Polish Theater and Drama (1956–1984)
E.J. Czerwinski

Child of the Earth: Tarjei Vesaas and Scandinavian Primitivism
Frode Hermundsgård

The Voice of the Narrator in Children's Literature: Insights from Writers and Critics
Charlotte F. Otten and Gary D. Schmidt, editors

"Our House Is Hell": Shakespeare's Troubled Families
Max H. James

Countries of the Mind: The Fiction of J. M. Coetzee
Dick Penner

The Devil's Advocates: Decadence in Modern Literature
Thomas Reed Whissen

James Joyce and His Contemporaries
Diana A. Ben-Merre and Maureen Murphy, editors

A Gift That Cannot Be Refused

THE WRITING AND PUBLISHING OF CONTEMPORARY AMERICAN POETRY

Mary Biggs

Contributions to the Study of World Literature, Number 34

GREENWOOD PRESS
New York • Westport, Connecticut • London

Library of Congress Cataloging-in-Publication Data

Biggs, Mary.
A gift that cannot be refused : the writing and publishing of contemporary American poetry / Mary Biggs.
p. cm. — (Contributions to the study of world literature, ISSN 0738-9345 ; no. 34)
Bibliography: p.
Includes index.
ISBN 0-313-26673-5 (lib. bdg. : alk. paper)
1. Poetry—Authorship. 2. American poetry—20th century—Authorship. I. Title. II. Series.
PN1059.A9B54 1990
808.1—dc20 89-11939

British Library Cataloguing in Publication Data is available.

Library of Congress Catalog Card Number: 80-11939
ISBN: 0-313-26673-5
ISSN: 0738-9345

First published in 1990

Greenwood Press, Inc.
88 Post Road West, Westport, Connecticut 06881

Printed in the United States of America

The paper used in this book complies with the Permanent Paper Standard issued by the National Information Standards Organization (Z39.48-1984).

10 9 8 7 6 5 4 3 2 1

Copyright Acknowledgments

The author and publisher are grateful to the following for granting permission to use their material:

"In Dispraise of Poetry" from *Monolithos: Poems, 1962 and 1982*. © 1982 by Jack Gilbert. Reprinted by permission of Graywolf Press.

"The Little Magazines Keep Coming" by Phillip Lopate in *The Little Magazine*, vol. 7, Fall 1973, p. 15. Courtesy of the author.

"Academic Publishing and Poetry" by Mary Biggs from *Scholarly Publishing* 17 (October 1985). Reprinted by permission of the publisher, the University of Toronto Press.

"Trade Publishing and Poetry" by Mary Biggs. Published by permission of Transaction Publishers, from *Book Research Quarterly*, Vol. 1, No. 3. Copyright © 1985 by Transaction Publishers.

From a letter from Morty Sklar to Mary Biggs, October 17, 1981. Courtesy of Morty Sklar.

From a letter written by Hart Crane in *The Letters of Hart Crane, 1916–1932*, edited by Brom Weber (Berkeley: University of California Press, 1952). Courtesy of the editor.

From a letter written by Robert Frost, in *The Letters of Robert Frost*, edited by Louis Untermeyer (New York: Holt, Rinehart & Winston, 1963). Courtesy of Henry Holt and Company, Inc.

From a letter written by Vachel Lindsay in *The Big Sea: An Autobiography* by Langston Hughes (New York: Alfred A. Knopf, 1940. Courtesy of the Estate of Vachel Lindsay by Nicholas C. Lindsay.

From a letter from James Grabill to Mary Biggs, February 6, 1989. Courtesy of James Grabill.

Every reasonable effort has been made to trace the owners of copyright materials in this book, but in some instances this has proven impossible. The publisher will be glad to receive information leading to more complete acknowledgments in subsequent printings of the book and in the meantime extend their apologies for any omissions.

In Dispraise of Poetry

When the King of Siam disliked a courtier,
he gave him a beautiful white elephant.
The miracle beast deserved such ritual
that to care for him properly meant ruin.
Yet to care for him improperly was worse.
It appears the gift could not be refused.

Jack Gilbert

This book is dedicated to the poets.

Contents

Illustrations

FIGURES

TABLES

Acknowledgments

I am deeply grateful to Abraham Bookstein, W. Boyd Rayward, and Howard W. Winger, all presently or formerly on the faculty of the University of Chicago Graduate Library School. They were infinitely patient and helpful. I am grateful also to Herman H. Fussler and Don R. Swanson, whose astute suggestions at two crucial junctures made more difference than they probably realize. Indeed, they transformed moments of panic into turning points. Terry Belanger of the Columbia University School of Library Service offered immensely useful suggestions for revision, as did my editor, Marilyn Brownstein.

Many librarians and other library staff members assisted me along the way. I should note in particular the library staff and collections of the University of Wisconsin-Madison; the University of Chicago; the Chicago Public Library Language and Literature Division; Northwestern University; Columbia University; the Gerber-Hart Library (Chicago); and the Coordinating Council of Literary Magazines (New York). I also obtained valuable assistance from the staff of Poets & Writers, Inc. (New York).

I am most grateful of all to the poets, who gave generously of their time and, in many cases, expressed enthusiasm for the study. Their interest and confidence meant more to me than they can know.

My sons, Nick and Nate Mancuso, tolerated my cross moods and inattention with good humor; I thank them.

To thank Victor Biggs is to say too little, to trivialize his contribution. He knows that if it were not for him, I would never have completed this book. Indeed, I would never have begun it.

Introduction: 203 Poets, 1950–1980: How Their Publishing Histories Were Studied

To address the question of how poetry reached the public between 1950 and 1980 is a formidable task. Clearly, such a study must include an examination of the role of little magazines. Often difficult to study because of their diversity, physical fragility, title changes, irregular periodicity, minuscule print runs and circulation, short life-spans, and editors' poor record keeping, these magazines have also become, since the 1960s, overwhelming in number.

In the littles' truly little world of the teens, a few magazines—*Poetry, The Dial, The Little Review*—had vied for the finest work while Ezra Pound, poet and ubiquitous promoter of poets, pulled the strings and the entire literary community of the United States, Britain, and expatriate Western Europe watched the show. There was no question about what had to be read, no wondering where the literary action was. When *Poetry*'s Harriet Monroe "discovered" a T. S. Eliot, Carl Sandburg, or Vachel Lindsay, when *The Little Review* championed the seemingly impenetrable work of an Irish experimental novelist or American dadaist, the literati followed these events, pondered their significance, took sides. Though the number of American literary journals grew, it grew slowly.

In the mid–1940s, a landmark study by Hoffman, Allen, and Ulrich detected about fifty existing literary titles of all sizes and degrees of quality and every aesthetic bias.[1] Poet/publisher Daisy Aldan recalled that in the early 1950s, there had been "about forty-two literary magazines in the whole country."[2] This was, of course, a guess based on remembered observation; the point is that, well-informed as she was, she did not perceive an abundance. A 1961 *Publishers Weekly* article estimated that by the mid–1950s, 180 literary magazines had ever been in operation.[3]

The first post-Hoffman little-magazine listing to attempt comprehensiveness was Len Fulton's Dustbooks directory of 1964.[4] Now, in a remarkably full twenty-fifth annual edition, the directory still misses a few enterprises, depending as it does on voluntary submission of information by editors and publishers. In 1964, unestablished and primitively produced, it undoubtedly omitted many more. Still, the change from an easily enumerable group of literary journals and a handful of book presses in the fifties, to the 260 periodical listings in the Dustbooks directory's first edition, to the estimated 1,307 literary periodicals and 1,230 literary presses of the United States and Canada alone included in the twenty-third, is stunning.[5]

A multitude of factors, the relative importance of each one endlessly arguable, contributed to this proliferation. The availability of cheap mimeo, photocopying, and offset printing technology, along with better typewriters and fast, keyboarded cold-typesetting hard to distinguish from linotyping, were the most obvious and practical causes. Also important was the swelling number of young adults and, concomitantly, college students—as the postwar baby boom aged to a youth boom, an affluent, upwardly mobile adult population sent more of its offspring to college, and student status carried a draft exemption during America's involvement in the Vietnam conflict.

Literate, energetic, politically impassioned, technologically aware, impressed with their strength in numbers, and seeking a public voice, young people turned inevitably to publication—and along with the handbills, the leaflets, the "underground" and alternative newspapers and journals (many of which used some poetry), came a plethora of mostly-literary magazines, often, though by no means always, with a discernible leftward bent. For this generation was marked not only by its size, politicization, and access to technology, but by experience in an educational system that stressed increasingly the validity of the individual vision and the necessity of self-expression, including creative expression. Many educators, at least in progressive colleges and universities, departed from traditional aesthetic standards, sometimes in an attempt to define new standards better suited to the times, sometimes in a humanistic or political rejection of the very notion of standards as elitist. Creative writing classes burgeoned (and continue to flourish), and everyone who wished to become a poet did so. Many observers, including poets Conrad Aiken, Jack Gilbert, and Gerald Stern, claimed that even among the more genuinely talented poets, a levelness was evident—that no group of influential innovators, no masters, took shape against the crowd as Eliot, Pound, Stevens, and others so clearly had in the modernist teens and twenties.[6]

Understandably, the only efforts to survey a broad area of contemporary literary publishing have resulted in two collections of editors' essays, one published first as an issue of *TriQuarterly,*[7] the other as an issue of *December*.[8] Though readable and often delightful, each amounted to simply a series of unintegrated, largely anecdotal papers of varying quality and purpose.

Given the obstacles to approaching the printed products directly, I started instead with the creators: the poets. The first task, then, was deciding whom to study. To examine tellingly a thirty-year period punctuated with changes and split at the center by the twin upheavals of the Mimeo Revolution and antiwar resistance required that the group studied be stratified somehow. Therefore, two poet groups were formed, one category consisting of living American poets who had published their first book-length poetry manuscripts in the 1950–65 period, a second of those whose first books had appeared between 1970 and 1981 inclusive. Each of these two categories, in turn, broke down into two subcategories: one of poets who had received prestigious writing prizes and a second of those whose careers had included at least one book publication and numerous appearances in literary journals, but, through 1980, none of the dozens of literary awards included in a standard listing.[9]

The winning of major poetry prizes is a highly questionable but often used measure of distinction. Although poets continue to seek and cite them, prize decisions are routinely said to be influenced by friendship or by generational, political, or aesthetic loyalties. The much-decorated poet Mark Strand declared bluntly while participating in this study: "prizegiving is determined by friendship," a view expressed or implied by many other participants, both prize-laden and prizeless. However, prize lists do offer a systematic means of identifying a manageable number of *recognized* poets, even if not necessarily the *very best*—a group that no method could yield.

Therefore, two groups of prizewinning poets were identified: those who had won at least two prestigious prizes designed for, or most often awarded to, well-established poets—and those who had received at least one of the most important prizes earmarked for newer poets. These are referred to throughout as the OP (Older Prizewinning) and NP (Newer Prizewinning) Groups (see appendix.).

However, examples abound of excellent published poets consigned for years to near-oblivion. And many writers of serious intent but modest gifts make worthwhile contributions. Any investigation of the publishing patterns of prestigious awardees alone would present a distorted picture, one hard to interpret. At best, in a country boasting thousands of published poets and hundreds of literary presses and magazines, a study concentrating on prizewinners could illuminate only a minuscule, elite corner. Therefore, two more lists of poets, labelled the NN (Newer Nonprizewinning) and ON (Older Nonprizewinning) Groups, were established by first randomly selecting names from a standard directory of living published poets and from that long list drawing much shorter lists of all poets who met my criteria.[10] It should be emphasized that the Older/Newer groupings correspond not to the poets' ages but to the ages of their book-publishing careers.

After this, citations were gathered to all of the writers' poetry books and to their periodical appearances at particular career points. The citations were classified by publishing sector (commercial or trade; academic; and independent [i.e., noncommerical and not academically sponsored]) in order to gain information about where poets published overall and at key career and time periods. In addition, basic biographical information was collected, and the poets were asked questions about their writing and publishing experiences.[11] Their responses drifted in from late 1982 to spring 1984, with most arriving in 1983.

Although many libraries and reference sources were exploited, records held by New York's Poets & Writers, Inc., examined, scores of poets' questionnaires analyzed, and thousands of unindexed little-magazine issues studied one by one, all that could be done, given the elusiveness of the subject, was to build a discussion leading to suggestive conclusions. While one cannot generalize with confidence about the entire realm of poetry publishing from 1950 through 1980 using this study as a base, it does bring systematically assembled evidence to bear upon questions that concern poetry writers, publishers, and readers. To assess the evidence sensitively, however, to appreciate what occurred during the thirty years studied, we must gaze briefly into the preceding decades and see how recent trends in poetry publishing originated.

A Gift
That
Cannot Be Refused

1

The Publishing of Poetry Before 1950

POETRY PUBLISHING BEFORE 1912

Modern American poetry is sometimes said to have begun in 1912, a date not accidentally coincident with the publication of *Poetry* magazine's first issue. Yet the authors who became early leaders of the modernist movement were not transformed into poets within a few months, one year, or even two. They had long been writing in near or total obscurity—sometimes known to other poets, sometimes not, but never known to a large public—and publishing where they could. But before *Poetry*, few opportunities awaited serious nontraditional poets. No market was perceived for their work, and no poetry-publishing enterprises that were willing to disregard the market factor had arisen.

The Place and Nature of Popular Poetry

The nineteenth century, and especially its early years, is sometimes recalled as a time when poetry held an honored place—recited in schoolrooms, at Independence Day picnics, and, during courtship, by moonlight—read at fireside by fathers and at bedside by mothers in quaint scenarios incongruent with the age of television and the dual-career family.

In a recent book that has attracted attention, Christopher Clausen argues that while poetry was in crisis from the late eighteenth century on, the size and enthusiasm of its readership began to decline only near the end of the nineteenth, plummeting with the advent of modernism.[1] Other scholars have tended to the view that serious (and, certainly, experimental or highly original) poetry has never commanded a substantial audience in proportion to total numbers of readers, while sentimental, formulaic, homiletic poetry has and does. In his study of nineteenth-century American literary publishing, William Charvat concluded that from 1800 to 1820, close to half of all published volumes of verse probably emanated from local print shops, their costs funded by their authors. He warned that, despite a superfluity of amateur poets and the tradition of commemorating significant events in verse,

> this does not mean that the living poet, or anyone else who made the writing of belles-lettres a primary occupation, was respected. . . . From that day to this, there has been an extreme ambivalence in the public's attitude—on the one hand, veneration . . . for greater names like Homer and Milton, and for old living poets who have made a reputation; on the other hand, contempt (expressed in such historic phrases as "beggarly poet" and "wretched rimester") for young and unsuccessful poets.[2]

On the nature of poetry that found wide favor in the nineteenth and twentieth centuries, popular-culturist Russel Nye is instructive and entertaining.[3] While the British Romantics were developing their brilliant and peculiar new poetry, and Whitman was creating works of genius and unprecedented character, Americans preferred the simple romantic narratives of Longfellow and Whittier, the country verse of James Whitcomb Riley, and the jingles, tearjerkers, and rhymed moral lessons of dozens of now-forgotten versifiers. There actually seems remarkably *little* difference in the fundamental values of poetry audiences of the 1800s; of the early twentieth century when, in the age of Pound, Eliot, and Hart Crane, the best-loved poets were Robert Service and Edgar Guest; and of the present, when Rod McKuen and the Lebanese prose-poet Kahlil Gibran eclipse John Ashbery and Galway Kinnell, and numerous poets with extraordinary ability but "strange" styles or discomfiting subjects remain little known even within the literary establishment. They draw sustenance instead from, if anywhere, narrow cultlike followings. Surveying Athie Sale Davis's subject-arranged annual anthologies of newspaper verse published from 1920 through 1942, Nye observed that the subject categories remained basically stable over that period, and that the majority of poems in the 1942 annual could "as easily have appeared in 1872."[4]

Clausen half-concedes the historical predominance of the simple and accessible in poetry, but draws back to proclaim unprecedented "the present situation, in which serious contemporary poetry has virtually no audience at all outside the English department."[5] Yet despite the minuscule sales of poetry volumes overall, with even major publishers' titles often selling but a few hundred copies, several serious, original poets have within the past few decades realized respectable sales of at least one of their books—among them Allen Ginsberg, Gary Snyder, Carolyn Forché, and Haki R. Madhubuti (né Don L. Lee). Certainly their audiences are not limited entirely to the professional literati, but have encompassed a somewhat larger slice of the population of serious readers.

It seems clear, in any case, that in the two or three decades before 1912, poets of highly unusual style and vision were as little valued by the general reading public as they have ever been. A major difference between then and now is that there existed virtually no publishing outlets through which they might be heard by the few who would listen, the few with whom they might have formed artistic linkings and developed a new literature.

Commercial book publication was hard to achieve, with self-publishing the only alternative. Few magazines devoted much space to poetry, and those poems that did see print were likely to be predictable works mined in old veins. Such journals as *Atlantic Monthly, Scribner's, Harper's,* and *Century,* though aesthetically timid and able to publish few poems, were most poets' beacons. Here, and in the spaces between newspaper articles, lay their only hopes for exposure. In retrospect, *Poetry*'s founder, Harriet Monroe, remembered these poets as "humbly content to sit on the door-sill of the established magazines, and serve as the butt of newspaper paragraphers . . . no favors were accorded the poets beyond an occasional page-end appearance; and their books, if anyone dared publish them, found indifferent critics and few readers."[6]

Maxwell Bodenheim, a poet-novelist never accused of being unduly content, was published first in *Poetry* and soon afterward in *The Little Review,* after eight years of "sending verse to American museums, hammocks, and cuspidors [periodicals], and had received an unbroken flow of rejection slips, some six hundred in all." In the two years following his small-magazine breakthrough, during which his renown among poets and serious poetry readers was growing rapidly, *The New Republic* and *The Century* each took two of his poems "out of the forty-odd sent to each magazine."[7]

How and Where Poets Published

Many other poets also grew restless on the doorsills. Young experimentalists had little hope of crossing the threshold oftener than occasionally and craved an audience for the new things they had to say. In a pattern that was to be reversed after 1912, when nonprofit literary magazines began to proliferate, many turned to book self-production as a best hope; at least they would see their words typeset on paper and handled respectfully, not shortened or revised according to an editor's whim. The number of volumes by later-illustrious modern poets that were printed, yet remained invisible to readers, is stunning and undercuts any assertion that an American poetry of originality and worth "began" in the second decade of the twentieth century. Like trees falling in deserted forests, these books made no sound, but their authors were *there,* ready to be heard. Edwin Arlington Robinson, alone of those who shaped the new poetry of the teens and twenties, had a commercially published book before the turn of the century, but it received little notice.

At age nineteen, Robert Frost had *Twilight,* his first book, handset and printed in a two-copy edition. In the following year, 1895, he enjoyed his first poem sale—to *The Independent,* a magazine he had run across in the library of Dartmouth College, where he was an undergraduate. Many years later, he recalled: "They bought it so easily I thought I could make my living this way, but I didn't keep selling 'em as fast as that."[8] Seventeen years after that first sale, Frost was still knocking on barred doors, with only eleven additional published poems to his credit (five of which were in *The Independent,* three in *The Youth's Companion*). That year, editor Ellery Sedgwick returned a batch of poems with this notation: "We are sorry that we have no place in the Atlantic Monthly for your vigorous verse."[9] A real break came only after Frost's move to London where, in 1913, the manuscript of *A Boy's Will* was accepted for publication by David Nutt; a full two years later, and after Nutt had brought out a second Frost volume, *North of Boston,* the poet finally found an American publisher, Henry Holt. The same year, the *Atlantic* found sufficient space for "vigorous verse" to publish two of Frost's most famous pieces, "Birches" and "The Road Not Taken."

In 1909, Vachel Lindsay also had his first book privately printed, but won notice and a commercial publisher only after his first *Poetry* appearance. William Carlos Williams, who, like Pound, would become a pivotal figure for both the influence of his style and his support of other poets and little magazines, brought out a booklet in 1909, having it printed by a family friend in Rutherford, New Jersey. Four copies were sold. It was, Williams admitted, an "obviously young, obviously bad" book and was reasonably enough no candidate for the New York press.[10] Twenty-five years later, however, long after he had found his distinctive voice and won acceptance by the intelligentsia and the small magazines, Williams had to help finance his *Collected Poems* and considered himself fortunate to have a publisher at all. He searched throughout his life for a dependable commercial house.

Indeed, of the poets to lead the "renaissance," only Amy Lowell had achieved any conventional success before it began—with four publications in the *Atlantic Monthly* (1910–12) and acceptance by Houghton

Mifflin of her first book manuscript. These triumphs must be considered, however, against a complex backdrop. Lowell's poetry, not yet touched by "Imagism," was fairly traditional; she was a legendarily insistent and formidable, yet charming, woman; and most important, perhaps, she was an immediate member of Massachusetts' "royal family," and the *Atlantic* and Houghton were both Boston-based. Book buyers, however, were not swayed by such factors, and *A Dome of Many-Coloured Glass* sold only eight copies in its first year.

The Role of Ezra Pound

For at least two decades, beginning in 1913, it would seem as though Ezra Pound had discovered, fostered, and tried to control every new poet and every poetic development of great importance in American and British literature. He is known justly for his own poetry, but his broader effect was inestimable. He turns up everywhere, his hand somewhere revealed in the careers of dozens of writers, magazines, publishing houses. Difficult as he could be, and controversial as he became because of his political stands, he had amazingly fine aesthetic judgment, courage, and generosity and was the architect of the literary renaissance.

Like the poets he sponsored, Pound paid for the printing of his first book in 1908. His second was published by a London bookseller whose shop was a gathering place for poets and who had taken Pound under his wing. This method of gaining publication through friendship networks, always of some significance, would pervade the poetry world in the twentieth century and was exemplified, of course, by Pound's own relations with his "discoveries." He would soon begin expending his enormous energy on their behalf, using as his vehicle an utterly unlikely partnership formed with Harriet Monroe, a genteel Chicago poet who in 1911 had written to ask if he would submit verse to a magazine she intended to publish.

Harriet Monroe and Poetry Magazine

If one were to rank in importance all twentieth-century literary enterprises affecting poets, the founding of *Poetry* magazine would clearly come first. As a result, the magazine's purpose and ultimate contribution have been recorded and analyzed from numerous perspectives and need not be discussed in depth here.

Hoffman, Allen, and Ulrich's authoritative bibliography of English-language little magazines through 1945 identifies nine United States predecessors (1891–1911), but none of these focused exclusively on poetry and only two used substantial amounts of it.[11] *The Chap-Book* and the leftwing *Masses* (1911–17), whose principal interest was not literary, are the only two of the nine journals remembered today. None of the nine survives. *The Chap-Book* existed as an island, neither creating a community of writers around it nor stimulating a proliferation of magazines with a like purpose, nor exposing a "new" literature.

Monroe was herself an earnest, likable poet of mild talent and derived her fundamental identity from her writing rather than the editing at which she excelled. Her autobiography, written when she was in her seventies, was entitled, tellingly, *A Poet's Life.*[12] Her attraction to poets, empathy with their problems, and devotion to the development of the art were those of a passionate creator, born of personal experience and commitment, and were absolutely unshakeable. The same might be said of Pound, Williams, Ernest Walsh (editor of *This Quarter*, 1925–26), and many other editors, but Monroe alone was distinguished by openness to virtually every style, every school.

While raging throughout the teens against her catholicity of taste (and the magazine's resultant lapses into mediocrity, as he saw it), at Monroe's death in September 1936, Pound singled out this quality as the basis of *Poetry*'s genius:

> An exclusive editorial policy would not have done the work of an inclusive policy (however much the inclusiveness may have rankled one and all factions). It is to Miss Monroe's credit that POETRY never degenerated into a factional organ. . . . No other publication has existed in America where any writer of poetry could more honorably place his writings. This was true in 1911. It is true as I write this.[13]

The fact remains, however, that Monroe's "inclusiveness," added to her need to fill the pages of a monthly magazine, resulted in the publication of some weak verse. This was especially true during the last fifteen years or so of her editorship, when numerous journals competed in a field where *Poetry* had briefly stood alone, Pound and several early contributors defected to new, zesty, inconoclastic magazines of their own or their friends, and Monroe fell out of touch and sympathy with much that was fresh in poetry. But some softness of judgment had always been evident in her uneasiness with elite, inaccessible verse and her affection for the craftsmanlike minor poet.

Poetry's greatest years—roughly 1913 through 1916—were the fruit of her collaboration with Pound, their strength as a team inherent in their drastic differences as people. An American living in London, Pound had responded to Monroe's request for submissions not only with poems but with an offer to serve as foreign correspondent, a suggestion she seized upon with characteristic acuteness. She announced his appointment in *Poetry*'s second issue and was rewarded with a stream of manuscripts from authors who would become the most illustrious in twentieth-century poetry: William Butler Yeats, T. S. Eliot, Dylan Thomas, Williams, Frost, Rabindranath Tagore, D. H. Lawrence, and Pound himself among them. "So far," Ernest Hemingway wrote from Europe,

> we have Pound the major poet devoting, say, one-fifth of his time to poetry. With the rest of his time he tries to advance the fortunes, both material and artistic, of his friends. He defends them when they are attacked, he gets them into magazines and out of jail. He loans them money. . . . He advances them hospital expenses and dissuades them from suicide.[14]

As Robert Frost later remembered, Pound "had to be first in everything. He wanted to discover, to break the way."[15]

Pound's erratic energy, intensity, insight, insistence on excellence, and poetic brilliance and Monroe's complementary stability, patience, and caution were joined by their shared devotion to art and merged to form a dazzling magazine. It was never as bright after he resigned in 1919, and none of his sporadic forays into publishing—under his own sail or as collaborator under others'—was enduring.

Poetry on Balance

Partly because of her association with Pound, partly because of *Poetry*'s fortuitous birth at a time when there was much adventuresome writing being done, partly because of her editorial wisdom, and very much because what *Poetry* provided was unique, Monroe succeeded beyond her anticipation in stimulating the development of a new poetry and providing a home for young writers of merit. Further, she had been convinced that a midwestern poetry might emerge to challenge the eastern and European cultural monopoly and had been vindicated by the voices of Lindsay, Sandburg, and other poets less remembered.

Her finest memorial is the little-magazine movement she set in motion, which remains vital to this day. It might well have started without her, but *Poetry* was a harbinger of such magazines. As new titles flickered into (and often out of) existence throughout the United States and the European centers of expatriatism, she applauded and promoted them generously. "Success to them all!" she exclaimed at the conclusion of an early editorial describing her competitors. "It is the little magazines which should be encouraged and subscribed for . . . POETRY, or one of these others, beginning in a dream, will end by freeing American literature."[16] Although it is impossible to tell what would have happened to American literature absent little magazines, the findings of the present study and the published observations of many authors suggest that in the case of poetry, at least, her grandiose prediction was realized. That is, because it could be published without depending on the narrow commercial-magazine market, poetry was free to be what its poets would have it be, obeying the imperatives of their creative needs.

The poetry, however, could not free its poets, nor bring them large audiences and income, nor liberate them from both drudgery and want. This Monroe had striven for, and she considered the continuing narrow appeal of the genre as signalling her worst failure. Directly, she tried to ease the poets' plight by paying her contributors more, and more consistently, than almost any other small magazine of that day or this, and she lamented the puniness of the amounts. She also found funding for several prizes to be administered through *Poetry* and urged that more be established. Yet she had expected to build not a reservoir of awards and fees for serious poets, but a popular readership, and she felt the defeat of this expectation as a profound failure. Not only is an accumulation of readers the only means of assuring a poet a steady income, it is the sole indication of the democratization of the art, the extension of poetry into the lives of the many. Seeing this as not only desirable but necessary, Monroe had adopted for her magazine's slogan a quotation from Walt Whitman: "To have great poets there must be great audiences too." She understood this to mean audiences great in number as well as capacity for appreciation. "We believe that there is a public for poetry," she asserted in the opening issue, "that it will grow, and that as it becomes more numerous and appreciative the work produced in this art will grow in power, in beauty, in significance."[17]

Pound, a frank elitist, infuriated some readers by referring in the same issue to Americans as "that mass of dolts" and opposed *Poetry*'s slogan as unrealistic and unbefitting the tradition of artistic genius. After simmering for nearly two years, his dissatisfaction boiled forth in an editorial: "It is true that the great artist has always had a great audience, even in his lifetime; but it is not the *vulgo* but the spirits of irony and of destiny and of humor, sitting within him." Monroe allotted to herself the last word, following Pound with her judgment that: "No small group today can suffice for the poet's imaginative audience."[18] Subsequent experience, however, confirmed Pound's view. Monroe's annual birthday editorials, when read consecutively, constitute a sad chronicle of progressive disillusionment. When *Poetry* turned twenty-one, she claimed that "the long fight for a public has availed a little. . . . At least today the poet is no longer a stock joke. . . . "[19] But this statement sounds feeble and joyless when measured against the goal she had once striven toward. It was a goal other editors and poets would set forth and, with few exceptions, fail to reach. The invisibility or nonexistence of poetry's audience, what this says about the nation's values and educational system, and its implications for the poet's and literary publisher's economic, emotional, and psychological survival—and for the very worth of poetry, the rationale for writing it—are recurrent themes throughout the modern history of the genre, as they are throughout this study.

FALLOUT: POETRY PUBLISHING IN THE TEENS

The Little Review

At the start of the teens, then, there remained for poets the old middlebrow magazines—outlets old-fashioned in stylistic preference and severely limited in the amounts of poetry they could handle; *Poetry*, which at once became the obvious magazine goal for serious writers and reviewers of verse; and book publication—hardest of all to achieve—through trade presses in New York, Boston, or London, or, failing that, through self-financed printing.

The little-magazine flood that would follow *Poetry* began as a trickle in 1913 with Alfred Kreymborg's short-lived *Glebe* and a few British efforts, notably Harold Monro's *Poetry and Drama* and Dora Marsden's feminist *New Freewoman*, which would soon be overwhelmed by Ezra Pound and his troupe of Imagists and reborn as *The Egoist*. But not until March 1914 did a second American little magazine appear. Like *Poetry*, it emanated from Chicago and was begun by a strongly independent woman who was motivated by love for ideas and the arts, blessed with great flair and a distinctive personality, and who took on as foreign editor Ezra Pound. As he had done for *Poetry*, Pound unearthed the best work the magazine would ever publish (Joyce's *Ulysses*) and for a time exerted strong influence. This was Margaret Anderson's *Little Review*. The resemblance between the two Chicago magazines was mostly superficial, however—*Little Review* being the brainchild of an editor barely out of her teens, prone to passionate but fickle enthusiasms, and possessed of an erratic brilliance, a highly literate, ornamental prose style, and terrific self-indulgence and snobbery. In 1917, Pound signed on, publicly explaining his decision via verbal swipes at *Poetry*, with which he remained affiliated. Echoing his earlier criticisms of Monroe's democratic idealism, he accused her magazine of "unflagging courtesy to a lot of old fools and fogies whom I should have told to go to hell" and complained that "my voice and vote have always been [those] of a minority."[20] Privately, he derided "that infamous remark of Whitman's about poets needing an audience."[21]

Contrasting with the Whitman quote was *Little Review*'s slogan: "making no compromise with the public taste." Explaining that this "came to us, among other precious things, from Ezra Pound," coeditor Jane Heap went a step farther: "I believe in peace and silence for and from the 'masses'—a happy undisturbed people."[22] Earlier, she had written in defense of Joyce: "All compulsion exists within the arts. . . . The only concern of the artist is to try in one short lifetime to meet these inner compulsions. He has no concern with audiences and their demands."[23] Clearly, Pound, Anderson, and Heap were ideological and to some extent temperamental counterparts. Out of their volatile partnership came perhaps the most memorable publication in little-magazine history.

Harriet Monroe viewed it ambivalently, admiring its editors' spirit and originality on the one hand ("a gallant adventure . . . all the audacity and flaming sincerity of youth"), decrying its arrogant elitism on the other ("the organ of a choice little group of superintellectualized ultimates and expatriates"[24]). Discussing the "rebel, combative" *Little Review* in their 1946 study, Hoffman, Allen, and Ulrich waxed sentimental: "There are many reasons for writers, now between forty and fifty years old, to remember gratefully *The Little Review*, and for their insistence that it was the best magazine of their youth."[25] It exerted and still exerts an extraordinary appeal.

Yet as a home, a showcase, or a source of income for the unknown writer without powerful contacts, it could not compare with *Poetry*. Predictably, the editors were inhospitable to offerings from the masses and published only a minuscule number of unsolicited manuscripts. Indeed, *The Little Review* was unashamedly the organ of a small group linked by aesthetic biases and often-tempestuous friendships. In this it resembled numerous successor journals, many of which one assumes it inspired or influenced. Comparison of *Poetry* with *The Little Review* reveals two fundamental polarities that have characterized little magazines down to the present: openness versus cliquishness; eclecticism versus stylistic exclusivity.

Others and The Dial

Having abandoned *Glebe* after a falling-out with its patrons—the publishing Boni brothers, who preferred European writers to obscure American experimentalists—Alfred Kreymborg established *Others* in 1915 as the first United States magazine to offer American poets a strong, home-based alternative to *Poetry*. It was conceived, as its title implied, as a magazine for the "others"—that is, those rejected by, or dissatisfied with, the periodical that for three years had virtually monopolized United States poetry publishing. This motivation became explicit with the publication of a special issue featuring poems rejected for publication by *Poetry*.

Again, Ezra Pound surfaced to offer a young magazine its most valuable asset: in this case, by recommending that Kreymborg, who lived in New Jersey, contact the then-unknown Jersey physician-poet, William Carlos Williams, who became *Others'* contributor and associate editor in his first of many affiliations with little magazines. Williams drew to

Others his friends whose work was too avant-garde for Monroe; who were disenchanted with her conservatism, which manifested itself, though very rarely, in attempts to edit distinguished poems; or who simply needed another vehicle. Later Williams would write that *Others* "took up the burden of publishing the newest work in verse where *Poetry* left off."[26]

Among the "others" flocking to the magazine that Kreymborg, "penniless," published year-round out of a "shack never meant for winter," were Eliot, Stevens, Maxwell Bodenheim, Marianne Moore, and Conrad Aiken—all promising new poets who had published for the first time in *Poetry*. *Others* was given all his poems at this time, Williams later recalled humorously, "and, of course, we—myself and my friends—owned it, so you see I wasn't really cutting much of a figure as a poet."[27] Self-publication through one's own small journal would become a commonplace for poets far too adventuresome, difficult, prolific, mediocre, or proud to win ready acceptance in established organs. Setting another precedent that would soon become common practice, Williams terminated *Others* in 1919, not out of necessity but because it seemed to have lost its spark, its cutting edge, to have become "just another little magazine."[28] Except for academically sponsored titles, few little magazines, devoid of profit motivation, would be allowed to outlive their own vivacity.

Under these circumstances, their demise has seldom been long lamented, for, once the movement was set on its apparently endless, everwidening course, new titles always sprang up to replace the dead, frequently borrowing some of their ideas, purpose, spirit, and recasting them in fresh forms. Occasionally, a magazine would shake off its anomie under new direction. Both cases are exemplified by *The Dial*, which, founded in (again) Chicago in 1880, had been for most of its years a conservative and in recent years reactionary force, launching a notorious attack on *Poetry* for its publishing of Carl Sandburg's idiosyncratic "Chicago Poems": "an impudent affront to the poetry-loving public."[29] In 1917, however, the elderly *Dial*, for which "the only good poet was a dead one,"[30] moved to New York to take on, under a new owner, advanced views and the work of such modernists as Lowell, Bodenheim, and Babette Deutsch. Late in 1919 *The Dial* again changed hands. One of its new editors chanced to meet the members of the group that had surrounded the just-disbanded *Others* and began publishing them in the again reconstituted *Dial*, giving it a tone reminiscent of *Others*. This similarity sharpened five years later when Marianne Moore, one of the most gifted "others," became editor of *The Dial*.

Many years later Williams would write: "The little magazine is something I have always fostered; for without it I myself would have been early silenced. To me it is one magazine, not several. It is a continuous magazine. . . . When it dies, someone else takes it up in some other part of the country."[31]

Book Publishing

While a network of magazines willing to print poems, both avant-garde and traditional, was developing throughout the decade, publication of a book of serious, unconventional poetry remained a near-heroic accomplishment—most feasible, perhaps, for someone of Amy Lowell's social standing. That many poets paid for their books to be privately printed or sought publishers abroad, has been noted. However, a third option was slowly taking shape as the small book presses, operated out of a love for literature and without hope of a profit, began to emerge, first abroad among the expatriates, later at home. These presses, which were essentially counterparts of the little magazine, would proliferate in number and significance throughout ensuing decades. Egoist, Inc. was the book imprint of *Egoist* magazine, one of whose most prominent supporters and contributors was Ezra Pound. Appropriately, Egoist issued in 1917 the first book by Pound's star discovery, T. S. Eliot: *Prufrock and Other Observations*. Despite the international stir caused two years earlier by the publication of the title poem ("The Love Song of J. Alfred Prufrock") in *Poetry*, the edition of five hundred took four years to sell out—a fact that underscored the futility of relying on a profit-driven industry to disseminate poetry.

THE TWENTIES

Little poetry except the most clichéd had ever found a welcome among mainstream publishers, and it was perhaps predictable that a movement of book presses fuelled by literary idealism would follow the similarly motivated magazine movement. Through the magazines, new writers had found their voice both individually and collectively, had had a chance to read one another's work, to learn, be inspired, make contact, form alliances. Enhancing their developing sense of community was the artistic expatriatism that flourished during the twenties, then declined in the thirties. American and British writers were drawn into tight-knit circles in Paris, circles welded by strong emotion, mutual commitment, and the need to create a community in a foreign place. Amazing amounts of sheer talent and energy were concentrated, then, in small pockets of a single exciting city, with the predictable twin results of great profligacy and great productivity. And still, all roads seemed to lead to Ezra Pound.

Out of this community of remarkable people—mutually supporting, mutually demanding and inspiring—sprang new presses and magazines and foreign offices of U.S.-based journals. Much of the literary history of the time amounts to the history of this group. This fact poses the now-familiar paradox of such circles. While they nurture many artists, focus the development of a literary movement, and serve as advocate for new and worthy writers, they become more or less closed systems, beaming their searchlights inward. It may be true that this century's finest writers of the third decade invariably were those humming around the lights of Pound and his colleagues in Europe, Monroe and the midwestern school, or the southern agrarians. Or it may be that, just as some tastemakers lionized mediocre writers from time to time, they also rejected or overlooked important talents. Literary cliques *will* form; they always did and still do. Their ultimate effect on literature and even on the development of the included—that is, those individuals whom they seek to foster—is debatable, but sometimes, certainly, it is stifling. This issue is as alive today, when there are thousands of magazines and book presses and, no doubt, hundreds of literary friendship groups, as it ever was. In the research reported here, it emerged repeatedly as a continuing cause of concern and bitterness among poets and is discussed in chapter 6.

The Market for Poetry

While a captivating national poetry was taking shape against a new and vital, if mercurial, poetry press, poets and publishers would continue to bemoan the failure of market development. There was no "great audience" and little money to be had as a reward for the strenuous work of creation. Poets lived on inherited or family money, professional income, a spouse's support, or hand-to-mouth on menial wages, sporadic editorships, or the largesse of friends. Only a very few modern poets, among them Langston Hughes and Edna St. Vincent Millay, realized much income directly from their writing, and this neither made them permanently comfortable nor necessarily reflected public acceptance of their most serious poetic work. Hughes, for example, also wrote the "Simple" stories and other prose, and the lighter and more sentimental of Millay's verses were extremely popular, though of trifling literary importance. A 1921 Bookseller's Poll had placed six poets, all of them modernists, among the forty "Leading Names in Contemporary American Literature," as manifested in bookstore sales.[32] While this is surprising from the perspective of today, when no poet at all would likely be named in such a poll, it was surprising then that so *few* were named, because imaginative literature dominated public taste and poems were still memorized in classrooms and orated routinely on public occasions.

Christopher Clausen claimed that even this relatively meagre audience decreased as the decade progressed, resulting in the "virtual extinction of the [always rare] self-supporting poet."[33] He attributed this to the serious poets' break with accepted forms and refusal to provide readers with the genre's traditional satisfactions. Other equally plausible reasons can be hypothesized; determining a full, final reason is outside this study's scope, though it would undoubtedly turn out to be a complex blend of several broad cultural factors. In any case, it is certain that poetry sales benefited little in the economically flush, newly sophisticated, postwar, pre-Depression decade.

At the start of the twenties, Bodenheim had characterized the alleged post–1912 "poetic boom" as "a floridly persuasive circus-barker shouting . . . to passers-by, but now and then wearily turning his back to look at the empty seats showing through the circus-entrance . . . inside of the tent, has the nation's appreciation of poetry increased more than an inch?"[34] At decade's end the respected poet Louise Bogan informed John Hall Wheelock: "Harriet Monroe writes me that she's sending out *Dark Summer* to the Poetry Clan (which numbers, I believe, two hundred members) as its sixth book. . . . Scribner's will like that, from the monetary point of view. Personally, I think that two hundred lonely, isolated Clan members is a picture to weep over." Seven years later, writing again to Wheelock, she expressed resentment that *Dark Summer* "fell into a deep dark well; it is never stocked in bookstores, and is known to a small group only," and declared that only by "running with some pack" could she promote it, "but this I can not and will not do."[35]

Alongside the small and possibly shrinking public demand for poetry grew, paradoxically, an expanding poetry supply. While large numbers of amateurs had always written poems, often for recreational or courtship purposes, the advent of free verse and apparently looser poetic structures, combined with the mushrooming poetry press (and, no doubt, other cultural and educational factors), encouraged unprecedented hundreds of poets to write with serious intent, seeking publications and a degree of fame. What was "so depressing," Monroe's assistant George Dillon concluded in 1927, was not the dreadfulness of the writing that resulted, but "its level of rather high mediocrity," achievable only by "largely appreciative and intelligent" people without "adequate talent." There was, he decided, a prevailing "mania for publication," which had surely reached its farthest possible extreme.[36] In this judgment he was proved wrong, as worry and bitterness about the burgeoning ranks of published authors grew through the following decades and exploded into outright incredulity during the 1960s and 1970s, when popular creative-writing classes and workshops multiplied, generating thousands of overnight "poets," some of whom had no literary background and read little or nothing—but possessed the common urges for self-expression and recognition. Far from having reached an extreme, then, this trend was born in the 1920s, but came to typify and complicate the poetry-publishing situation.

Book Publishing

Whether even those who wrote poetry often bought it was questionable, and most established book publishers stayed shy or became shyer of poetry manuscripts. But poets whose writing now appeared regularly in little magazines and those who admired their work would not long tolerate the scarcity of opportunities for book publication. Some New York houses, propelled by both a profit motive and love for literature, were founded at about this time and offered new chances for poets. Among these was Boni & Liveright (later Liveright), which, before going bankrupt in 1933, published major poem anthologies as well as Pound's work, which the house persisted in supporting despite the money losses it brought. On Pound's recommendation Liveright also published H.D. and T. S. Eliot. Instructed by Pound to leave Eliot's *Wasteland* untouched, the publisher abandoned apparent common sense out of respect for his judgment and issued the first edition of the poem, unedited, in 1922.[37] Liveright also took early books by Robinson Jeffers, Hart Crane, and e. e. cummings (who claimed the ubiquitous Pound as mentor).

A more durable new publisher blossoming at the same time as Liveright, with much of his affinity for good literature and noncommercial impulse, was Alfred A. Knopf, like Liveright a liberal, cultivated young Jew on the fringes of New York society. Knopf was Eliot's first United States publisher (*Poems*, 1920), Langston Hughes's first (*Weary Blues*, 1925) after many years of magazine appearances, Stevens's first, and Bodenheim's second. His imprint continues to be found on books of fine poetry that lack obvious market appeal.

Despite such oases the New York-based for-profit publishing industry was a desert for poets, and they despaired of it as they had despaired of finding a place in the slick periodicals. Numerous independent, usually short-lived, literary publishing enterprises were founded, the best documented and perhaps most important being in expatriate France. For example, Robert McAlmon, who was rich by marriage, became Hemingway's first publisher (*Three Stories and Ten Poems*, 1923) under his Contact Editions imprint. At Black Sun Press, Harry Crosby, rich by birth, brought out the first edition of Hart Crane's *The Bridge* after housing the poet at the Crosby's mill-home, enduring his mad antics, and at last virtually imprisoning him to force him to work on what would be his masterpiece. After Crosby's suicide in December 1929, his widow Caresse, scarcely missing a beat, carried out publication plans for *The Bridge*.

Small magazines, meanwhile, continued to be born. Again, these were often inspired or fortified by Pound, though by the conclusion of the decade, his value as mentor and literary judge was being mitigated by the passion of his opinions and by his hypersensitivity and ill temper.

Among the many twenties' magazines were *The Double Dealer* (1921–26) and *The Fugitive* (1922–25), both emanating from the American South and heralding a regional literary renaissance in the work of the agrarian poets; Williams's and McAlmon's *Contact* (1921–22), founded before McAlmon's financially advantageous marriage and funded by his wages as an art-class model; Ford Madox Ford's Pound-influenced *Transatlantic Review* (1924–25); *This Quarter* (1926–27), which survived for three legendary issues, dying with the death of its editor; and Pound's four-issue *Exile* (1927–28). Perhaps the finest new magazines of the twenties were two founded in 1927: *Hound and Horn* (1927–34), begun at Harvard; and *transition* (1927–38), which encouraged experimentalism, wielded huge influence, and assembled a brilliant list of contributors. That same year saw the birth of the University of Nebraska's *Prairie Schooner,* an early, enduring example of the academic little magazines that would become omnipresent and controversial in years to come.

As the 1920s drew to a close, the stock market crashed and worldwide Depression followed, ending an era that, while not making poets rich, had at least offered overseas havens, a few family fortunes to subsidize publishing ventures, and a strong sense of possibility. The thirties would have a drastic effect not only on poets' economic prospects, but on the character of poetry itself.

THE THIRTIES

As the decade opened, poet Edward Dahlberg and his friend John Dos Passos could deplore the fact that, in their opinion, too many literary periodicals existed, but as the nation's economic crisis took its toll, writers worried more about an opposite problem.[38] One after another, magazine offices closed, deflating the market, wrote Harriet Monroe, "like a toy balloon."[39] On the occasion of *Pagany* magazine's demise, fiction writer Julian L. Shapiro (later John Sanford) lamented, "Everywhere one hears the same sad slow music."[40] The editors of both *Prairie Schooner* and *Poetry,* wounded by their own financial shortfalls, wondered aloud whether the little-magazine movement could survive its afflictions. Publisher James Laughlin, who was studying at Harvard in 1935 and forming literary aspirations, later recalled it as a curiously empty time, with poetry readings "practically unheard of," few writing schools or programs or groups, the house of Liveright and the most exciting small magazines of the twenties already defunct.[41]

In a sense, however, poets suffered less from the Depression *as poets* than other workers did—for economic distress had always been their lot. To fail to earn money from the profession that constituted his source of identity was an accustomed predicament for the poet, causing no fresh psychic stress, though the loss of an expatriate haven, of family money, of jobs that had paid the bills and released energies for writing poetry, did, of course, cause poets practical anxiety. Since writers—and certainly poets—weren't thought of as workingmen even in good times, their difficulties evoked relatively little public sympathy when hard times arrived. In 1938, for instance, a St. Louis editorialist argued that the writer was "supposed to go hungry and ragged and cold, to drudge at chores he loaths. . . . It MAKES a writer and weeds out the poseurs."[42]

An alleviation for some was the Federal Writers' Project (FWP), begun in 1935 and aimed principally at writers who could qualify for relief. Ironically, the Project probably favored some poets with the fattest, steadiest paychecks they had ever enjoyed.

Meanwhile, many thoughtful Americans, artists and writers prominent among them, were re-examining their country's economic and class structures and the assumptions underlying them in light of their apparent collapse and were affiliating with left-wing groups. From these new affinities sprouted numerous lively journals—some strongly literary, others mostly political, many a (frequently unsuccessful) blend. That Laughlin did not perceive these as filling the literary gap left by the deaths of older journals can be explained by their frank ideological bias, which led them to advocate (and often demand) a different content, play a different role, fulfill another purpose.

These remarkably prolific efforts included, for example: *Front* (1930–33), an international magazine with Communist Norman Macleod heading its United States offices, concerned with literature as a means of arming "the workers against the bourgeoisie"[43]; *Smoke* (1931–37), a fine poetry journal hospitable to experiment; *Leftward* (1932–33), *The Left Front* (1933–34), *Left Review* (1934), and *Red Pen* (1934), all sponsored by John Reed Clubs; *Dynamo: A Journal of Revolutionary Poetry* (1934–36); Laughlin's annual *New Directions in Prose and Poetry*, publishing nearly every major writer of the later thirties; and Reed Whittemore and James Angleton's feisty *Furioso,* which would eventually print virtually every prominent contemporary American poet and many Britons. The best of the batch, and the only title that survives (although with profoundly altered outlook and diminished interest), was *Partisan Review,* founded in 1934 and publishing an array of distinguished (or soon-to-be-distinguished) poets: Eliot, Stevens, Allen Tate, Delmore Schwartz, John Berryman, Karl Shapiro, Randall Jarrell, and dozens more.

The politics of journals had a way of delimiting the ideas, even in creative pieces, and there grew up a proletarian, radical, or left poetry—never as pronounced or dominant as the same movement in fiction, but significant nonetheless. Characterized by straightforward language and themes of revolution, war, and social criticism, many of the left poems seem dated and quaintly self-conscious today when the specific crises generating their political bent are long past.

A second publishing trend, sown earlier but beginning to blossom now, was the sponsorship by academia of literary journals far away from northeastern publishing centers. These journals were usually quiet and eclectic rather than doggedly experimental or political, were free of direct profit motivation and relatively financially stable, and commenced with a regional bias that was eventually shed. Various purposes fuelled them, including devotion to providing a platform for good literature, or more specifically for regional writing, or *most* specifically for local professors. Sometimes the administrators of a small college or obscure university hoped to enhance the institution's visibility and student-faculty appeal; sometimes a single determined instructor initiated the magazine, fought for funding, and ran it single-handedly. Whatever their reasons and idiosyncrasies, these academic journals offered then and would increasingly offer a steady sometimes paying outlet for new verse in a variety of styles and lengths. Joining *Prairie Schooner* in the 1930s[44] was *Southern Review* (founded at the University of Mississippi and later moved to Louisiana State University); *University Review* (University of Kansas City); *American Prefaces* (University of Iowa); and *Kenyon Review*, a journal started in 1939 at a sequestered Ohio college enrolling roughly 300 students. In the 1950s and 1960s, the number of academic magazines would increase until, by the late 1970s, many colleges and almost every university would be or would recently have been host to one or more.

There was, then, by the end of the 1930s a bewildering quantity of magazines, stimulating in their differences from their predecessors and from each other, usually flickering in and out of existence within months. Among them the indomitable *Poetry* was a rare island of stability. Yet poets still faced a dearth of book-publishing options. The poetry book market, always minute, shrank with the Depression. Liveright and many expatriate presses were dead or faltering, and those publishers once guardedly receptive to poetry were forced to be even more cautious in the changed environment.

As the decade opened, Pound had decried the reluctance of American patrons and publishers to subsidize the printing of books for their sheer intrinsic value and had seen hope only in the "*cheap* book trade": "Let three or four chaps get a . . . press . . . and print off what they believe in. There would be no money in it."[45] Soon to step into the void, once again, were dedicated independents such as Pound had visualized. Representative of them were two wealthy young writers who established book presses—one short-lived, the other still existing today. And just behind each of them stood Pound himself as advisor and profound influence, which had been for twenty years his accustomed role in dozens of publishing ventures, but which he would soon vacate, swallowed up by his economic and political preoccupations and personal trials.

George Oppen, himself a gifted poet, joined with the 1930s' Objectivist school of writing and formed the Objectivist Press. A striking trio of writers made up his Advisory Board: Pound, Williams, and premier Objectivist Louis Zukovsky. Early publications included Oppen's own first book (1933) and Williams's first *Collected Poems* (1934), preface by Wallace Stevens. "Needless to say," Williams wrote later, "it didn't sell at all."[46] Oppen himself later remembered "how small a public even those I looked up to as established poets had at this time."[47]

A second publishing house founded in this difficult decade would become the most successful and enduring American press committed exclusively to experimental literature. Its ultimate progenitor was Pound, who, shown some poetry by the twenty-two-year-old James Laughlin, told him he would never succeed as a writer and might better do something "useful": namely, close the gap left by Depression-killed publishers. Laughlin took up the challenge, established New Directions, and quickly built a glittering list made up of Pound and his acquaintances who had been stranded by the loss of their publishers. Other friendship networks garnered more authors: Laughlin's Harvard school friend Delmore Schwartz, who in turn recommended *his* friends John Berryman and Randall Jarrell; and Kenneth Rexroth, who brought in Denise Levertov, Jerome Rothenberg, and Gary Snyder. Linkings meant everything, and Laughlin had forged brilliant ones; timing was critical, and Laughlin's was perfect for a new publisher unconstrained by the need immediately to win sales. Later on, in the mid-forties, he *would* worry about money, writing one of his authors that half his time was spent running a ski hotel to subsidize New Directions: "You see we have grown in length of list but not in volume of sales. There will never be a large public for this sort of stuff and there is no use kidding ourselves about it. . . . For six years I have worked four or five nights a week till 12 and dropped eight to ten thousand dollars a year in deficits."[48]

The theme had never changed and never would. Though the "audience" had perhaps become smaller than usual, it had never been "great" and was not to be. So the forties arrived with the nation pulling out of the Depression, but there were continued economic straits for publishers of poems, a new source of social chaos, and still another set of editorial demands for poets to meet.

THE FORTIES

The new climate for writers was augured by a 1941 remonstrance from Edward Weeks, *Atlantic*'s editor, to Richard Eberhart: "It seems to me in this crucial year when people are searching more earnestly for truth and guidance than at any time these past two decades, the curse which above all a poet must avoid is that of unintelligibility. . . . This is not a time for art to be esoteric." The poet retorted: "I appreciate your problem as an editor, but I have the profoundest respect for poetry as a vital resource of life. . . . I suppose a cranky idealism may be at the back of this."[49] If many others shared his aesthetic idealism, it was increasingly eclipsed by nationalism. In a time of grave foreign threat, poetry must be seen by many as frivolous, an unjustifiable luxury, unless distorted to serve a patriotic goal. In 1941 production costs skyrocketed, universities lost funds, many writers and young potential writers entered military service or became preoccupied with volunteer support work, and such readers as poetry might have had were distracted by thoughts of war. The expatriates were at last home from abroad; Paris, London, and other foreign cities no longer offered safe, cheap sanctuary. The American presses and magazines that they had once run had all been halted within the past few years. Eileen Simpson, engaged to the then little-known John Berryman, remembers his walking the New York streets "from river to river, from Battery to Inwood" in 1941, railing that "he had been born at the wrong time and in the wrong country. 'Pushkin could count on railway workers to know his poems. *Think of it!* Who reads poetry in America?' "[50]

Though *Poetry, Partisan Review, Furioso,* many of the university publications, and a few other journals hung on through the war, others faltered. *Southern Review*'s editor claimed that its parent university, long hostile to the magazine, used the war as "a plausible excuse" to shut it down. Other journals were founded—notably *Accent* in 1940, which struggled on for twenty years, buoyed by its determined editor Kerker Quinn and, after 1951, a small university subsidy; it was always "just this side of collapse." Despite *Accent*'s general high quality and early publication of many famous writers, its circulation probably never exceeded 1,400—making it a typical, even relatively affluent, case.[51]

After Pearl Harbor, however, new literary journals were scarce, and those that did commence were often defensive in tone, traditionally inspirational in content, or both. *Poetry Chap-Book,* for example, an old-fashioned magazine featuring solid but conventional poets, felt called upon, in its first issue, to justify its very existence: "It is as an affirmation of faith in the inspirational value of poetry that the Editors of *The Poetry CHAP-BOOK* launch their magazine at this time. When war engulfs a nation, the need for artistic sustenance becomes greater than ever."[52] Hoffman, Allen, and Ulrich's bibliography shows a yearly average of five new United States little magazines for the years 1942–45, as compared with an annual average of nineteen in the Depression-ridden thirties.[53] Only four academic journals were founded. With the war's end the poetry-book market remained depressed, though its upturns and downturns had always, of course, been merely ripples in an ever-shallow pond. At the same time production costs remained high, and serious poets, always victims of customer apathy, were stressed additionally by inflation.

Discussing this state of affairs in an intriguing *Poetry* magazine symposium, poets and publishers on both sides of the Atlantic echoed conclusions reached by Pound almost two decades earlier: "poetry does not sell to any considerable audience in our culture," and this is irremediable through book promotion; the only hope for poetry publishing, therefore, lies outside the commercial sector, in donated "wealth" and "work"—in "individual dedication."[54]

The fifties arrived, then, with poets facing the same problems and publishers proffering the same answers. There were, in the memory of poet Daisy Aldan, "about forty-two literary magazines in the whole country . . . most . . . controlled by the academic poets" and hostile to the "so-called avant-garde."[55]

The next thirty years would witness changes more radical than even a poet could imagine.

2

Who Was Published and When

Not only the study's seventy-four prizewinning poets but also their 129 nonprizewinning peers belong by definition to a poetry elite of writers who have managed to accumulate substantial periodical publishing records and bring out at least one book. While an informed guess is that at least one thousand American poets constitute this substantial elite, there must be thousands more attempting to publish with less or no success. What, then, can be told about those who do break into print repeatedly, and how do those of great reputation vary from those less known?

In the first place, published poets are distinguished by the possession of poetic gifts or at least inclinations. This must have a profound effect on how their time is spent and is sometimes imagined to imply certain personality characteristics. There are, for example, popular stereotypes of the poet as social pariah, effete versifier, sheltered academician, romantic adventurer, tortured youth, or daring defier of middle-class mores. To discover, albeit in superficial terms, whom we are discussing when we speak of the poet, biographical data sheets registering year of birth, state of residence, education, and occupation were compiled for each poet and reviewed by those who cooperated in the study. In addition, several survey questions were written to gain information about the poets' writing lives.

Through these varied data can be drawn the broad outlines of poets' most characteristic personal circumstances and writing and publishing histories during the three decades examined.

THE QUESTION OF BIAS

How these histories are affected by certain personal characteristics—especially sex, race, region, and sexual preference—has been the subject of much discussion. While many poets, editors, and readers hold strong opinions about this, sometimes amounting to absolute convictions that indefensible biases exist, solid evidence of widespread discrimination against any group is not available. This does not mean that such discrimination does not occur, but any effort to prove that it does would be fraught with problems. Not only is quality of submissions impossible to determine objectively, but there is no way of obtaining an accurate, complete description of the population of poet-submitters. Still, both the reality and the perception of discrimination against specific groups could have an impact on where and whether work created by members of those groups would be submitted and published.

Although no firm evidence perfectly shed of confounding variables could be amassed, those poets belonging to groups that have been said to suffer from editors' or publishers' biases were asked whether they considered themselves to have been the subjects of (positive or negative) discrimination and whether they made submission decisions accordingly. Also, contributor counts were carried out for a few key periodicals in order to shed light on the question of bias and add brush strokes to a picture of the publishing environment in which poets function. If it is true that people tend to feel most appreciated, or at least most likely to be understood, in situations where other people of their sex and race are sharply visible, then it is a somewhat poignant picture for women and minorities. They may quite easily conclude that bias exists and perhaps become reluctant to submit work to many of the better-known journals.

Sex

That women have more difficulty winning awards and finding publishers and that this was even more true before the advent of the contemporary feminist movement and women's presses have often been suggested. Several women writers whose careers spanned much of the three decades have cited experiences that seem outlandish from a present perspective. For example, poet-publisher Daisy Aldan, who does not consider herself a feminist, once recalled that in the fifties, male editors and writers "spoke about 'women's poetry' as if it had a special sentimental romantic quality. . . . An editor once said to me, 'If I didn't know that you, a woman, had written these poems, I would like your work.' And once an editor wrote me, 'Your poems are dynamic, colorful, exciting, but too strong for a woman.' "[1]

Three of the four responding women poets in the Older Prizewinning group—Ruth Stone, Maxine Kumin, and Mona Van Duyn—spoke of sex prejudice experienced early in their careers. Kumin elaborated: "Until the Women's Movement, it was commonplace to be told by an editor that he'd like to publish more of my poems, but he'd already published one by a woman that month . . . this attitude was the rule, rather than the exception, until the mid–60s. It was just generally harder to gain credibility as a woman. Highest compliment was to be told: 'You write like a man.' " In a published interview, a fifth OP-group woman, Adrienne Rich, described contemporary sexual bias among literary editors and publishers.[2] We cannot know how common such experiences and opinions were or are. However, the fact that they existed and were discussed publicly even by respected, long-experienced, and relatively successful women poets at least admits the possibility of past sex bias. Equally important, they evince a publicized *perceived* reality that, real or not—and if real, significant or not—may bear on what other women poets believed and did with regard to writing and publishing.

In her questionnaire response, Mona Van Duyn added that women had been and still were less likely than men to be anthologized. Anthologies are important in teaching literature and thus in the development of new audiences for poets. It is not surprising that their editors' openness to all types of writing should be monitored and any appearance of sexual exclusiveness bitterly resented. Poets as diverse as Marjorie Fletcher, a young feminist activist,[3] and the long-established, relatively apolitical May Swenson,[4] who was included in the present study, commented for print on the disproportionately small numbers of women selected for general anthologies, a point borne out by contributor counts of both trade-press and small-press American poetry anthologies purporting to be sex-general in coverage—that is, not expressly emphasizing one sex over the other.[5] Most of these show men as sole or senior editors.

The dominance of male editors may lead to unfair neglect of women's work, but whether or not this is so, it may entail a *perception* that such neglect is likely, generating reactions from women and resulting in printed products similar to those that would follow actual neglect. This observation is even more clearly pertinent to literary magazines, which use new submitted work, than to literary anthologies of reprints.

Women poets frequently allege that these magazines allot scant space to women. The most resentment about this is directed, quite naturally, against those periodicals perceived as most prestigious, though the problem is seen as not being limited to them. Since periodical publication almost always precedes book publication and is a poet's primary means of gaining visibility initially and establishing contacts in the literary world, the criteria employed by periodical editors is a matter of keen interest to poets. In the 1970s dozens of writers of both sexes joined in protesting the domination by white males of *The American Poetry Review,* a widely read, influential bimonthly that had received substantial amounts of public money and, as shall be seen, was very highly valued by poets in this study.

Marie Harris and Isabel Glaser were among several of this study's women poets who noted the predominance of men in journals, although, Glaser observed, "In schools and poetry organizations, females who write well have always seemed to me at least as numerous as comparable males." Although this cannot be confirmed, it *is* possible to determine the sexes of editors and contributors in the types of prestigious journal thought to promote poetic careers and to trace any changes over time. Nine respected periodicals were analyzed in this way, all founded in the early 1950s or before.[6]

Men completely dominated poetry editing responsibilities at the selected independent and general-interest magazines, a fact the more striking when one understands that, in titles of the latter type, none of the poetry editors is a founding editor; all were deliberately *hired* for their prestigious posts. Only among academic titles were any female editors found, and only a single periodical—Stephens College's *Open Places,* founded in 1966—had been edited by a woman (Eleanor Bender) throughout its existence. Because the number of female editors was so small, no firm statements can be made. However, there was an overall tendency for proportions of women poets included in these journals to decline slightly from the early 1950s to the early 1970s, then rise in somewhat greater degree over the following decade. Nonetheless, numbers of women contributors relative to men had always been low: well below half and usually less than 40 percent. The poetry in only two of the fifty-six volumes examined was authored *primarily* by women. Both were volumes of academic titles, published in the early 1980s and edited by women: *Prairie Schooner,* 1982, edited by Bernice Slote and comprising 51 percent women poets, and Bender's *Open Places,* 1982–83, with 65 percent women poets.

The results of a *Ploughshares* analysis were especially striking. A well-regarded independent literary journal, *Ploughshares* used a different guest editor for each issue. Eight issues from the early 1980s—four edited by men, four by women—were analyzed by sex of contributors. The women editors selected much higher proportions of women poetry contributors, and there was no overlap in proportions between male and female editors. That is, the man choosing the *largest* number of women proportionately (James Randall: 44 percent) still selected fewer than the woman who chose the *smallest* number of women proportionately (Lorrie Goldensohn: 47 percent). However, women editors did not demonstrate as much preference for their sex as men editors did for theirs. On average, the men published 71 percent men poets and the women published 55 percent women poets. The *most* female-dominated issue, edited by Joyce Peseroff, included 68 percent women poets, while the most male-dominated issue, Seamus Heaney's, included 93 percent men. Following this was Alan Williamson's issue (75 percent male) and Donald Hall's (72 percent male). Only Randall's issue had a smaller proportion of men than Peseroff's did of women. This analysis certainly raises questions about sex bias, but, because of other factors that may affect selection, cannot serve as a basis for hard conclusions. For example, editors of forthcoming issues were announced by *Ploughshares* in advance; possibly women poets were more likely to submit to a female than a male editor, thus providing the women editors with a differently composed submissions pool. Also, of course, what is *generally* true cannot be universally particularized. For example, there was a difference of only three percentage points in the proportions of women contributors selected by Lorrie Goldensohn and James Randall.

The point to be made here, and discussion of many figures may have obscured it, is not that men are obliged to establish sexual quotas or alter their poetic preferences, but that a situation existed, and was perceived to exist, where many of the best-established, most prestigious anthologies and journals of all types were edited by men and published many more male than female poets. A strikingly male literary environment presented itself to girls studying poetry in school and women poets seeking exposure for their work. This could be discouraging or embittering and it may *actually* have reflected, and may very well have been *thought* to reflect, extra-literary bias built on sex. During the 1970s, it gave rise to a discrete, feminist-oriented (though not necessarily overtly political), literary publishing sector.

Some women took the more radical viewpoint that sex discrimination works subtly from childhood to defeat creative motivation and ambition, and that this, not outright editorial bias, is its most powerful manifestation. Said Karen McKinnon, a poet in this study who began writing at the late age of thirty-three, "The only woman poet we ever read or studied was Emily Dickinson. . . . we read no women in prose either, with the exception of Jane Austen. . . . I just assumed I couldn't be a writer because I was female." (This recalls the point just made regarding sex composition of the authorship of classroom anthologies.) On the other hand, McKinnon was given violin and ballet lessons that would have been denied her as a boy and helped develop a "love of rhythm, cadence," which she carried into her poetry. Anne Hazlewood-Brady spoke likewise of having to "*unlearn* much of [her] education," and noted that women writers must "juggle" peculiarly conflicting demands or choose solitude, because "friends and relatives rarely understand." Naomi Clark echoed this last complaint: "Perceiving myself through others' ideas of what it means to be a woman has made it difficult for me to achieve the necessary commitment."

On a concrete level, the lives of women who do *not* "choose solitude" typically allow little time or privacy for meditation and creative work. This is more true than ever in an age of gainfully employed women and single-parent families, that parent most often being the mother despite a trend toward paternal and shared custody. Only three women in this study did not work for money (and one of these was over eighty), relying instead on spousal income. Most of the others, like most men, were juggling jobs and writing and seemed also to take primary responsibility for care of their homes and dependent children. While many of the men undoubtedly devoted time to family and domestic chores, only three mentioned such constraints, and none of them noted these responsibilities as a significant problem. Indeed, no man linked barriers to writing with his sex, but a number of women did.

Barbara Harr, who was for many years an evangelical minister's wife, eventually found intolerable the tensions between the careful respectability required by that role and her need as a writer to explore freely whatever subjects gripped her attention. Another poet took an eleven-year "leave" from poetry while raising her family, occasionally sending out poems written years before in graduate school—and a middle-aged divorcee with a large family of grown children noted that when they return home for the holidays, "all I can [write] is . . . lists." Sandra McPherson, a well-known poet in the Newer Prizewinning group and wife (since divorced) of another poet, Henry Carlile, explained that the demands of parenthood, poetry, and paid work combined to form fourteen-hour workdays. "[Poets] need babysitters!" she exclaimed.

Aware of these conflicts and discouraged by what she had read of the lives of women poets, Jane Shore told an interviewer that she once decided she would have to choose between poetry and motherhood, but had since met "women writers who have jobs and children and survive . . . it works itself out in a life and although you never have all . . . you can have *parts* . . . which is not a terrible trauma if you're a writer, for that struggle may feed the writing."[7] Struggle may "feed" poetry's richness, but is likely to reduce volume and may in some instances discourage women from writing at all. The special pressures of women's lives must be taken into account when assessing the openness of editors and publishers. It cannot be assumed that in a fair literary environment women would appear in print in the same proportions as they appear in the population.

Some observers believe that if bias existed, it was directed more at subject matter than at all the work by any individual or by all women. "There is still the feeling," said Erica Jong to a *New York Quarterly* interviewer, "that women's writing is a lesser class of writing, that . . . what goes on in the nursery or the bedroom is not as important as what goes on in the battlefield . . . that what women know about is a lesser category of knowledge."[8] Maxine Kumin once said that "Women are not supposed to have uteruses, especially in poems," and noted in response to this study's questionnaire that one simply did not send "childbirth poems" to *The New Yorker*.[9] A number of other people have cited cases of men's resistance to subjects drawn from typically female experience. Although one might expect this from editors of magazines aimed primarily at readers of one sex, customary rejection of themes related to women's experience is much harder to defend in periodicals designed for sex-general audiences. It is especially problematic in noncommercial journals of this type, which certainly draw both male and female readers, are subscribed to primarily by institutions, are by policy not for profit, are usually committed to publishing simply "the best," and, in the late 1960s through the early 1980s, very often were kept alive, or at least strong, with public money.

Some women, while not encountering open hostility, had found women editors more receptive to writing from an explicitly female perspective and so tended to concentrate their submissions on women-staffed publishing ventures. Elaine Starkman and toi derricotte both mentioned doing so, and a Newer Prizewinner who had published widely noted the difficulty of proving reasons for rejection: "I suspect the 'slicks'—*New Yorker, Atlantic*—or maybe just Howard Moss [since deceased] of the *New Yorker*, of feeling 'above' my writings and of not understanding my woman's point of view. I have no evidence of this."

Because all writers yearn to be read, women's subjects may be lost through not only editorial indifference but self-censorship. Certainly this was true in the past, when poems dealing frankly with some aspects of women's existence were rarely printed. A perusal of virtually any serious literary journal published before 1970 and of most published later discloses few or no poems focused, for example, on childbirth, motherhood, or on relationships between women, family members, friends, or lovers. Adrienne Rich began publishing extensively in the 1950s and once recalled that in early career, when her children were young, she wrote her motherhood experiences into private journals rather than poems "because by the male standards which were all I knew, motherhood was not a 'major theme' for poetry."[10]

The contemporary women's rights movement that began in the late 1960s insisted on the legitimacy of women's experiences as themes for art. Interestingly, most prominent feminist activists were writers, many of them poets, a fact that led author Jan Clausen to label the women's rights cause "a movement of poets."[11] Women poets, including Ruth Stone, Nona Nimnicht, Karen Snow, and others in this study, have cited feminism as the force that set their writing free and permitted full artistic development. The validation offered by feminism sparked an explosion of writing on formerly unacceptable topics, as well as strident criticism of the attitudes and enterprises that had branded them unacceptable. Results included defensiveness as well as conscious accommodation on the part of those criticized and the proliferation of publishing ventures run by and for women.

As the feminist press developed and aged, and its diverse practitioners wrestled with intra-movement ideological differences and tried to resolve tensions between art and politics, it at times imposed its own restrictions and revealed hardened attitudes leading to attacks from the women it claimed to serve. Tess Gallagher, now a highly praised poet, explained that in the movement's early days, she was negatively affected: "The mood was highly inflammatory—*for* very 'hot' feminist writing. . . . My book was turned down because I was not woman enough for the times." Karen Snow pointed out that, ironically, her narrative poetry had sometimes met with resistance from feminist editors because her lesbian characters were considered too stereotypical, hence not politically "correct."

In the mid–1970s some radical feminists argued that publishing with the women-controlled press was not so much an option as a political obligation. Given the relatively meagre resources of this publishing community, and the fact that, having proven their commercial viability, many women writers were being courted by trade presses, this position drew more fire than adherents.[12] Although women in the present study at every level of renown had published through women-only endeavors, only two said that they screened potential publication sources according to sex-related factors: Ellen Marie Bissert, who rarely sent work to a male editor, probably because she feared that her characteristically lesbian subject matter would trigger automatic rejection; and one older poet, who scanned journal contents pages to see whether at least half the contributors were women.[13] Still, the idea that women writers must be loyal to women's presses lived on in various guises, and some writers built and maintained reputations among almost solely female audiences. "I'm distressed by the 'ghetto' aspect of feminist publishing," wrote *13th Moon*'s editor (since resigned), the widely published poet Marilyn Hacker. "There are [writers] very well-known within those boundaries, unpublished outside—often, I think, because they don't submit their work elsewhere. I don't find this salubrious for writers *or* audiences."

Given the often-expressed reservations about women's chances to publish and be recognized, the poets in this study were analyzed by sex. Of the 203, sixty-six, or 32.5 percent, are women. Proportions range from a low of 21 percent among Older Prizewinners, the most prestigious group, to a high of 39 percent among Newer Nonprizewinners, perhaps the least prestigious group overall. The smallest percentages of women are found in the older groups, the largest percentages in the newer, but only among Newer Nonprizewinners are as many as one-third women. These figures suggest that younger women were writing for publication more and/or finding editors more receptive than did women who began seeking print in the 1940s and 1950s. But they suggest also that both older and younger women were less likely than men to receive major prizes, although this discrepancy may have been diminishing.

Appended to each woman's survey form was the following question: "As far as you *know* or *believe*, has being a woman ever affected—positively or negatively, directly or indirectly—your ability to publish your poetry?" Only among Older Nonprizewinners were there no complaints of discriminatory treatment. In all other groups the percentage of women claiming to have experienced at least some negative effects was half or more. Two women with sexually ambiguous names, Siv Cedering and Bennie Lee Sinclair, mentioned that they established publishing histories before editors realized they were women. In the sixties, when she first began submitting poetry, Sinclair was told by "several editors" that "they might not have accepted my work if they'd known I was female." A few additional respondents who believed they had suffered because of their sex quoted overtly sexist editorial remarks, but most simply noted domination of anthology and journal space by men or spoke vaguely of the inevitable influence of the larger sexist society. Some pointed out the virtual male monopoly on influential editorships. One thing that must be taken into account is the effect of post-sixties feminist analyses on individual women's interpretations of their own experience. As we have seen and shall see again, rejection is a fact of most poets' lives, at least in early career and often forever. Reasons for this are many and usually not objectively determinable, leading poets to cast about for likely causes.

Women considering their sex an advantage cited special opportunities afforded by women-only anthologies, journals, and presses. However, exclusively women's enterprises were insignificant overall and emerged as important for only a small handful of individuals when publishing data were compiled. Also mentioned was the timeliness of female concerns in the seventies, leading in some quarters to an almost faddish pursuit of women writers.

The evidence is soft, but does not allow us to discount the possibility that there were some special hurdles for women poets. That less than half the women in this study were conscious of having had to surmount these and that 21 percent actually had found their sex advantageous suggest that the hurdles, deplorable though their existence may have been, were usually rather low and likely not insuperable barriers to the talented and determined woman.

Race

Minority race, like female sex, is frequently cited as an obstacle to publishing. Because white males generally fill the editorial chairs at all but special-interest journals and publishing houses, minorities, like women, must often send work to editors who are unfamiliar with their subject matter, attitudes, and perhaps even their poetic style and language or dialect.[14] Again, then, if bias exists, it is hard to say whether it is directed against the author as a person or the poetry's content. A striking example of possible race bias against the person, not the work, was provided by Jitu Tambuzi, né Richard Byrd, who had sent out the same poems under his chosen African name first, then under his birth name, and found acceptance only as "Byrd." Like Maxine Kumin, who was complimented for "writing like a man," Tambuzi had been told that "most of my poems read 'white' when editors learn I'm Black."

Black poets Gwendolyn Brooks and Dudley Randall have noted the complete absence of minorities from most classroom poetry anthologies, including those from which they themselves tried to learn and teach. In 1984, Randall, founding president of Detroit's Broadside Press, told an interviewer that after the 1960s' fad interest in black writing had dissipated, publishing opportunities for black men declined, though the feminist movement fuelled demand for black women's work.[15]

Members of racial minorities, like women, have when necessary satisfied their desires to publish and edit by founding literary journals and publishing companies. Some have been devoted exclusively to the work of a particular group, with Broadside an outstanding example, but others simply have been determinedly multi-cultural, not necessarily excluding the work of whites: for example, black poet Quincy Troupe's *American Rag; Black Box,* a poetry "journal" on tape cassette coedited by two men, one black and one white; and *A,* published in New Mexico and favoring Native Americans. Another small group of editors and publishers has offered special encouragement to prisoner-poets, many of whom belong to racial minorities. Prominent examples are Native American Joseph Bruchac's Greenfield Review Press, publisher of some of the minority and prisoner poets in this study; Cardinal Press, operated by Mary McAnally, ex-wife of the poet and former prisoner Etheridge Knight; and *Gravida,* a literary journal coedited by the married poets Lynne Savitt and Gary Allan Kizer, who was serving a life sentence when he participated in this study. Savitt's second book of autobiographical poetry, published by Cardinal and entitled *No Apologies,* was dedicated to Kizer and revolves around her experiences as a lifer's wife.

The number of minority poets in the present study is unfortunately so small that little useful information about them can be gleaned, save the interesting fact of their meagre numbers. Only fifteen poets, or 7 percent of all those studied, were identifiable as minority, and it is unlikely that any were misidentified as white. Eight of the fifteen are black; the others are black/Asian-American (1); Asian-American (2); Hispanic-American (2); or Native American (2). The largest proportion of minorities is found among Newer Nonprizewinners (twelve, or 11 percent), followed by Newer Prizewinners (three, or 7 percent); neither of the older groups includes any poet belonging to a racial or ethnic minority. Only seven of the fifteen minority poets completed questionnaires: three blacks; both of the Asian-Americans; one of the two Hispanic-Americans; and one of the two Native Americans.

Native American Minerva Allen had appeared only in Indian publications and seemed not to have submitted to others largely because of her aspiration to help "retain the Indian tradition, culture and history for the younger generations." One senses that she would have welcomed, but did not really seek, a cross-cultural audience. One black poet mentioned tokenism, and another, Primus St. John, wrote that while racism might conceivably have worked against him at some point, "I don't worry about it. If I can write good poems, I'll be able to publish them someday." Neither Asian-American poet considered race an issue in his publishing.

More minority people began writing and publishing poetry after 1960–70 than did earlier. Beyond that, however, little can be concluded about the publishing chances of nonwhite poets. Their disproportionately small numbers among published, and especially prizewinning, poets were puzzling. Blacks constitute 4.5 percent of the poets studied and less than 3 percent of the prizewinners. Even among younger poets, they comprise only 6 percent of the total and 4 percent of prizewinners. Yet in 1980, 11.7 percent of the United States population was black. Similarly, Hispanics are 1 percent of the poets studied, but were 6.4 percent of the population. Only Asians, who comprised 1.5 percent of the population in 1980, and Native Americans, who were .6 percent, are represented proportionally in the study. Editorial prejudice is a possibility, but other plausible reasons for these discrepancies can be hypothesized. As will be shown later in this chapter, virtually all the poets are college-educated, and a majority were connected professionally to higher education. Excepting Asian-Americans, the minorities mentioned were receiving less education, on average, than whites. Family values and needs may also be significant. Though demanding of time and energy, poetry brings little remuneration and may seem a frivolous, even indefensible, activity to minorities attempting to gain an economic foothold in a competitive society. Also, the literary arts may not be valued equally by all minority groups. There is also the possibility that for some, the usual requirement that work be written in English posed difficulties.

Sexual Preference

Because homosexuals have complained of editorial bias and developed their own publishing enterprises, an attempt was made to evaluate the effects of sexual preference on publishing options. A poet was designated "gay" or "lesbian" only when that seemed indisputably true through deliberate self-identification. Altogether, five poets of each sex, or almost 5 percent of those studied, could be termed openly gay or lesbian; the verse of only seven or eight actually reflected this characteristic, and of the seven completing questionnaires, only five used gay content regularly in their writing. Three of these, one woman and two men, said that they had faced theme-based rejection. Lesbian publication was touched on briefly in the preceding discussion of women poets, and indeed lesbians' publishing experiences are likely to be more analogous to women's generally (especially feminists') than to gay men's. This section, then, is limited to consideration of the gay male poet.

In 1976 Daniel Halpern's influential *American Poetry Anthology* (1975) was attacked by veteran gadfly Richard Kostelanetz for omitting experimental and gay poets.[16] "Conversation around the community of poets never ceases to tell of 'unpublished gay poems which are really XYZ's best stuff,' " declared Kostelanetz, "and this suggests that in the battle for unashamed, 'free' expression, there are still some distinct frontiers to be crossed." He named Ginsberg as one of two exceptions to the rule that gay sexuality is smothered out of print, yet in responding to this study, Ginsberg wrote that despite his celebrity, he remained unable to publish "some major work [with gay content] in major media (newspapers, mags, TV, radio)."[17] Given his enormous literary reputation and proven commercial strength, it seems surprising that he should have had trouble placing any of his work, regardless of its quality. By staying, until 1985, with Lawrence Ferlinghetti of City Lights Books, an iconoclastic small publisher who was also a personal friend, Ginsberg insulated himself to some extent against mainstream mores and commercial exigencies.

Like women and ethnic minorities, gays have since the 1960s been founding their own publishing outlets, whether in response to prejudice or the simple desire to impose their editorial tastes on contemporary literature. Echoing women's responses to sex-related questions, Allen Ginsberg noted the benefit of his sexual preference in opening such markets to him although it simultaneously closed others, those others being both more visible and more lucrative. Lyle Glazier, an emphatically gay writer as well as a widower who was heterosexually married for several decades, paralleled the plaints of feminist poets like Ellen Marie Bissert and Karen Snow, who had found feminist editors ideologically rigid: "Gay editors of gay magazines can be terribly touchy about any taint of bisexuality unless it resolves into exclusive homosexuality," wrote Glazier. He emphasized, however, that he also considered many straight enterprises intolerant: for example, "I read gay poems for an audition for [the Vermont Council on the Arts'] Touring Artist series. I was rejected at the first audition but accepted after a year when I did not include any gay poems for the second audition."

Casual perusal of general literary journals turned up almost no openly gay/lesbian content, but a number of authors known to be gay, though not detectable as such through the poems published, did appear. Almost certainly, theme rather than personality was the key to most of the editorial biases that existed. This is borne out by Glazier's audition anecdote and by the responses of two frankly gay poets, both experimentalists, who rarely wrote of homosexual experience and had perceived little prejudice. "I have not much sought gay-identified publication as such," explained one. He added, however, that while "gay material hasn't ever been explicitly discouraged by any colleagues whom I respect," it was not received enthusiastically by heterosexual men.

Gay and lesbian poets who were publishing seemed able to continue, albeit with some setbacks—yet the ranks of the openly gay were rather small given the usual estimation that between 5 and 15 percent of the total population is primarily homosexual. Deliberate "closeting" may have been a factor, as may unwilled closeting caused by editorial rejection of only the gay portion of a person's work.

As was the case with women's and minority enterprises, gay journals and presses turned up only occasionally, being seldom seen even in the bibliographic data of assertively gay and lesbian poets. This could simply reflect the paucity and limited capacity of special-interest publishing outfits, or it may indicate that although they served a purpose, they either were not essential to the exposure of most women and minority poets or were important mainly as publishers of work that was directly subject-linked to sex or minority status.

Region

In the past observers guessed that editors and grant-givers might favor city dwellers, easterners, or, more specifically, New Yorkers. From the 1950s through 1980, publishing ventures sprouted from coast to coast, generated by technological advances permitting cheap typesetting and printing; availability of government grants for small journals and presses; and the growth of higher education and the attendant need for journals to enhance institutional visibility and publish the swollen numbers of job-seeking graduate students and tenure-striving faculty. Thus plaints of regional bias became rarer but were still voiced at times, especially with regard to publication by trade presses and mass magazines.

The states of residence of all but one poet in this study were discoverable. In 1982–84, when the data were compiled, they were scattered over thirty-eight states and the District of Columbia, but the largest number lived in New York State (22.5 percent; 10 percent in New York City alone); California (15 percent); and Massachusetts (10 percent). Interestingly, the small and relatively rural state of Maine ranked fourth, with nine poets, or 4 percent of the total. Each of the other thirty-four states and D.C. housed one to seven of the poets.

Nearly half of the Older Prizewinners were residing in New York State, a fifth in New York City alone, while their younger counterparts were much more widely dispersed. No more than five NPs, or 11 percent of the group, lived in any one state. In fact, the only other disproportionate concentrations by state were among Older Nonprizewinners, five (21 percent) of whom lived in New York State, and Newer Nonprizewinners, with twenty-four (22 percent) in New York and twenty-two (21 percent) in California.

When states are compressed into regional categories, northeastern prominence becomes clearer. More than half of all poets lived in the Northeast, but this tendency was much stronger among the older groups, approximately 70 percent of whose members were northeasterners, as compared with 39 percent of NPs and 46 percent of NNs. Nonprizewinners of both age groups were more likely than awardees to live in the Northeast, which undercuts any suggestion that contest-judging arrangements and commercial and academic editorial practices were giving short shrift to writers outside the tight arc of trade-press influence. On the other hand, the poets' regional distribution suggests that northeastern (and, perhaps, West Coast) residence may have helped them get published *at all.* (What is not known, of course, is where the poets grew up and where they lived when launching their writing careers.) It could also be that the large amount of publishing activity in the Northeast and the access it offers to other writers fuels writing ambitions among its residents. Alternatively (or in addition), the area may draw aspiring writers who hope to be benefited by proximity to publishing houses, fellow writers, poetry readings, and like events.

As we shall see, those writers who had succeeded in building reputations were likely to be offered teaching positions by one or more of a number of colleges and universities that value the presence of published poets on their faculties. A handful of these institutions is in New York, but others are scattered across the United States. Thus, while lesser-known writers may have congregated in certain geographic areas, in the

1960s and 1970s, success probably had the effect of dispersing them somewhat.

OTHER PERSONAL CHARACTERISTICS

Age

Fifty-four years of age separate the oldest poet, Dorothy Lee Richardson, born in 1900, from Zack Rogow, the youngest. Despite this great range, the Keatsian image of precocious brilliance and early fame was nowhere reflected. In 1981 no poet studied was under twenty-seven. For both groups of older poets, median birth year falls in the mid–1920s; poets in both newer groups show median birth years at the start of the 1940s.

A peculiarity is evident in Older Prizewinners' age distribution. In other groups age is spread rather evenly, with no single five-year period accounting for more than 28 percent of birth years and no single decade for more than half. However, in this group of most renowned writers, there is a remarkable generational concentration, with 83 percent born in the years 1921–30, inclusive. This could reflect important generational connections, with friendships and contacts based partly on age, college class, and so on, facilitating the development of reputation and, eventually and perhaps very indirectly, the winning of awards.

Education

The poets studied are most strikingly similar in their educational backgrounds. Of the 175 poets for whom this information was available (86 percent of the total), only six (3 percent) had never attended college. Another 6 percent attended but did not graduate, and two, or another 1 percent, held only two-year associate degrees. A remarkable 90 percent had at least the baccalaureate; 72 percent had master's degrees; and 23 percent had Ph.D.s. The image of the romantic, impractical autodidact, writing poetry against the grain of his background in the tradition of Hart Crane and, more recently, Charles Bukowski, is reflected in this study only by the extraordinary "beat" poet Gregory Corso.

An interesting note is the markedly stronger tendency of Older Nonprizewinners to hold a doctorate. Forty-eight percent of them do, as compared with 34 percent of Newer Prizewinners, 15 percent of Newer Nonprizewinners, and only 11.5 percent of Older Prizewinners. Since they had persisted in writing poetry for almost forty years, on average, they had demonstrated dedication to the art and would value employment that afforded time to write and read and awarded recognition based on publishing: namely, college or university teaching. Faculty appointments could be won by prestigious prizewinners who lacked a Ph.D., and this had perhaps been even more common some years earlier; examples included the nondoctorate-holding academicians John Ashbery (Brooklyn College), Galway Kinnell (New York University), and James Dickey (University of South Carolina). For less famous writers a doctorate was probably more important or even necessary.

It is interesting that the poet group most prestigious by far (the OPs) was also the least likely, by a notable margin, to have earned graduate degrees, especially the Ph.D. On the other hand, Newer Prizewinners may be termed the best educated group overall. All were four-year college graduates, and 90 percent had master's degrees.

Claiming the highest proportion of graduate-degree-holding alumni was the University of Iowa, home of the oldest and most famous creative writing program in America. Of the forty poets holding Ph.D.s, six (15 percent) earned them at Iowa. Seventeen of the thirty-five M.F.A.s, or 49 percent, were also conferred by Iowa, and two of the M.A.s. Younger poets were much more likely than their seniors to have earned M.F.A. degrees, NPs and NNs accounting for thirty-two, or 91 percent of them, with the remaining three held by OPs. Among younger poets as well as older, prizewinners were more likely to have a degree than nonprizewinners. M.F.A.-holding prizewinners were also far more likely than nonwinners with the same degree to have acquired it at the University of Iowa. Of eighteen M.F.A.s held by prizewinning poets, thirteen (72 percent) were awarded by Iowa; only four (23.5 percent) of the nonprizewinners' M.F.A.s were Iowa degrees. While the Iowa experience may have been variously profitable—through the craftsmanship and professionalism it taught, as well as the prestige and connections it afforded—its power should not be overstated. Only ten of the last several years' M.F.A. graduates showed up in the Newer Prizewinners' group, and only 22 percent of the entire NP group had ever worked for any degree at Iowa. Also, it seems clear that the proliferation of highly enrolled creative writing programs in the 1970s caused an oversupply of M.F.A.s, leading to a loss of status and marketability for poets holding this degree, including Iowa alumni.

Employment

As is consistent with their academic credentials, 87.5 percent of the 184 poets for whom occupational data could be found were employed as professionals (including those in business). The great majority of these—82 percent (or 71.5 percent of the total 184)—were dependent on the educational system. Forty-nine percent of the poets occupied regular academic faculty positions. Altogether, 70 percent were teachers at some level, almost invariably of writing or literature. The nonprofessional 6 percent were semi- or unskilled laborers, unemployed, office workers, prison inmates, or a fulltime housewife (only one woman). Just twelve people (6 percent) were fulltime authors and only two-thirds of these fulltime poets, the other four devoting more of their time to prose.

Fitting a fantasied ideal of selfless poetic dedication, but extremely unusual in reality, was the handful of poets who found ways to survive—perhaps marginally by usual standards—without taking conventional jobs that consume writing time and energy. Exemplifying this ideal were two Older Nonprizewinning poets: John Stevens Wade, a poet-translator with a long writing history, and Theodore Enslin, who had published forty-six poetry books, more than any other person in the study. Wade was digging for diamonds in Arkansas when first contacted (after much difficulty), and wrote that he would soon be off to prospect for gold in the West. Enslin, on the other hand, was firmly rooted in Maine, but managed to survive without regular employment, raising his own food and devoting his full intellectual energy to poetry: "I am responsible to nothing but the art itself," he wrote.

Another popular stereotype, until this century common in reality, is that of the moneyed poet whose inheritance, family allowance, patron, or spouse permits leisure for unpressured creativity. Of respondents to this study, only one had been favored with an inheritance that made work for pay unnecessary. At least three others had been saved by working spouses from the need to be self-supporting, though not from homemaking and parenting tasks. Actually, only one had refrained entirely from paid work.

Given that more than 90 percent of the poets were gainfully employed at work other than writing, and that, excepting the Older Prizewinners, three-quarters or more of their income was generated by activities not related to writing,[18] their responses to the following question were unexpected: "What do you regard as your *primary* occupation? That is, if you were asked what you 'do' and could give only one answer, what would you say?" Almost 55 percent of the 143 respondents identified themselves as solely "writer" (29 percent) or "poet" (26 percent). When compared with the tiny percentages of poets writing full time, these responses are startling (Figure 2.1). Another 8.5 percent insisted on claiming two "primary" occupations and listed a paid job in addition to "writer" (5 percent) or "poet" (3.5 percent). Prestige seemed to be a factor only in the case of the clearly best established, most prestigious group (and the group best-remunerated for poetry writing): the Older Prizewinners. Ninety-three percent (fourteen) of the respondents in this category called themselves "writer" or "poet," compared with insubstantially different proportions of Newer Prizewinners (60 percent), Newer Nonprizewinners (55 percent), and Older Nonprizewinners (62.5 percent).

Figure 2.1
Poets' Occupational Self-Identifications
(Mean percentages of poets self-identified as primarily "writer" or "poet" compared with mean percentages of those who were full-time writers.)

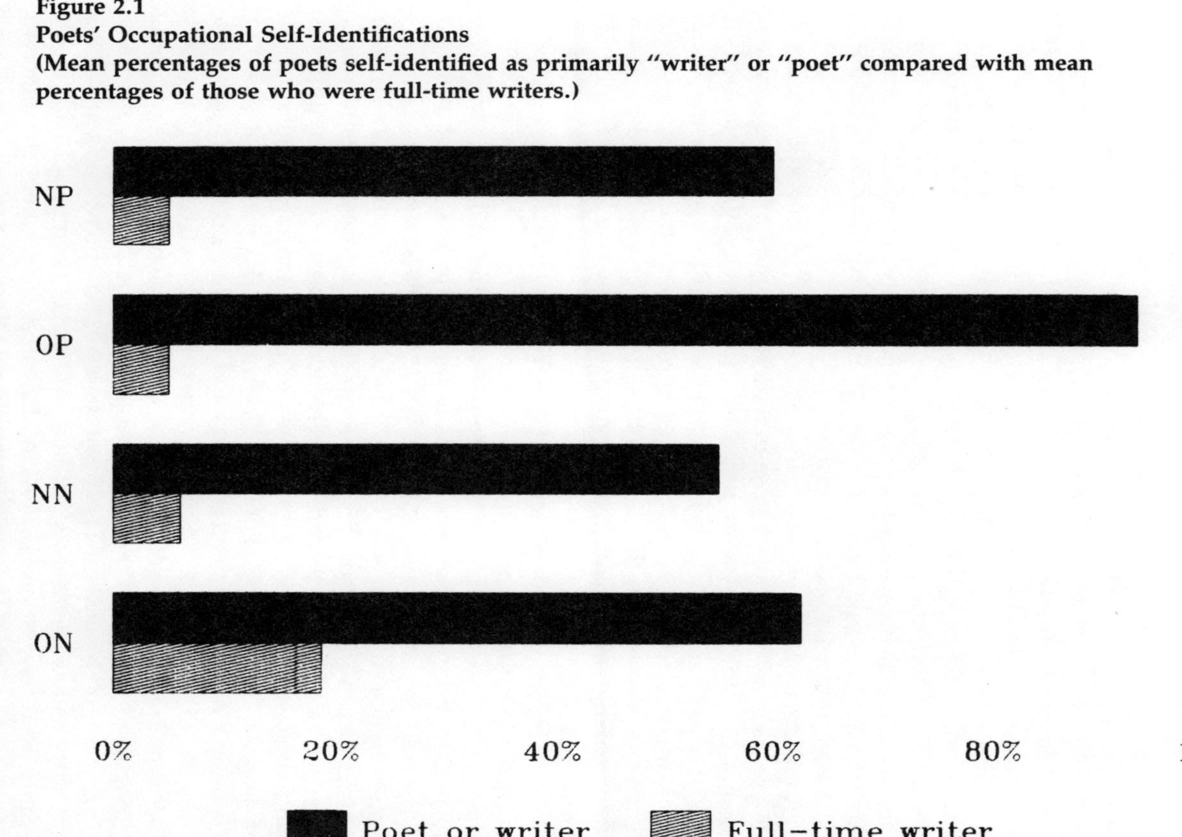

It may be conjectured that the study structured a writing-oriented response to this question because the subjects were approached *as poets*. On the other hand, the number of "writer" and "poet" answers may underrepresent respondents' true degree of identity as authors. Charles Martin explained: "When people ask what you do, they usually want to know how you earn your living. If you answer such a question with 'I'm a poet,' they will usually say something like, 'No, but what do you *really* do?' I usually tell people that I'm a teacher and a writer." This was borne out by answers such as Diana Ó Hehir's: "I suppose I would, because of the economic factor, say that I teach. But poetry is to me, my most important activity."

Another inhibition results from the nebulousness of the terms. Because one is not typically defined by employers as "poet" or even "writer," thus confirming in concrete public form the fact of it, and because "poet" carries with it twin associations of challenging figures of intimidating greatness on the one hand and mediocre amateurs on the other, some may find it hard to accept the label as suitable for them. The successful poet Richard Howard once told an interviewer that he had "always found that a hard thing to say—*I am a poet*. . . . I put 'translator' on my passport for years, but never 'poet' or 'writer'. . . . But I can do it now—I can deal with that amount of real panic when it is necessary to say 'I am a writer.' "[19]

For many poets the experiences of writing and publishing worked powerfully to mold identity. Rare indeed was William Stafford, a much-honored, extremely prolific poet of advanced years who maintained an oddly detached relationship to his writing. He explained in an interview: "In some ways . . . I can say I never have decided seriously to become a poet . . . poetry has been my involvement with the world of the arts. But I still feel that maybe, primarily, I'm something else. In my real self."[20] To another interviewer, he said: "I'm still a kind of dilettante as a writer. . . . My vocation is teaching; my avocation is writing."[21] (On his questionnaire Stafford identified himself as "writer," perhaps because he had recently retired from his professorship.)

It seems safe to say that at least 54.5 percent of respondents saw writing as their primary occupation, and another 8 percent as one of two such occupations. Although only 9.5 percent were without other jobs, not a single poet derived as much as half his income from poetry royalties and publication fees, and more than half the income of 78 percent came from sources entirely unrelated to their writing.[22] Since these sources are so often academy-based—a relatively new phenomenon for poets—and the vast majority of poets are college-educated, controversy has arisen over whether the influence of academia is salutary for poets themselves and for literature generally. Chapter 4 is devoted to discussing these issues.

THE WRITING LIFE

To find time, in conjunction with uncluttered mental space that allows free imagining and invention, is poets' greatest challenge and worst frustration. Since fulltime paying jobs are a necessity for almost all, writing is perforce a part-time activity even if a fulltime preoccupation and the cornerstone of a poet's identity. College faculty jobs, which typically allow flexible scheduling, alleviate the problem somewhat, but may burden the poet with piles of student papers to grade and dozens of aspiring student writers to advise in addition to teaching. Also, a succession of temporary appointments, common among writers, may offer modest pay without benefits and require frequent moves, which can be devastating to a poet's concentration and need for a sense of community. In any case, despite the academy's newfound generosity, it cannot accommodate all poets.

In a 1927 issue of *Poetry* magazine, Margery Mansfield identified scarcity of time as "the crux of [a poet's] artistic problem," and despite the support now allocated to poets through grants and teaching work, it remained so half a century later.[23] An occasional author admitted fighting inner battles to use even the time available for writing, which is among the most demanding and least externally disciplined of all tasks. Maxine Kumin, for example, once confessed in an interview,[24] and implied in her questionnaire, that she let physical chores distract her from more taxing creative work, and respondent Jack Barry said that for years, he was diverted from writing poetry to merely reading it, "something I am beginning to realize was costly indeed. . . . I have begun the task of simply writing again and . . . getting in touch with that part of me that should be most alive." While he was unusually candid, other poets' comments confirmed that it could be all too easy to let the poetry slip away, often at severe psychological cost. What seems an opposite situation, but can be the same one differently analyzed, is simply a superfluity of unavoidable chores that drive out the poetry or force it into corners of the workday.

The average proportion of working time devoted by the study's poets directly to writing poems was 22 percent, with an even lower median figure of 15 percent.[25] Newer Prizewinners claimed to spend 28 percent on average and both prizewinning groups about 20 percent. While Older Prizewinners' ability to attract grants might have been expected to free more of their time for writing, this was not the case—perhaps because their fame also garnered more requests to conduct readings and workshops, give interviews, and judge contests. Only 10 percent on average of OP poets' time was devoted to writing poetry, while their average time allocation to other poetry-related activities was 18 percent.[26]

Although on the average poets were spending about one-fifth of their working time writing poetry and arranging for its publication, 23 percent of them, including five prizewinners, spent less than one-tenth of their time this way, and nearly 75 percent one-quarter of their time or less. Only six of 136 respondents were spending more than half their working time directly on new poems and only one of these 100 percent. In contrast, just over half of the poets' time, on average, was absorbed by neither writing nor readings nor workshops nor dealing with editors and publishers but by other tasks, mostly regular paying jobs. Newer Prizewinners' mean percentage was slightly below the average, as would be expected, but the only significantly asymmetrical figure was the surprisingly high mean proportion of Older Prizewinners' time spent this way: 69 percent. Again, while literary distinction might boost income and morale, it did not have that effect on the responding poets' time for writing poetry.

The frustrations implied by these figures are well documented in the literature, as well as in comments added to study questionnaires. James Dickey, who completed his first two poetry books while building a successful career in advertising, later wrote vividly of the personal price these efforts exacted.[27] Even academicians often must relegate poetry writing to early mornings and evenings. For example, before retiring from his college faculty position, William Stafford said that he wrote every morning for an hour or so while his family was still asleep.[28] Reg Saner, Bin Ramke, and Jack Myers, among other professor-poets studied, also were concentrating their writing at odd hours of the day, and Charles Martin was committing "perhaps one day out of seven" to poetry, "but this day is of course broken up into tiny little slices stretched out over the week. . . . Much more time goes into being a husband and father and principal wage-earner of my domestic menage."

Special problems plague the rare poet who achieves some measure of celebrity and financial solvency through his writing. Perhaps the prime living American example of this most elusive circumstance is Allen Ginsberg. Though not subject to an employer's demands, Ginsberg was frazzled by the attentions of admirers, mail, phone calls, readings, meetings, constant public appearances, and travel. "I'm probably too much dispersed in time and energy," he told an interviewer in 1973. "I'd probably do better if I were in an ivory tower."[29] Several years later he was complaining of headaches induced by too much, too fragmented, work.[30] To his generously complete questionnaire he appended an apology: "Sorry I can't be more extensive—no time—1:30 AM." While it is true that much of Ginsberg's activity was extra-literary and could have been resisted if he had reordered his priorities, he received pay for some of these activities, and, more to the point, his high reading charges and book sales probably depended in large part on his flamboyant reputation, which was built and sustained as much through his counter-cultural visibility as his writing. For this study Ginsberg estimated that only about 10 percent of his time was devoted to writing poetry, another 20 percent to music (he often performs with blues musicians), with the remainder parcelled out to readings, paid and volunteer teaching, formal "meditation" (which he perceived as necessary to his work), and "who knows?" Only 14 percent of his income was derived directly from poetry writing in the form of royalties and fees, despite his status as a best seller among poets. Another 60 percent, however, was yielded by public readings.

Because poetry royalties alone could not command sufficient steady income, even when that poetry had the brilliance and shock value of a *Howl* or a *Kaddish*, virtually every serious poet had to find another money source. Except for those few who could write creatively within the terrible discipline of regular twelve-to-sixteen hour workdays, that source consumed voraciously the poet's best hours. Making time still more precious was the sheer amount of it required by creative work and the often devastating effect of interruption. Private time is needed for writing, but also for "waiting," which, Philip Levine has pointed out, is "as much a part of writing as anything"[31]: "You have to let [the muse] open the door and come into your brain, into your hand, wherever it comes. And I do a lot of that. . . . I do nothing. I've learned that you have to do nothing. You have to be silent and see if the voice will enter you."[32]

Others have emphasized the poet's obsessiveness. For example, several questionnaire respondents, among them Robert Pinsky and Theodore Enslin, explained that they "wrote" constantly, even while doing other things. For them and many of their colleagues, creativity was an ongoing process, inherent in existence, and could not be isolated into discrete blocks of time. "There are very few hours or even minutes in the day when I'm not turning over some poetic problem in my mind," James Dickey once wrote. "The poetic process . . . is something that simply goes on all the time, even when I'm sleeping. It never stops."[33] Although he usually held a job, and for several years a university teaching post, Dickey said many times in different ways that poetry had been "the central concern of my being and my character all my life."[34] The grip of poetry on the writer's psyche is often so compelling that other obligations, however time-consuming and essential to survival, are secondary.

Age at Which Poets Begin Writing

Many poets begin writing as children. William Stafford believes juvenile poesy is so widespread that the frequent interview query—"When did you start writing?"—makes no sense, as it assumes the activity to be exceptional. He wonders instead why most youngsters *stop* writing.[35]

Diana Ó Hehir once declared: "Almost every poet I have ever talked to has been a childhood versifier."[36]

In 1981 the "newer" poets studied had been writing "seriously" for five to thirty-two years, with a median of fifteen years for nonprizewinners and twenty for prizewinners. Both groups of older poets had been writing, on average, for nearly forty years. When average length of serious writing career is superimposed on average age, both older groups are shown to have begun in their very early twenties, both younger groups in their mid-twenties. However, the ranges are great and group differences insubstantial. If it is true that most of the poets had been versifying since childhood, the assignment of a starting point by "seriousness" may have been arbitrary. What does seem clear is that the average Newer Nonprizewinning poet began writing at a slightly later age than those in other groups. However, there were no important differences in length of time writing or age begun between poets with and without major awards.

While some poets, like Stafford, seemed to have started writing in response to an unexamined urge and never stopped, others recalled a specific event or circumstance that propelled them into poetry. Some wrote to escape isolated or unhappy childhoods, while some were inspired by parental encouragement. Others began after a wrenching change in environment caused, for example, by military service or prison confinement. Loneliness, an onslaught of new experiences, and (often) slack time characterize such changes and may combine to create opportunity and need for self-expression and the discovery of elusive meanings. The reading of poetry often inspired writing, as did any number of different types of individual event—as substantial and complex as a loved one's death or new romance, or as simple as the announcement of a poetry contest. William Hunt recalled an early experience of writing itself as the crucial event launching his serous efforts: "Just before my 21st birthday . . . I had a deeply affective experience writing something; I didn't until then know what a poem could be, how demanding it could be of the spirit, how fulfilling and how daring in the act of creating."

While there is evidence, then, that writing seldom has its genesis in early adulthood, that may be when it most often takes hold as a commitment, with, as we shall see, public recognition coming still later, after months or years of editorial rejections.

How Much Was Written

To assess volume of writing by counting poems written can tell only a limited amount: a single verse may be three lines or hundreds of pages long. Indeed, Aram Saroyan once attracted attention with a one-word poem, and Theodore Enslin is the author of a multi-volume verse. Still, the poem is the most convenient unit of measure, and poets studied were asked to estimate how many they had written. Several emphasized that their estimates were rough, and some said merely "innumerable," "many," "hundreds," "thousands," or in one case, "godzillions"; prolific poets may lose control of record keeping. Charles Martin listed additional obstacles to making accurate estimates: "Would the number include poems unfinished? Poems finished but later discarded? Poems forgotten about? Translations of poems?"

Despite such problems, 117 respondents, ninety-seven newer poets and twenty older ones, did essay a poem count. Numbers of poems ranged from fifty to 7,000 among the younger poets (with a prolific writer in the short haiku form giving the high number) and seventy to 2,000 among the older—an enormous variation reflected in great gaps between mean and median figures within all age groups save Older Nonprizewinners. Median number of both younger groups was 300, with means of 509 (NP) and 645 (NN). Only six Older Prizewinners offered an estimate, for a median of 650 poems, a mean of 1,520. Their nonprizewinning counterparts' median was a comparable 700, but their mean was much lower: 742. Because the very prolific poets had the most trouble formulating a response, these numbers are probably low.

To gain an idea of how many poems were written, by group, per year of "writing seriously," mean and median numbers of poems written were divided by corresponding numbers of years writing. Not only had nonprizewinners written for about as many years as prizewinners, but they had written at least as much. This challenges the commonsensical expectation that these two groups of generally less recognized poets would—as cause or effect of nonrecognition, or a combination—be less active as writers. "Hidden" explanations of intergroup similarity can be imagined. For example, prizewinners may indeed have written *more*, but revised more heavily, thus producing more finished and better poems. However, the evidence mentioned earlier, regarding percentage of working time devoted to poetry writing, argues against this. No notable differences in amount of time spent on poems or number of poems written could be discerned by group. The poets' quantifiable levels of commitment to their creative work were amazingly alike, especially considering the dramatic intergroup differences in worldly recognition achieved.

Whatever differences obtained among the groups with regard to publishing experiences and history, the explanation could not be found in how much or how long they had written.

PUBLISHING HISTORIES

Achieving First Publication

Except for those few poets so well established that they can publish virtually at will, writers must endure, year in, year out, the stress of having editors return their poems. Judith Steinbergh remarked poignantly that "it takes incredible detachment and perseverance not to lose confidence after so much rejection." Edward Field saw his first book, *Stand Up, Friend, With Me,* win the prestigious Lamont Poetry Prize in 1961 after having tried for years to find a publisher willing to handle it and being rejected by twenty-two houses: "I had come to accept failure," he wrote.[37] For self-protection against the pain of repeated early rebuffs, Galway Kinnell trained himself so well not to care, he told an interviewer, that when editors finally began to take his work, he couldn't enjoy the triumph: "If you accept that it doesn't matter when they don't, you have to accept that it doesn't matter when they do."[38]

Maturity, self-confidence, and emotional resilience were needed to cushion poets against these editorial blows, which were usually unexplained and unceremonious and occasionally flatly rude. "I kept sending poems in and I kept getting back these form rejections," James Dickey reminisced in an interview. "In 1948 or 1949 I remember with what wonder I saw a true human hand-writing on the rejection slip. It said, 'Not bad.' "[39]

Asked whether editorial rejections had preceded first acceptance, 130 poets responded, 63 percent of them in the affirmative. Since the struggle for first publication tends to be taken for granted as a required rite of passage for the poet, this figure is strikingly low.[40] When responses were analyzed along older and newer lines, however, the older poets' rate turned out to be considerably higher—78 percent in contrast to 60 percent for newer poets—perhaps because publishing outlets were fewer and self-publication less feasible in the 1940s and 1950s than in the following two decades, when most of the younger poets were first seeking print. Another factor may be the greater tendency of the newer poets to have attended formal creative writing classes, where, very likely, contacts were often acquired and advice about how to publish dispensed.

Of the eighty-two respondents who were unable to publish at once, twenty could not remember how many rejections preceded first acceptance. The sixty-two who could give a figure had received an average of twenty-three rejections, a median number of eighteen. Here, the differences between those who would become prizewinners and those who so far had not were very large: medians for Older and Newer Prizewinners were nine and ten, respectively, the medians for Older Nonprizewinners more than triple the OPs' and the median for Newer Nonprizewinners twice the NPs'.

Sixty-three poets could estimate the time span over which they had submitted work unsuccessfully. Median periods of time spent awaiting first acceptance were the same for future prizewinners: one year. Newer Nonprizewinners had waited two years and Older Nonprizewinners four years for first publication. Numbers ranged as high as 200 rejections over as many as fifteen years, and averages may be low because much-rejected poets may have been the least tenacious record keepers overall and may have had the most trouble recollecting facts years later.

Nonprizewinners' similarity to prizewinners in time spent writing and amount written contrasted, then, with their sharp difference in length of time spent seeking first publication and number of rejections received. At the commencement of their professional careers—before any prizes had been won, any public praise lavished—those who would one day claim major awards were already being distinguished from those who would not. The data cannot show whether differences in rejection experience were due to quality of the work submitted or causes unrelated to quality: for example, insensitive methods, on the poet's part, of choosing where to submit, or lack of connections. What *is* clear is that future prizewinners were distinguished from the very start as writers with comparatively strong potential for success. Their early histories of editorial rejection and acceptance were, simply, very different. So were their patterns of early publication.

Time of First Publication

For almost every poet who embarked on a serious literary career, the first published book was preceded by periodical appearances. The work of only five poets in this study, or 2 percent, appeared first in book form.

Generally speaking, those who would win major prizes began publishing younger. Only 11 percent of all the poets published in magazines while still teenagers. Of those few, 52 percent are in the two older groups, although these groups account for only 25.5 percent of the poets whose ages at first publication are known. Although the number of poetry periodicals in existence forty or fifty years ago was a small fraction of the number publishing in 1980, and although creative writing programs, which have been criticized for overemphasizing publication, were far less numerous, to publish in adolescence was more likely several decades ago than it was in the 1960s and 1970s. Twenty-three percent of Older Prizewinners and 22 percent of Older Nonprizewinners had publications to their credit before turning twenty, but only 5 percent of Newer Prizewinners and 8 percent of Newer Nonprizewinners. A possible explanation is the encouragement of college student writing by the post-fifties plethora of poet-professors; this may sometimes have engendered serious poetic interests in people who were already in their twenties or older. Before that time, there were surely fewer poets with professional intent, and their emergence may have depended more upon sheer internal drive, which might manifest itself very early in some people. Alternative, equally plausible interpretations abound. For instance, television, that convenient villain, may distract children from reading and writing and even impair the power of concentration, which is crucial to creative writing. So may the pressures of our more urbanized lives. On the other hand, post-World War II educational emphases may fall more heavily upon science, technology, and socially "relevant" literature at the expense of traditional literatures that might be more likely to awaken dormant poetic impulses.

It was even less common for the poets to have deferred publication until middle age. Only 10 percent were thirty-six or older at first publication, and only two poets, or 1 percent, were in their latter forties.

A poet's first book generally followed first magazine appearance by five to ten years. Poets in all but the Older Nonprizewinners' group tended to have ushered their first books into print sometime in their early thirties. Older Nonprizewinners' first books came out somewhat later, but usually before the poet's fortieth birthday. While no poet was older than fifty when the first magazine poem came out, eight people (4.5 percent), all nonprizewinners, waited this long to publish a book, and one was past sixty. In all, 35 percent of the poets were older than thirty-five when their first books were issued. Only one had published a book as a teenager and only another 11 percent while in their early twenties. The average gap between first appearances in periodical and book formats was nine to ten years for both older groups, seven to eight years for Newer Prizewinners, and five to six years for Newer Nonprizewinners, presumably because of this group's greater reliance on self-publication.

Amount of Publication

Poets vary greatly in their relative emphases on sheer amount of publication, quality of what is published, and proportion of what is published to what is written. While poet-respondents in each group had offered, on average, over half their work for publication (with a range by individual of from 7 to 100 percent), Newer Nonprizewinners were notably more reticent than others, sending out an average 54 percent of what they wrote (the median was 50 percent), as compared with 60 percent or more for all other groups. Unsurprisingly, those poets who had written longest were most satisfied with the quality of what they wrote (or else most resigned to its limitations) and most likely to seek its publication. However, prizewinners from both age groups were most successful in achieving print.

Asked how many of those poems offered to editors had actually been published, Older Prizewinners claimed the most success, with 85 percent published, Newer Nonprizewinners the least, with 64 percent published. Yet fifty-three individuals, or 44 percent of respondents, had found print for only half or less of the work they had submitted to journals and book presses. Even one Newer Prizewinner showed an acceptance rate as low as 14 percent. Generally speaking, however, the poets were remarkably successful in finding print *somewhere*, even if not always through the most desired sources. Interestingly, the modal rate for all four groups was 100 percent, and voluminous self-publication hiked one Older Nonprizewinner's rate to 375 percent! That is, by heavy use of self-publication he had brought out almost four times as many poems as he had ever submitted to editorial judgment. (His answer was not included in the calculations of mean and median.)

Once a poet had broken into print, then, subsequent publication seems to have been relatively easy. The very low acceptance rates of a few poets probably reflect unwillingness to appear through any but a narrowly selected group of outlets, a tendency to send out unfinished work, or lack of persistence. Still, there were no guarantees. One Older Prizewinner, who is among the most honored writers of our age, had placed only three-fifths of the poems he would have liked to see in print. Indeed, only four of the eleven OP respondents to this question had placed everything they had sent out.

All of the 203 poets' books that are eight pages or more long, came out before the end of 1981, and are not prose, translations, anthologies, or published outside North America, were included in publishing analyses. Total numbers of books per poet ranged from one to forty-six, Theodore Enslin being the most prolific. For all but the Older Prizewinners, average numbers of books published fell below five. Not all OPs published so heavily. One had only three books to her credit, one only four. However, it can be said that overall, poets in the Older Prizewinning group had published many more books than had their nonprizewinning counterparts, while Newer Prizewinners had published only slightly more than Newer Nonprizewinners. Very possibly a book-publishing gap between the more and less recognized poets widened as time elapsed and the former group accumulated honors and the attendant benefits. As we have seen, this study suggests that the differences cannot be attributed to such apparently likely factors as discrepancies in time spent writing and amount written.

Because private printers sometimes ask poets whom they admire if they may gather a few of their verses into a special limited edition, it seemed that Older Prizewinners' output might be inflated by small books comprising poems that appeared also in standard-sized volumes. Book lists were analyzed and citations grouped by size: eight to fifteen pages; sixteen to thirty-nine pages; and forty pages or more. While Older Prizewinners registered more very short books than did the others, these still amounted to an individual average of only one-half book, compared with one-fifth book for ONs and one-tenth book for both newer groups. Only thirty-seven authors (18 percent) had ever published a poetry book of eight to fifteen pages. Older Prizewinners and Nonprizewinners alike claimed an average per person of 2.4 books in the middle category (sixteen to thirty-nine pages), compared with less than one for both newer groups. The isolation of short books did help explain Theodore Enslin's amazingly long bibliography—only twenty-seven of his forty-six books contained forty pages or more, the others only sixteen to thirty-nine pages—but his productivity was still remarkable. (It is probably significant that Enslin was among the twelve poets writing fulltime).

No category of poet was especially prone to concentrate publication in pamphlets or special small editions, though both groups of prizewinners were slightly more likely to publish a few of these. However, when mean proportions of books published, by length, were compiled, the two groups of prizewinners were revealed to have nearly identical bibliographic patterns. Nonprizewinners had brought out slightly higher proportions of their books in shorter lengths, perhaps because they depended more heavily for publication on small presses, which often favor or even specialize in chapbooks.

SUMMARY

Who got published? What were the superficial, easily definable, aspects of the poet's life? Profiles can be drawn from what was learned about poets in this study, always remembering that the Older Nonprizewinning group is small and Older Prizewinners' level of questionnaire response even smaller. The profiles are, then, suggestive in outline, not definitive.

Bearing these limitations in mind, we can say that the image evinced by this study of the typical published poet in 1980 is a white college-educated man with at least one graduate degree. While published poets of any age and degree of fame were most likely to be white and male, women and minorities were found least often among older poets (that is, those who had published at least one book before 1966) and among winners of important poetry prizes.

Regardless of the strength of his reputation, the poet could not subsist on money reaped from his writing and held a professional job, probably teaching literature or creative writing in higher education. Only 20 percent of his working time could be devoted to writing unless he was a prestigious younger prizewinner, in which case he might spend closer to 30 percent writing. Despite the time consumed by other work, his primary self-identification was as "writer" or "poet." If he was twenty years or more past his first book publication, he probably resided in the Northeast; if he had a younger career, he was still more likely to live in the Northeast than in any other single region, but his location was much less predictable, as more than half of all newer poets lived elsewhere.

He was a childhood versifier but began writing seriously only in his twenties. Twenty to thirty editorial rejections over two and one-half years preceded his first poem acceptance, though if he eventually went on to win major awards, his number of early rejections was smaller. If he was an older poet who had never won a prize, he had probably had to persevere through four to six years of rejection slips before his first acceptance.

His work appeared in magazine format before he brought out a book, his first poem reaching print when he was in his twenties. However, if he was an older poet, with or without prize recognition, he was almost four times as likely to have published for the first time while still in his teens. Roughly seven to eight years after his print debut, his first poetry book had been published. The publication of poetry in the well-known and historically important chapbook and pamphlet formats had meant little to him, as most or all of his books were of more substantial length.

His ability to attract prestigious prizes had no impact on the time he devoted to his poetry or the amount that he wrote, although it did affect, from the very start of his career, his ability to win acceptances from magazine editors; as time passed, his volume of book publications was also affected. Yet if he persisted in writing and publishing any appreciable amount, he wrote on with deep seriousness and commitment, virtually regardless of his work's reception by award committees and prestigious publishers.

He was committed to his art although it was time-consuming, solitary, intellectually and emotionally demanding, and at best could offer him only minimal financial reward or fame, forcing him to toil at other work as well in order to earn his living. For there were few readers, thus little money.

How, then, in a profit-driven society, was poetry publication possible?

3

Where the Poets Published

> Poetry takes chances, without hope of immediate gain. Curiously, editing . . . partakes as much of chance-taking as poetry does. We launch a new book the way a poet launches a poem or a spider launches a web—into the void, across the abyss that separates one reader perusing a text in a room from another reading the same book a thousand miles or years away. The energy that transforms itself into a word between reader and writer is as mysterious, as chancy, as the spider's first filament.
>
> Peter Davison[1]

Two basic possibilities offer themselves to poets desiring an audience: to read their work publicly or to seek print. Uniquely among literary genres not written primarily to be performed, poetry may find a contemporary audience through oral "publication." Practically speaking, however, print publication remains the condition for preserving literary work and achieving extra-local repute. Theoretically, tapes and recordings could also serve these functions, but in actuality they do not. Records of poets reading their work have been available for decades but are generally seen as adjuncts to print publication and usually comprise poems that have been in print for some time and "proven" themselves as the poets' best or most popular. *Black Box*, the only regularly published poetry "magazine" on tape as far as could be discovered, endured from 1975 into the 1980s without spawning imitators. The popularity of readings is probably partly attributable to the social nature of these occasions and the audiences' pleasure in seeing live poets. Most contemporary serious poetry is so compressed and carefully crafted that it cannot be absorbed entirely by ear; it must be read.

Virtually all poets, therefore, even the small minority who stress performance, put considerable effort into winning acceptance from journal and book editors. Essentially, four avenues to print publishing exist: those leading to the trade (or commercial) press, found impassable by most poets; the academic press; the independent noncommercial (or small) press and little magazines; and self-publication through one of several means. As we shall see, most poets in all groups found print initially via one of the last two routes. Subsequent journeys were less predictable.

In practice, self- and small-publishing are often hard to distinguish. The most obvious and notorious way in which authors support publication of their own work is by using one of the few established commercial subsidy (or vanity) presses. This kind of publication differs in important ways from self-publishing: all publishing functions—editing, design, production, promotion, distribution—are handled by the subsidy house for a substantial fee, and the book appears under its imprint. Only four authors in this study could be identified as having used subsidy press services. Windy Row and Dorrance had each been patronized by two poets, but only one of the four had used the press for more than a single book.

Examples of truly self-publishing poets include Charles Haseloff, whose *Ode to Susan* came out through his Penumbra Press, and Ellen Marie Bissert, whose sole book was published under the imprint of her literary journal, *13th Moon.* Self-publishing and other small-press publishing are often difficult to distinguish between. Many small presses have inbred lists, with friends and relatives publishing one another. Furthermore, small publishers often publish their own books, but, unlike Haseloff and Bissert, those of other poets as well—for example, from this study, David Lunde of Basilisk Press and Douglas Messerli of Sun & Moon. Self-published works by serious poets almost never appear with the poets' own names used as imprints.

A variation of self-publishing is publication by a cooperative of which the poet is a member. In these cases, the manuscript usually has to win approval of the collective's members before acceptance, so editorial screening may actually be more rigorous than at many conventional small presses. Among poets in this study who had published via collective were Pat Parker (Women's Press Collective), Mindy Aloff and Marina LaPalma (Kelsey Street Press), and Marie Harris and Joyce Peseroff (Alice James Books). Both cooperative and self-publishing were grouped with other small-press ventures in the "independent noncommercial" category when analyzing poets' bibliographic citations.

Poetry publication data were gathered and tabulated in order to test three sets of assumptions about the roles played by the various segments of the literary publishing industry and the shape of poets' publishing histories. These assumptions have commonsensical bases and are often encountered in printed opinion pieces and statements; they also cropped up in poets' narrative responses to questions asked in this study.

Small Presses, Little Magazines, and Lesser-Known Poets

The first widely held belief to be examined is that during the three decades studied, independent noncommercial publishing played the greatest role in exposing the work of new poets and of experienced poets who were not well known.

It was, of course, the perceived inadequacy of commercial presses—with respect to poetry in general, but especially the work of experimental and obscure poets—that sparked the early twentieth-century small press movement. Repeatedly Harriet Monroe, Ezra Pound, and other poets employed the editorial pages of the early *Poetry* to denounce publishers' neglect, ignorance, and subscription to commercial values. Small magazines and presses unconcerned with profits sprang up here and among literary expatriates in Europe.

It was assumed that while such ventures had been important to little-known and unknown poets throughout the three decades explored in this study, they had become even more so since the late 1960s and early 1970s—when the proliferation of little magazines and small presses occurred simultaneously with conglomerate takeovers of trade publishing houses and a sharpened focus on profits in the trade sector. The attendant assumption was that with the passing of the 1950s, the trade press and mass-distributed magazines played a *reduced* role in new poets' careers. It was speculated further that the academic publishing sector, university presses and college- and university-sponsored journals, might also have moved into the lacuna left by withdrawal of the trade, to emerge as more important in printing new poets' work during the latter 1960s and 1970s than it was in the 1950s.

New Poets

To judge the truth of the first of these common beliefs—that is, that the small presses and little magazines had, throughout the contemporary period, borne heavy responsibility for ushering new poets into print—

citations were compiled to the older poets' first ten periodical appearances and the newer poets' first five and to poetry books by all poets. These were then analyzed by publishing sector.

Independent little magazines were shown to account for the majority of poets' earliest periodical appearances by thirty-seven more percentage points than the next most prominent type, academic journals (63.8 percent contrasted with 26.8 percent). General-interest magazines with larger audiences, such as *The New Yorker* and *The Atlantic*, ushered only 9.3 percent of these early creations into print.[2]

As publishers of poets' first books, commercial houses were somewhat more notable than were the general magazines in publishing early poems. This type of house brought out nearly 14 percent of poets' initial books, compared with over 19 percent from university houses. The small presses' role in publishing new poets' work was comparable to little magazines'. Slightly over 62 percent of first books were brought out by small presses, compared with just under 64 percent of earliest periodical appearances in little magazines.

It is not surprising that academic journals were so much more active than academic book presses as publishers of early work. Ever since they began to be founded in the second quarter of this century, academic journals had accommodated poetry. Most university book presses, however, had considered issuance of poetry and fiction incongruous with their mission to promote scholarship. While *criticism* of poetry was thought publishable, poetry itself was not, except at a very few houses with (usually extremely limited) poetry programs. In more recent years, however, poetry series had been initiated at a number of university presses, including those sponsored by the University of Chicago (reintroducing poetry after a long hiatus), Princeton, Carnegie-Mellon, Louisiana State, Johns Hopkins, Central Florida Universities, and the Universities of Illinois, Alabama, Georgia, and Arkansas.

Lesser-Known Published Poets

Not only new poets but also poets of less repute, regardless of length of career, were thought to rely on the independent press, which was believed more immune than any other to influence by sales potential or authors' fame. To see if this was so, Older and Newer Nonprizewinners' book publications overall, as well as their first and last books, to permit comparison, were analyzed by publishing sector. Also analyzed were their early and late periodical appearances.

As expected, small presses proved overwhelmingly important to the exposure of lesser-known poets' work throughout their careers, bringing out nearly 84 percent of all their published books and slightly over 79 percent of both their first and their latest books. For book publication at either period in their careers, commercial presses offered these nonprizewinning poets almost negligible service. The university press, while more active, was also eclipsed by the overwhelming predominance of small presses. It seems fair to say that without the small press, many of the less celebrated poets would scarcely have found public voice.

By examining the same data for prizewinning poets, comparisons can be made. Taking all book publications into account, nonprizewinners were revealed to be almost twice as reliant on small presses as prizewinners were. Prizewinners had nearly twice as many university-press books and six times as many trade-published books. Thus both poet categories, prizewinning and nonprizewinning, published more through small presses than through any other type of press, confirming small presses' high importance in poetic careers generally. But they were much more important, overall, to the nonprizewinners. (As indicated earlier, prizewinners' career-long dependence on the small press could be explained partly, though by no means entirely, by their periodic return to it in order to have a limited edition or an atypical work specially printed.)

An examination of first and more recent books, divided by publishing sector, is particularly revealing. While nonprizewinners' acceptance by the trade, always minimal, had declined slightly in recent years, more (by nine percentage points) of prizewinners' latest than earliest books were trade-produced, and at *both* career points they were somewhat more likely to publish with commercial than with small presses. The decline experienced by nonprizewinners may be attributable to one of two factors or a combination of them. First of all, difficult as it is to find a publisher for one's first book, it has often been declared that getting a subsequent book published is even more difficult unless the first one has sold well. This may be because the attraction to the publisher of taking a risk on an interesting unknown is replaced by the perceived likelihood of taking a loss on a proven poor seller. Another explanation is that commercial presses had been tightening their operations. By the late 1970s, they less often accepted poetry unsupported by mass appeal or a famous name that might bring, if not spectacular sales, at least a prestige benefit. Some amplification of this point may be appropriate here.

Peculiarities of industry reporting made it impossible to determine exact numbers of poetry books issued per publishing sector or even overall. Poetry and drama were collapsed into a single category, and many small-press and self-published works were probably overlooked. Still, the often-expressed belief that trade presses became increasingly resistant to good poetry and other commercially unpromising material is borne out by a great body of anecdotal evidence and by a good deal of the bibliographic data gathered for this study.[3] It is almost unthinkable that a serious poet lacking personal connections, a prominent prize, or some other distinction extrinsic to the poetry itself could have made it onto a trade publisher's list in 1980.

Criticism of trade presses was most often voiced by poets citing their neglect of poetic work generally and of poetry newcomers in particular. Almost never was it suggested that the apparent prime cause of this neglect, the typically small market for poetry books, was a fictitious or even remediable situation. Implied, therefore, was an assumption that even self-defined commercial houses had the cultural obligation to sponsor worthy literature whether or not it sold. Indeed, poets often commented negatively on the trade's elevation of economic considerations above literary contributions, and the presses themselves retained a perhaps anachronistic notion that they had some responsibility to publish meritorious fiction and poetry regardless of their saleability. Witness, for example, trade-press spokesmen's defensive claim that low-quality books of "blockbuster" potential, which they were criticized for publishing and supporting with huge author advances and promotion budgets, actually "subsidized" and permitted the publication of books likely to show loss. The latter were sometimes referred to as "conscience books." In the competitive 1970s' publishing industry, however, with basic values often set by conglomerate parents and carried into practice by a new breed of managers who were more businesspeople than book lovers, the price exacted by conscience was low. The recent history of one large house once known for its poetry is illustrative.

In 1975, Diane Matthews of Doubleday stated publicly that that huge house had cut back to between seven and ten poetry titles per year, plus anthologies. No more than four new poets could be signed up annually. Even at that, each volume was being published at a loss of between $10,000 and $15,000. Marge Piercy's *To Be of Use* (1973), one of Doubleday's "best-selling poetry books," had still not broken even two years after its publication. "I hope we can continue to publish poetry," Matthews said, but her tone was pessimistic.[4] In 1983, a year when Doubleday issued 500 new titles on all subjects and had a total of 4,000 in print, the company's 1983–84 catalog listed seventy-one titles under "Poetry." At least ten were multi-author anthologies of reprints. No more than twenty of the rest were by living poets. And none was new. Thus, under 2 percent of the company's in-print works were books of poems; under .05 percent of these were by contemporary poets; and no poetry book was among those being listed for the first time. Matthews's pessimism was well advised.

Poets with no books or a very few small-press volumes to their credit told repeatedly of regretful letters from trade editors pronouncing their work publishable but, because of commercial pressures, not by *their* enterprises. For example, one poet in the study had received many "complimentary" rejections from big houses: "Basically they said they could publish few [poetry] books, and if this had not been the case, if this had been several years earlier, mine would have been taken." Such rejections are sometimes euphemistically phrased form letters intended to let poets down gently. But the fact that many poets in the study, including some who were long-experienced and sophisticated, mentioned receiving *obviously* personal letters of this type suggests that many editors were expressing genuine regret.

Somewhat less intergroup difference emerged when data on early and later periodical publications were compared. Yet the same basic pattern held with regard to commercial and little magazine outlets. Again, nonprizewinners had always received and continued to receive little attention from mass-distributed magazines. And while both prizewinners and nonprizewinners relied on little magazines for more than half of both their earliest and most recent periodical appearances, this proportion *increased* slightly in nonprizewinners' later period, but decreased substantially for prizewinners. The 2.5 percentage points between the two groups with regard to early periodical publications had widened by 15.5 percentage points in the later period. Differences between the groups that were negligible in the poets' early careers became substantial and took the predicted direction as time went on. Interestingly, although the early differences were too small to allow for conclusions, they too were of the character one would expect—that is, with nonprizewinners a bit *less* likely to publish in mass magazines, a bit *more* likely to publish in the littles.

As we have seen, the situation with regard to first and latest books was quite different. From the very beginning future prizewinners were much more likely to be handled by trade or university enterprises, and a plurality of their latest books—almost half—were published by the trade. In contrast, nonprizewinners' publishing experiences changed little, with nearly eight out of ten of both their first and last books bearing small-press imprints.

Interestingly, and somewhat counter-intuitively, commercial and academic periodicals were slightly less likely to publish nonprizewinning poets later in their careers than at their commencement, the little magazines commensurately more likely to do so. Clearly, the independent noncommercial sector was relied upon heavily by this study's nonprizewinning poets at all stages of their careers, bearing out the second part of the hypothesis.

Changes over Time

It was also thought that the noncommercial sector (academic as well as independent) played an *increasingly* important role in publishing new poets during the later 1960s, the 1970s, and the start of the 1980s, when many trade presses were beginning to be run in more traditionally businesslike, profit-conscious styles. To determine whether this was true, the early publishing records of older- and newer-poet groups were analyzed by sector and compared. Most older poets began appearing in magazines in the late 1940s or early 1950s. Their first books, it will be recalled, by definition appeared in the 1950s or early 1960s. The work of most newer poets first saw magazine print in the 1960s or early 1970s; their first books came out between 1970 and 1981, inclusive.

Immediately evident when one compares the first-book publications of Older and Newer Nonprizewinning poets is the greater importance of small presses in publishing the newer poets' earliest books, with a slight decline in support by the commercial press, and a much more notable decline on the part of the academic presses. However, when Older and Newer *Prizewinners'* records are isolated and compared, the difference with regard to independent press publication is unimportant: just over one percentage point. As predicted, older poets in both groups were more likely than newer poets in corresponding groups to have won first-book acceptance from commercial presses, this difference being dramatic among prizewinners. Almost twice as many Older as Newer Prizewinners had first published with the trade. By contrast, twice as many Newer as Older Prizewinners saw their first books come out through the university press; almost half of NPs' first books bear university imprints. Thus, for poets who would go on to win major prizes, the most notable shift seems to have been from commercial to university presses as publishers of first books.

It seemed possible that this could be explained partly by the fact that the 1970–80 choices of the Yale Younger Poets series, which guarantees Yale University Press publication of winners' first books, were automatically included in the NP group (see the appendix). However, inclusion in the same group of Walt Whitman Award winners, whose first books are handled by trade presses, and Swallow prizewinners, relatively few in number, who were published by the small Swallow Press, might offset the impact of the Yale award. To assure that selection criteria for the Newer Prizewinners' group did not skew book publication data, the twenty-one Yale, Walt Whitman, and Swallow winners were removed temporarily, leaving in the NP group only the twenty-four post–1970 winners of the Lamont, Guggenheim, and American Academy of Arts awards. The university press now emerged as even *more* dramatically significant, while small presses' contribution shrank to less than it had been twenty to thirty years earlier.[5] Again, the major shift had been from commercial to academic publisher. When one recalls that very large proportions of Newer Prizewinners held advanced degrees and were working in academia, this does not seem surprising.

Constant throughout all comparisons is evidence of commercial presses' decline as publishers of new poets. This is particularly striking in the histories of those established poets who were recognized as the most distinguished of their publishing generations. While over 41 percent of Older Prizewinners were sponsored first by the trade press, the same can be said of only about half as many of their younger counterparts. The academy's role had been enhanced correspondingly because of its success in ushering into print new poets who later attracted prize notice. Whether this happened because university press editors had a genius for identifying and signing the finest new poets, or because academic imprimatur tended of itself to lend prestige and capture attention, or because gaining acceptance from these presses necessitated contacts that also facilitated prizewinning, or because of several or all of these reasons is probably impossible to determine firmly. It seemed at least incidentally interesting to identify presses responsible for two or more first books by Newer and Older Prizewinners. Except for Yale and Swallow, which were bound to head the Newer Prizewinners' list because of criteria for inclusion in the NP group, only the University of Pittsburgh, with its relatively large Pitt Poetry Series, and Wesleyan University, which had long published poetry, were prominent.

Earliest periodical publications were compared for the same groups for whom first book publications were compared, and again, the commercial sector proved to have taken a markedly less active role, the academic sector a more active, in publishing new poets in the 1960s and 1970s than in the 1940s and 1950s. Contrary to expectation, however, little magazines were much less significant conduits for the early poems of Newer Prizewinning poets than for the early poems of Older Prizewinners. Almost 70 percent of Older Prizewinners' earliest periodical appearances were in the littles, contrasted with only 53 percent of the Newer Prizewinners'. Academic journals made up the difference.

Nor did any single journal dominate the new poetry horizon in the more recent period as *Poetry* had done during the earlier. Over 17 percent of OPs' early exposure was provided through the pages of this venerable little magazine (Table 3.1). While in the more recent period it remained, technically, the most important periodical publisher of future poetry names, its leading position was now tenuously held and essentially insignificant, as it accounted for only eight, or fewer than 4 percent of Newer Prizewinners' earliest citations. *The New Yorker*—the second most prominent magazine publisher of Older Prizewinning poets in the days before they achieved fame, claiming seventeen, or about 6 percent, of their early citations—appeared only once among all early citations on Newer Prizewinners' bibliographies.

Possible reasons for the almost threefold increase in academic journals' sponsorship of young future award winners are many and interrelated. Whatever the reasons, however, many poets' enthusiasm for this de-

Table 3.1
Titles Accounting for Five or More of Older Prizewinners' and of Newer Prizewinners' Early Periodical Publications

Older Prizewinners		Newer Prizewinners	
Title	Number of Publications	Title	Number of Publications
Poetry	51	Poetry	8
New Yorker	17	Intro	7
Hudson Review	13	December	6
Western Review	12	Chicago Review	5
		Poetry Northwest	5
Accent	10	Prairie Schooner	5
Beloit Poetry Journal	10	Nation	5
Furioso	9		
Paris Review	8		
Kenyon Review	7		
Atlantic	6		
Partisan Review	6		
Perspective	5		
Sewanee Review	5		

velopment would likely be rather restrained. College and university literary periodicals, which usually emanated from English or creative writing departments and were almost always produced independently of the institutions' formal presses, were often maligned with such adjectives as "conservative" and "establishment-oriented."

The root of the problem was located, naturally enough, in the journals' origins. They were founded to make neither money nor aesthetic waves, both of which are purposes that at least inspire action and at best imaginativeness and creativity. Academic journals were usually motivated by reasons related only tangentially, if at all, to literature. Two of the most common motives were to lend a relatively obscure institution visibility or a mediocre one prestige (or at least a literary image). Such motivations did not lead inevitably to the dull and commonplace. For example, the vigorous, influential fifties' magazine *Black Mountain Review* was published at Black Mountain College after Charles Olson, the college's rector, "proposed to the other faculty members that a magazine might prove [an] active advertisement" for the nature and form of the college's program.[6] Yet this "program" was passionately experimental (the college has long since collapsed), and Olson was an avant-garde poet with a charismatic gurulike appeal. If the academic journal is meant to publicize and reflect its parent institution, Black Mountain's was bound to be vivid, aesthetically sophisticated, and unlike any other college publication. For the most part, charges that academic journals were characteristically traditional and conservative, favoring known names and familiar styles, and were comparatively hostile to newcomers seemed credible on their face and were partially supported by this study's findings. (Much less, pro or con, had been written about university presses' poetry-book publications, probably because there had until fairly recently been so few. One imagines, however, that eventually they might generate similar criticisms.) Quite clearly the academics' independent counterparts, small presses and little magazines, remained, as in Harriet Monroe's day, the group most hospitable to the new.

Indeed, one reason for the independents' oft-noted vitality may have been their receptiveness to literary experimentation and unfamiliar writers. Almost as frequently expressed by their editors as the desire to print the best was the hope of helping the new, unknown, or underappreciated author. This was to be expected, given the counter-cultural stance of little magazines and presses (in a sense, to start one at all was to register protest) and the fact that so many were founded by authors who had faced frequent rejection themselves early in their careers. While some editors stressed above all exposure of authors who as yet lacked reputation, those committed primarily to breadth or to experimentalism also remarked their special feeling for obscure poets. This was partly empathy; partly a logical necessity, given the competition of established journals; partly the drive to discover great talents, as their editorial ancestors discovered Frost, Eliot, and others (always an intoxicating prospect for literary editors); and partly the commonsensical perception that if a new poetry was to emerge—with new understandings, themes, uses of language or form—then it would most likely emerge through the work of new poets.

Data from the present study, it will be recalled, confirmed the primary importance of independent noncommercial enterprises' importance in publishing complete unknowns, as well as experienced but unsung poets. At the same time, however, a substantial contribution to the exposure of new poets was made by the much-maligned (and much-admired) academic sector as well. In chapters 4 and 5, strengths and limitations of these two sectors and poets' ambivalent attitudes toward them are explored more fully.

BIG PRESS/SMALL PRESS AND PRIZEWINNERS' CAREER-LONG PUBLISHING PATTERNS

The second major set of assumptions to be tested was that poets who had achieved success as measured by prizewinning tended to publish increasingly often with the trade press and widely distributed general-interest magazines and to a lesser degree with academic literary journals, largely ignoring small presses and little magazines.

To assess patterning over the long publishing careers typical of older poets, four periods were spotlighted—for books: (1) the first book in each poet's career, all of which were published in the 1950s or early 1960s; (2) all publications for 1961–63; (3) all publications for 1968–70; and (4) last book through 1981—for periodicals: (1) ten earliest publications in each poet's career, typically falling in the 1940s and/or early 1950s; (2) all publications for 1961–63; (3) all publications for 1968–70; and (4) ten most recent publications through 1980. The periods demarcated by 1961–63 and 1968–70 fell roughly equidistant from the mid-sixties' commencement of the "Mimeo Revolution" when little magazines and, to a lesser extent, small book presses proliferated. Also, these were reasonable periods to use as midpoints for most older poets' publishing careers, which usually commenced in the 1940s or very early 1950s.

Changes in Prizewinners' Book Publishing over Time

With regard to the question of whether the prizewinning poets tended to move away from independent noncommercial publishers and toward commercial and university houses as their careers aged and their fame grew, it is clear from the data already presented that commercial presses took a much more active role in the later careers of poets who had the characteristics that attracted prestigious prizes. However, when these data are compared with those for Newer Prizewinners, we also see that in the 1970s commercial presses were only about half as likely to publish the first book by a new poet destined to win prizes as they had been in the 1950s. Over 41 percent of Older Prizewinners, but just over 22 percent of Newer Prizewinners, saw their initial volumes issued through the trade. This proportion had increased by sixteen percentage points for NPs' most recent books despite the poets' relatively short careers and still somewhat modest reputations. Older Prizewinners, whose last books had followed their first by as many as twenty-five to thirty years, had seen trade press involvement increase by about half. Sixty percent of OPs' last books and almost 70 percent of their last full-length books bore trade imprints. At the same time, it must be noted that small presses continued to play an active role in Older Prizewinners' careers, accounting for the publication of one-fifth or more of their most recent books. When citations to short books as well as long are considered, there is a trade press drop and independent press leap in the 1968–70 period, when small publishing firms were being founded and struggling for a foothold, and attracting poets' hopes, admiration, and political sympathy. By the late 1970s and the start of the 1980s, when Older Prizewinners' last books tabulated for this study were published, the small presses' role had declined, and the trade presses' increased proportionately. This was a logical development. The now more established small press may have lost some of its glamor, novelty, aggressiveness, and underdog appeal; and the trade press may have been drawn to the real, though comparatively modest, sales potential of poets with long bibliographies and lists of honors.

Prizewinners' Periodical Publishing over Time

Periodical publication, however, presents a much different picture. While there was an increased tendency in the later period for both Older and Newer Prizewinners to publish in such widely distributed magazines as *The New Yorker* and *The Atlantic*, two other facts are more striking. First is the reduction of these magazines' involvement, over the period from roughly 1950 to 1970, in exposing the early work of new poets who went on to win major awards. They accounted for 15 percent of Older Prizewinners' earliest periodical appearances, but only 4 percent of Newer Prizewinners'. Although newsstand-distributed magazines' prominence in Newer Prizewinners' bibliographies increased threefold between the earliest and latest periods of their publishing careers, the fact remains that a higher percentage of Older Prizewinners' earliest appearances than of Newer Prizewinners' latest were in them: 15 percent contrasted with 12 percent. (On the average, NPs' latest periodical appearances postdated their earliest by about ten years.)

The second striking fact is that, although Older Prizewinners' rate of commercial periodical publication increased by more than 73 percent (from 15 to 26 percent) in the two to three decades separating the end of the 1970s from the commencement of their publishing histories, these highly renowned poets still relied upon noncommercial magazines for nearly three-quarters of their magazine appearances, with the independent littles responsible for over half. When one considers that new poems typically are placed first in magazines to gain exposure and feedback and are only later collected into books, the little magazine contribution, which was obviously enormous, is magnified dramatically.

The gross outline of Older Prizewinners' career periodical publishing patterns was as might be predicted, with an overall decline in little-magazine, and increases in academic- and commercial-magazine, appearances. However, the most significant finding is the career-long dominance of little magazines.

Newer Prizewinners, by contrast, showed a much slighter decline in publication by littles, though fewer than half of their total late publications were in this type of magazine. Perhaps the most conspicuous revelations of the data are (1) that except for commercial magazines' much increased though still modest interest in these young poets, their publishing patterns remained relatively stable over their first decade or so in print; and (2) that they were much more actively involved with academic journals than was true of their older counterparts. (This is especially striking in the earliest career period, when 43 percent of Newer Prizewinners' appearances could be traced to academic journals, while only 15 percent, or about one-third as many, of Older Prizewinners' early appearances could be. This is probably partly explainable by the increased number of poetry-publishing academic journals during the three decades examined without a similar increase in the numbers of general-interest magazines that published poetry. Correspondingly, Newer Prizewinners were far *less* dependent on the little magazines early on than were the older poets.

Still, of course, both groups published substantially more heavily in the littles, which also increased numerically, than in any other type of magazine, a most important fact that should not be obscured. For example, although the gross career outlines of Newer Prizewinners confirm the hypothesis that with time (and prizewinning), they moved to mass magazines, other revelations supported by the data are far more interesting and important—notably the fact that after several years of publishing and the winning of at least one national literary award almost 88 percent of their magazine appearances could still be found in noncommercial publications of rather small circulation.

Finally, we can say that the second set of assumptions was partially supported. Having achieved repute (that is, major prizes), poets tended to move away from small-press and little-magazine publication. However, they remained much more dependent on it than anticipated and certainly never came to ignore the independent, noncommercial sector. Emerging vividly from the data are the reduced role of trade presses in publishing poets' first books and the dominant importance, among *all* groups of poets, of the independent little magazine as an avenue of exposure for new work. This last finding is finally, perhaps, the most important, and it is somewhat surprising. It seems generally true that the poets, no matter how long established or highly respected they became, never ceased to rely on the independents to usher their poems, and especially their new poems, into print. The little magazines were able to do this partly because they were so numerous.

THE EFFECTS OF LITERARY MAGAZINE PROLIFERATION

The little magazines keep crawling
under the door like deformed hands on wheels
they can't help it if they whine and their paper skulls

are battered in by childabuser mailmen
the little magazines keep coming.

Phillip Lopate[7]

The third and last major set of assumptions to be examined is centered in the remarkable proliferation of noncommercial literary magazines—both academic and independent, but especially the latter. The extent of this, its history, the consternation it caused, and its potential impact on postwar literature require explanation to set the stage for discussion of these last findings and enable appreciation of their significance.

That the sheer numbers of small magazines and presses have climbed throughout the past seventy years, and dramatically in the last twenty-five, is well documented.[8] Their growth in quantity over recent decades can be traced through the editions of the annual directory published by Dustbooks. Accompanying the increases have been accelerating, closely linked complaints about this deluge and the mediocrity of its content, particularly in relation to periodicals.

As long ago as 1931, Edward Dahlberg wrote Richard Johns, who had just founded the little magazine *Pagany*, that in his opinion, shared by a number of his writing friends, "there are so many goddam mushroom halfassed periodicals around town that one is leery of them all."[9] Nearly half a century later, poet and ex-editor Charles Haseloff, who participated in the present study, would employ the same metaphor in an opposite spirit: "Magazines were sprouting everywhere else—magic magazine mushrooms producing psychedelic visions of indescribable beauty, love, wisdom and glory."[10]

This divergence of opinion surfaces whenever the subject of numbers is raised. For example, a 1975 *Prairie Schooner* symposium asked six editors whether there were too many little magazines, and received "yes" responses from two (Glenna Luschei of *Cafe Solo* and Robert Bly of The Seventies Press), "no's" from three (Virginia Elson and Beverlee Hughes of *Yes* and James Boatwright of *Shenandoah*), and a somewhat qualified "no" from Ira Sadoff of *Seneca Review*.[11] After considering, in a rhetorical mode, and then rejecting abandonment of her own journal, Luschei playfully proposed founding one entitled *Save the Trees*, which would bring out no issues and, presumably, lead by example.[12] Boatwright, on the other hand, considered "too many" preferable to "not enough" and declared it "no coincidence that America has hundreds of literary magazines and an extraordinarily fertile and inventive literary culture."[13]

Those who found the mushrooming of books and magazines more troubling than magical, and even some of those who sensed the magic, fretted that good work was being buried in the avalanche, as it was, at least theoretically, dispersed among hundreds of titles. No longer was it possible, the argument went, as it had been in the teens, to keep up with the best in current poetry writing by reading three or four magazines and a few books each year—or even by reading forty or fifty magazines, as in the years immediately following the end of World War II. Allen Ginsberg of this study, who is certainly no small-press foe, spoke of the "overload of poetic information" with which even the most diligent scholars could not keep current, a problem mentioned also by respondents Charles Martin and Ron Overton.[14] Overton speculated that getting published might have become easier than getting read.

Certainly the proliferation of literary magazines can throw up barriers to scholarship, or even to following the new work of a single interesting poet, though this depends partly on the poet's opportunities and publication decisions. Barbara Holland, for instance, claimed a decade ago to have appeared in "some 800 magazines quick and dead in the Americas and Overseas," and several other prolific poets must hold comparable records.[15] To make a decision against publishing at all or in favor of concentration in a few magazines could be difficult for poets with a desire for expanded readership and loyalty to the editors and publishing sector that first recognized them. Danny Rendleman, for instance, wrote that "while I damn the glut, I almost always send stuff to new mags."

There were so many magazines by the end of the seventies, and so many more survived than would once have been the case—a phenomenon due partly to recently established grant funds—that, inevitably, the majority of them published weak poetry most of the time. Among the dozens of voices that joined in criticism after the publishing explosion commenced were those of small publisher Alan Brilliant (Unicorn Press); William Virgil Davis; poet Charles Bukowski, a prime beneficiary and benefactor of the small press; and poet-editor Hayden Carruth.[16] Numerous poets in this study, responding to a questionnaire invitation to write any additional comments they wished, castigated small-book presses or little magazines for the poor quality of their selection and editing.

The struggle against mediocrity was a tough one, however, for the little-magazine editor who had no special access to a gifted clique, or even for the editor who did. One is reminded of Margaret Anderson's famous blank issue, and her partner Jane Heap's quiet admission that *The Little Review*'s fifteen years, which had cost them so dearly in time, money, and emotion, had brought forth only one masterpiece.[17] Repeatedly, literature lovers who began publishing adventures with high enthusiasm and bright ideals were disillusioned as they found that the neglected geniuses they wished to help were very few, and most did not wander their way.

Poet-editor Ira Sadoff once made the intriguing suggestion that when publishing is easy, "it becomes impossible to equate the quantity of publications with one's worth as a writer," leading serious poets to put their energy into writing instead of publishing.[18] That even this benefit followed, however, was not borne out by the respondents. Many poets described the struggle to publish, its sapping of drive, enthusiasm, and self-confidence. It is more likely that as doors to publication multiplied and swung wide, the value of publishing *per se* was degraded, but the importance of appearing in prestigious organs was enhanced. This probably increased stress rather than reduced it as, after months and years of publishing, some poets continued to be turned away from the doors they most wished to enter.

In light of the foregoing, it was assumed that since the mid–1960s, all poet groups' periodical publications would be more widely dispersed, with few or no individual titles emerging as publishers of all or most prizewinners. Further, it was thought that there would be little agreement among poets as to which magazines and perhaps which book presses were publishing the best work and little uniformity in their reading habits—thus giving them no solid base of shared cultural understanding and discovery. It was also thought likely that there would be little agreement as to who were the best living American poets. Should these assumptions be borne out, fears of diffusion, confusion, scholarly inconvenience, impediments to the establishment and development of a coherent, elite national literature, and even the burial of extraordinary talents might have some justification.

To test them, two classes of information were compiled: concentration and dispersion of poets' most recent periodical publications (through 1980) compared with pre–1965 periods; and poets' responses to the following survey questions:

Of all U.S. and Canadian magazines which are publishing poetry today and with, which you are familiar (including both the bigger commercial magazines and the literary journals): which, in your opinion, publish the best, or most significant, poetry? (List as many as you wish.)

Which U.S. and Canadian poetry-publishing periodicals do you read regularly (if any)?

Of the book publishers bringing out poetry today (commercial, university, and "small" publishers) in the U.S. and Canada, and with which you are familiar: which, in your opinion, publish the best, or most significant, poetry? (List as many as you wish.)

Of the living U.S. poets with whose work you are familiar, whom do you consider the best or most interesting? (List as many as you wish.)

As noted above, two time-based categories of publication data were examined to assess amount of dispersion of poets' periodical appearances: (1) pre–1965 citations, comprising all older poets' earliest and 1961–63 publications; and (2) post–1965 citations, comprising older poets'

1968–70 and most recent publications (through 1980), and all younger poets' publications (again, only through 1980).

That there had been somewhat more scattering of periodical publication since the 1960s was suggested by the "concentration" figures. Every group except Newer Prizewinners showed some reductions in concentration of periodical publication over time—that is, fewer citations per periodical cited. This change was fairly striking among the older poets, but insignificant among the Newer Nonprizewinners, who, like their prizewinning generational counterparts, began publishing, as a rule, during or after the great magazine boom in the 1960s. (Interestingly, the degree of concentration in the most recent period was almost exactly equal for prizewinners—at 2.3 citations per cited magazine for both OPs and NPs, and for nonprizewinners—at 1.5 and 1.6 for ONs and NNs, respectively.) Perhaps nonprizewinners were less successful at establishing ongoing publishing relationships with particular journals, and while this could have been because their work was of lower or more uneven quality, it could also have been because they lacked friendships, contacts, connections, which facilitate both the winning of prizes and the development of secure publishing relationships. Another possibility is that nonprizewinners were less satisfied to stay with magazines where they had already appeared and kept seeking new avenues of exposure, perhaps in search of more readers or enhanced prestige.

Most notable, however, was the remarkably high number of magazines cited and low number of citations per title for all groups at all times. Only OPs' earliest publications were significantly concentrated. Clearly, when the older poets were first publishing in periodicals, their poems were less widely dispersed and easier to find, their new work easier to follow, than would be true of poets who began publishing two decades later. No single magazine published work by over half of the Newer Prizewinners at the beginning of their careers, as *Poetry* did in the case of Older Prizewinners. Indeed, no single periodical was responsible for any of the earliest publications of as many as 20 percent of Newer Prizewinners. By contrast, nine separate journals printed work by at least 20 percent of the Older Prizewinners at the beginning of their careers (Table 3.1).

More recently, neither group was heavily dependent on any one periodical. Excluding *Tendril* (whose prominence in the poets' bibliographies is attributable almost entirely to one special 1980 anthology issue comprising reprints of previously published poems), only seven periodicals appeared on 20 percent or more of the Older Prizewinners' recent publication lists and only three on the same proportion of Newer Prizewinners' lists (Table 3.2).

Dispersion figures reflect in a different mirror, from a different perspective, the tendency toward reduced concentration. While biblio-

Table 3.2
Periodicals Appearing on the Most-Recent-Publication Lists of 20 percent or More of Older Prizewinners and of Newer Prizewinners

	Older Prizewinners	
Periodical	No. Poets	% Poets
American Poetry Review	13	45%
Atlantic	12	41%
New Yorker	12	41%
Tendril	10[a]	34%
Antaeus	9	31.5%
Poetry Now	9	31.5%
New Republic	8	28%
Poetry	7	24%
	Newer Prizewinners	
Tendril	16[a]	35.5%
Poetry	12	27%
New Yorker	10	22%
Poetry Now	10	22%

[a]**Mostly reprinted poems in special "Poet's Choice" issue.**

graphic data for the Older Prizewinners reveal an overall increase in dispersion of publications in periodicals from these poets' earliest to latest career periods, there were slight *decreases* in dispersion during both of the spotlighted three-year clusters in the 1960s (that is, 1961–63 and 1968–70). Most recent publications were the most dispersed and those from the 1961–63 period were the most concentrated. However, the fact that the earliest period was characterized by the second highest rate of dispersion demonstrates that no strong conclusion can be based on the data.[19]

In the Older Prizewinners' earliest period, 5 percent of the magazines cited accounted for 32 percent of all the citations, 25 percent for 66 percent of citations, and just half for 84 percent. Corresponding figures for most recent publications were 5 percent of the magazines accounting for 30 percent of the citations, 25 percent for 64 percent, and half for 79 percent—or very slightly less concentration, more dispersion.

In the case of Older Nonprizewinners, there was more dispersion in both periods, with acceleration rather than decline of this trend during the 1960s as well. For example, half the journals cited on the Older Nonprizewinners' bibliographies accounted for 78 percent of all citations during the earliest period, but for only 66 percent in the recent period. The newer poets' patterns warrant some separate analysis, which will be provided in the next chapter. The point here is that the periodical publishing of neither newer group showed the *increased* dispersion over time that that of both older groups did. Instead, both newer groups in both time periods showed dispersion comparable to the Older Nonprizewinners' in late career.

Those people who deplore increased amounts of publication often express a quite reasonable concern that it has become much harder to find the work of unknown but promising new authors. When older and newer poets' data are compared, this is shown to have been a possible problem by the end of the 1970s, and there is no reason to think it has vanished. Older Prizewinners' early publications were considerably more concentrated than Newer Prizewinners' and Older Nonprizewinners' somewhat more concentrated than Newer Nonprizewinners'.

It seems clear that poetry publications in periodicals became more dispersed over larger numbers of journals after the onset of the mid- and late-sixties' proliferation of noncommercial periodicals, both academic and independent. In the following ten to fifteen years, however, the rate of dispersion apparently stabilized. There was no reversion to the earlier situation of more concentrated publishing. Unlike some other counter-cultural activities of the sixties and early seventies, noncommercial publishing and editing did not decline in amount or acceptability to authors. As some ventures failed for lack of money or enthusiasm, others started up, with a result of net growth rather than shrinkage of numbers, as examination of the annual Dustbooks directories confirms. Still, there is obviously a limit to the amount of dispersion that can occur, and it seems to have been reached, or nearly so, by around 1970.

While the assumption of greater dispersion after the early sixties is borne out by the data, the increase does not seem to have been sufficient to support dire warnings that excellent poetry might be getting buried under an avalanche of print, unless it always had been. Since World War II, at least, there seems never to have been such a high degree of predictability in the location of fine new work that it was easy to follow, with the best poets' names surfacing inevitably in one eminent magazine, or even one of a few. For example, while *Poetry* published nineteen of twenty-nine to-be-acclaimed young postwar poets (that is, those in the Older Prizewinning group) very early, it missed another ten and in any case was responsible for only fifty-one of the 287 OPs' earliest citations used in this study. Indeed, the eight journals that published the largest number of Older Prizewinners in early career were together responsible for only 129 of those citations. That seems a lot in one sense, but not many at all when one considers that well over half of these poets' earliest publications were scattered among a great variety of journals, numbering seventy-seven in all. Still, it is true that Older Prizewinners' early periodical appearances showed a concentration figure exactly twice as high as Newer Prizewinners'—OPs having 3.4 citations per journal cited, NPs 1.7.

Also, to show that dispersion had not increased as much as might have been expected is not to deny that *any* increase may have been problematic. Indeed, the most critical implication of these data may be that an injuriously high level of dispersion had existed throughout contemporary times, and that the expansion of publishing activity in the sixties exacerbated an already untenable situation. Certainly, the information can be interpreted this way by those who place a high value on the concentration of new poetry in a small number of excellent journals.

Best Periodicals, Book Publishers, and Poets and What Was Read

Poets' answers to several survey queries shed light on the complicated question of what poetic work and which publications were read and valued and to what extent those experiences and attitudes were shared by the poets. Respondents ranging in number from 140 to 150 declared 178 different poetry-publishing periodicals and 159 poetry book publishers to be "best or most significant" and 171 periodicals to be "read regularly" (Tables 3.3–3.5). Astonishingly, 139 respondents named 405 different living American poets as "best."[20] Although all twenty-nine Older Prizewinners were named by at least one respondent, as would be expected, four were named *only* once, one only twice, and another only three times. (On the other hand, every one of the twenty-four poets ranked one to fifteen, and four of the five ranked sixteenth had been either included in the prizewinning groups or disqualified from inclusion only by their first books' publication dates.) Despite the surprisingly large number of poets cited as best, they included only twenty-four, or just over half, of Newer Prizewinners.[21] Among those whose names did not appear were some who were very new or had published little since their first books, but also such well-known writers as Peter Everwine, Maura Stanton, and Leslie Ullman, some of whom had been publishing in little magazines since the 1960s.

The sheer number of poets named implied little agreement about which, if any, were the masters of our age, an implication supported

Table 3.3
Twenty-one Periodicals Cited Most Often as "Best or Most Significant"[a]

Periodical	No. & (Percent) of Respondents Citing		Rank
Poetry	56	(39)	1
New Yorker	46	(32)	2
American Poetry Review	41	(28)	3
Antaeus	29	(20)	4
Field	29	(20)	4
Ploughshares	25	(17)	5
Georgia Review	21	(14.5)	6
Ironwood	21	(14.5)	6
Iowa Review	18	(12)	7
Paris Review	17	(12)	8
Poetry Northwest	16	(11)	9
Atlantic	15	(10)	10
Hudson Review	15	(10)	10
New England Review	15	(10)	10
Ohio Review	13	(9)	11
kayak	12	(8)	12
Missouri Review	10	(7)	13
Kenyon Review	9	(6)	14
Poetry Now	8	(5.5)	15
Prairie Schooner	7	(5)	16
Virginia Quarterly Review	7	(5)	16

[a]Total number of respondents = 145.
Total number of periodicals cited = 178.

by the data in Tables 3.6 and 3.7. Lack of consensus was everywhere the rule. In none of the four categories about which preferences were asked and in no single poet group did more than 60 percent of respondents agree on any one name or title. For example, while Adrienne Rich was the poet most often labelled as being one of the "best or most interesting," she was named by just over one-quarter of all respondents, rendering any strong statement about her pre-eminent prestige impossible.

Table 3.4
Twenty-one Book Publishers Cited Most Often as "Best or Most Significant"[a]

Publisher	No. & (Percent) of Respondents Citing		Rank
Atheneum	39	(28)	1
University of Pittsburgh	38	(27)	2
Ecco	34	(24)	3
Wesleyan University	32	(23)	4
New Directions	30	(21)	5
Farrar, Straus & Giroux	29	(21)	6
W. W. Norton	28	(20)	7
Harper & Row	26	(19)	8
Graywolf	24	(17)	9
Alfred A. Knopf	20	(14)	10
Houghton Mifflin	19	(14)	11
North Point	17	(12)	12
Black Sparrow	16	(11)	13
Yale University	16	(11)	13
Princeton University	15	(11)	14
University of Georgia	15	(11)	14
Random House	11	(8)	15
David R. Godine	10	(7)	16
Copper Canyon	9	(6)	17
University of Illinois	9	(6)	17
Viking	9	(6)	17

[a]Total number of respondents = 140.
Total number of presses cited = 159.

Only among Newer Prizewinners, when questioned about which periodicals they read regularly, did more than one-half of respondents in any group concur in anything. Sixty percent of NPs read the *American Poetry Review* regularly, and 53 percent *The New Yorker*. It is not surprising that this group, which was more consistent in educational background and profession than were other groups, would tend to show some con-

Table 3.5
Twenty-one Periodicals Cited Most Often as "Read Regularly"[a]

Periodical	No. & (Percent) of Respondents Citing		Rank
American Poetry Review	55	(39)	1
Poetry	51	(36)	2
New Yorker	45	(31.5)	3
Antaeus	25	(17.5)	4
Georgia Review	21	(15)	5
Field	17	(12)	6
Ironwood	17	(12)	6
Ploughshares	16	(11)	7
Atlantic	15	(10.5)	8
Paris Review	14	(10)	9
Poetry Northwest	14	(10)	9
Poetry Now	12	(8)	10
Iowa Review	11	(8)	11
New England Review	10	(7)	12
Hudson Review	9	(6)	13
Kenyon Review	9	(6)	13
kayak	8	(6)	14
Ohio Review	8	(6)	14
Nation	7	(5)	15
Black Warrior Review	6	(4)	16
Missouri Review	6	(4)	16

[a]Total number of respondents = 143.
Total number of periodicals cited = 171.

sistency in literary reading habits. Even here, however, agreement was not strong.

It is true, then, that even among poets who seemed professionally comparable, there was a rather low degree of accord as to which existing poetry magazines, publishers, and writers were best—and which periodicals one had to read in order to keep up with the most significant

Table 3.6
Twenty-four Poets Cited Most Often as "Best"[a]

Poet	Rank	NP Rank	OP Rank	NN Rank	ON Rank
Adrienne Rich (OP)	1	2	4	1	3
Galway Kinnell (OP)	2	1	4	2	3
Denise Levertov	3	3	3	4	3
Gary Snyder (OP)	4	6	3	3	NA
W. S. Merwin (OP)	5	4	2	8	2
Richard Wilbur	5	6	1	11	1
Robert Bly (OP)	6	4	NA	5	NA
William Stafford (OP)	7	2	4	6	3
Louise Gluck	8	2	4	9	NA
Robert Hass (NP)	8	3	5	7	NA
John Ashbery (OP)	9	3	2	10	3
Philip Levine (OP)	9	5	1	8	4
Maxine Kumin (OP)	10	7	5	8	3
Robert Creeley (OP)	11	6	5	9	3
Allen Ginsberg (OP)	11	8	2	10	3
Howard Nemerov	12	7	1	15	3
Louis Simpson	12	3	5	13	4
A. R. Ammons (OP)	13	6	5	13	2
Stanley Kunitz	13	7	5	11	3
James Merrill	13	NA	1	14	3
William Meredith	14	7	4	12	4
Robert Penn Warren	14	6	3	13	NA
Donald Justice (OP)	15	5	NA	13	4
Charles Simic	15	6	3	3	4

[a]Total number of ranks for each group is: NP = 8; OP = 5; NN = 17; ON = 4. "NA" indicates that only one respondent in the group cited the poet.

new work. It would indeed seem to be an age without identifiable masters.

All three of the study's major sets of assumptions were essentially confirmed by the data. Some demand closer attention, however, and

Table 3.7
Poets Cited Most Often as "Best" by Each Group[a]

Poet	No. of Cites and (Percent) of Respondents Citing		Rank
Newer Prizewinning Group (Respondents = 30; Total Ranks = 8)			
Galway Kinnell (OP)	9	(30)	1
Louise Gluck	8	(27)	2
Adrienne Rich (OP)	8	(27)	2
Robert Hass (NP)	6	(20)	3
Denise Levertov	6	(20)	3
Louis Simpson	6	(20)	3
Robert Bly (OP)	5	(17)	4
W. S. Merwin (OP)	5	(17)	4
Donald Justice (OP)	4	(13)	5
Philip Levine (OP)	4	(13)	5
A. R. Ammons (OP)	3	(10)	6
Robert Creeley (OP)	3	(10)	6
Charles Simic	3	(10)	6
Gary Snyder (OP)	3	(10)	6
Robert Penn Warren	3	(10)	6
Richard Wilbur	3	(10)	6
Older Prizewinning Group (Respondents = 19; Total Ranks = 5)			
James Merrill	6	(32)	1
Howard Nemerov	6	(32)	1
Richard Wilbur	6	(32)	1
John Ashbery (OP)	4	(21)	2
Allen Ginsberg (OP)	4	(21)	2
W. S. Merwin	4	(21)	2
Donald Hall	3	(16)	3
Anthony Hecht (OP)	3	(16)	3
Denise Levertov	3	(16)	3
Charles Simic	3	(16)	3
Gary Snyder (OP)	3	(16)	3
Mark Strand (OP)	3	(16)	3
Mona Van Duyn (OP)	3	(16)	3
Robert Penn Warren	3	(16)	3

Table 3.7 (continued)

Poet	No. of Cites and (Percent) of Respondents Citing		Rank
Newer Nonprizewinning Group (Respondents = 82; Total Ranks = 17)			
Adrienne Rich (OP)	27	(33)	1
Galway Kinnell (OP)	22	(27)	2
Gary Snyder (OP)	20	(24)	3
Denise Levertov	18	(22)	4
Robert Bly (OP)	16	(19.5)	5
William Stafford (OP)	14	(17)	6
Robert Hass (NP)	12	(15)	7
Maxine Kumin (OP)	11	(13)	8
Philip Levine (OP)	11	(13)	8
W. S. Merwin (OP)	11	(13)	8
Robert Creeley (OP)	9	(11)	9
Louise Gluck	9	(11)	9
Older Nonprizewinning Group (Respondents = 19; Total Ranks = 4)			
Richard Wilbur	7	(37)	1
A. R. Ammons (OP)	3	(16)	2
W. S. Merwin (OP)	3	(16)	2
John Ashbery (OP)	2	(10.5)	3
Robert Creeley (OP)	2	(10.5)	3
Allen Ginsberg (OP)	2	(10.5)	3
Galway Kinnell (OP)	2	(10.5)	3
Maxine Kumin (OP)	2	(10.5)	3
Stanley Kunitz	2	(10.5)	3
Denise Levertov	2	(10.5)	3
James Merrill	2	(10.5)	3
Howard Nemerov	2	(10.5)	3
Adrienne Rich (OP)	2	(10.5)	3
William Stafford (OP)	2	(10.5)	3

[a]Only poets in the top several ranks are listed on this table.

some unanticipated findings and some suggestions embedded in the data tempt analysis. Therefore, the following chapters probe deeper and look closer at noncommercial publishing sectors: the academic and the independent.

4

Poetry and the Academy

A major disclosure of unusual interest was the trend toward the academic institutionalization of contemporary poetry. The academy began to intervene in two ways: as publisher of poetry—a function it had performed for many years but increasingly in the 1970s and the beginning of the eighties—and as the agent and employer of poets.

ACADEMIC TRAINING AND EMPLOYMENT

As explained in chapter 2, the prizewinners invariably had at least some college background, while the nonprizewinners usually did but might not—Older Nonprizewinners being likeliest to have ceased their formal education at high school graduation or before. Newer poets were more likely than older to hold any advanced degree, and in particular the M.F.A., which might be termed the creative writer's professional degree. While no Older Nonprizewinner had the M.F.A., the only group for which this was true, they comprised the group *most* likely to hold what until recently was its scholarly counterpart: the literature Ph.D. Establishing a contrast that continues throughout their employment and publishing histories, members of this study's Newer Prizewinners' group were far more likely than the other poets to have M.F.A.s from, and other connections with, the University of Iowa's writing program. More than one-third of NPs for whom educational data were found had

M.F.A.s, and alomst two-thirds of those had earned the degree at Iowa (that is, almost one-quarter of the entire NP group). Their incidence of M.F.A.-holding was at least three times that of any other group. (In addition, three NPs were Iowa Ph.D.s.)[1]

Newer Prizewinners were also likeliest to work at regular academic teaching positions—"regular" here meaning appointments that carried a presumption or possibility of permanence, as distinguished from visiting-poet jobs, the conducting of temporary or occasional workshops, and so forth. Although Older Prizewinners were less likely by only 7.5 percentage points to have such jobs than Newer Prizewinners were, and Older Nonprizewinners were less likely by twelve percentage points, these figures demand further analysis. Information about poets' previous employment was not gathered systematically. However, it is clear that several Older Prizewinners—due probably to the passage of years, mounting frustration with financial insecurity and paid work that allowed no time for poetry, and the accumulation of honors and fame qualifying them for adequately remunerated faculty slots with light teaching loads—settled into academia on a full-time basis only quite late in their writing careers. They were often sharply critical of higher education and not strongly identified with their working environment and teaching colleagues. Professors Galway Kinnell and Philip Levine, both OP-group poets, exemplified such academicians. When asked their primary occupation, Older Prizewinners very seldom categorized themselves as "professors" or "teachers," though most were earning the largest portions of their income from such work. Because this group had a relatively low questionnaire response rate, only fifteen, or just over half, of their responses to this query are available. However, there is no reason to think that nonrespondents would be *more* academically identified; indeed, one would expect that these poets willing to fill out a long research questionnaire would include the most consciously academic poets of the group. By contrast, one-third of Newer Prizewinning respondents considered themselves educators first. For another 10 percent, the profession of "poet" or "writer" was shared with that of "teacher" or "professor" as primary self-identification.

While over 50 percent of Older Nonprizewinners were, also, academically employed, it must be remembered that almost half of this group held Ph.D.s. The degrees were scholarly, not "creative," and their work seemed to be the conventional instruction of literature; none was employed by an institution emphasizing fine arts degrees in writing. It seems safe to assume that they had acquired and held their jobs by virtue of their Ph.D.s and were regarded by their institutions more as literary scholars than practitioners. While no attempt was made in this study to determine exactly why so many randomly selected Older Nonprizewinning poets also held doctorates, one strong possibility suggests itself. It may be that after many years of writing and publishing with little formal recognition, people tend to lose or downplay their formal identification as poets, de-emphasize publication if not writing, and thus fail to arrange for listing in the creative writers' major professional directory—that is, the Poets & Writers directory from which the sample of nonprizewinning poets was drawn. Literature faculty, who are likelier than people in other lines of work to derive some status (and perhaps personal satisfaction) from simply *being* published poets, probably are also more motivated to keep creating and submitting work and to attend to directory entries, which afford at least a small measure of visibility and prestige.

In any case, Newer Prizewinners were definitely, and perhaps dramatically, more closely associated with academia than were older poets or young poets of less repute. Furthermore, they seemed more identified with writing as a profession for which one receives specific academic training culminating in a narrowly focused credential.

The implication is that more than ever before, poetry writing was taking place within universities and colleges, supported by academic resources and inevitably influenced in content and style by academic values and the events of academic life. It is even possible and credible, though neither obvious nor provable, that university-established connections and academically conditioned literary preferences shaped by the modernist tradition increasingly determined who would win both prizes and jobs. That is, as creative writing programs and attendant teaching opportunities grew and academe concerned itself more and more with poets *as* poets, one could question whether those in the Newer Prizewinning group were necessarily the best of their writing generation or simply the most compliant with institutional tastes and expectations. By the early 1980s considerable and strident concern had arisen about the thickening link between poets and the academy. To place this study's discoveries in context, the controversy should be examined.

The Controversy

Taking a long, dark view of the literary situation, poet-professor Hugh Kenner wrote in 1957: "I cannot help thinking that a civilization is in very perilous condition when all its writers have been driven into the universities."[2] Subsequently, the movement of poets into the academy swelled to an onrush, and debate over its implications became lively and apparently endless.

Academic poetry has been characterized by anti-establishment activists as lacking in "esthetic surprises," and as "a mess of pottage . . . substituted for the birthright of free speech and direct communication."[3] Charles Bukowski, who was mentioned earlier, is a West Coast cult hero renowned for his confessional poetry packed with descriptions of drinking, gambling, sex, poverty, hollow relationships, and personal failure. A few years ago he announced proudly, if unnecessarily, "I am no tidy professor with a home in the hills and a piano-playing wife."[4] And according to Robert Bly, a widely admired, traditionally educated poet (Harvard B.A., Iowa M.F.A.) who had chosen not to accept a faculty appointment, "Academic poetry . . . is recognizable by fake French surrealism and emotional anemia." We were, he warned, "living in a swamp of mediocrity, poetry of the Okefenokee, in which a hundred and fifty mediocre books are published each year."[5] Gary Allan Kizer—the little magazine coeditor and prisoner mentioned earlier, and a poet whose work often features left-political themes—on his questionnaire labelled academic poetry "trash with all the precision and neatness of Hallmark greeting card jingles."

Those who challenge such categorization object that the label "academic poetry" makes no sense because the poems of academically employed authors are indescribably diverse, on occasion including work that is daring in style and content and, presumably, anti- or non-"academic." What is more, said poet William Harmon, writers located outside academe are perfectly capable of being " 'academic' in the bad sense—pedantic, perfunctory, formulaic, dogmatic, predictable, preachy, partisan, political."[6]

In 1984 *The American Book Review* ran a special section comprising several articles written from different viewpoints on academic poetry. It is interesting to read this section alongside a debate about the same subject between senior poet-critic Yvor Winters (pro-academy) and the young poet-editor Hayden Carruth (anti-academy), which had been published in *Poetry* thirty-six years earlier, just before universities began admitting poets as faculty members with any regularity. Carruth anticipated many 1980s' concerns, and Winters offered many 1980s' defenses.[7] Indeed, the debate seems to have been running on a circular track ever since, coming no closer to resolution.

Alarmists' predictions were never quite borne out by events, but some did have bases in logic. The academy *is*, as teacher and chili-con-carne entrepreneur William Joyce pointed out, an extremely seductive, reliably remunerative "warm stall," relatively secure and comfortable for the published poet, and generous in its allowance of that invaluable treasure: time to write.[8] At the same time, universities are fairly traditional, imposing—admittedly with flexible limits—codes of behavior and aesthetic judgments. This sanctuary from tough living, combined with the requirement to publish (which carries the temptation to write what is easily publishable), and the subtle inhibitions on experimentation imposed by received critical ideologies, are what anti-academicians fear. A mild, conservative literature can be pleasant to read, but is not dynamic, strikes no sparks, cannot grow. Roger Mitchell called anti-academicism "cultural machismo" because of its characteristic insistence that poets encounter the "real world," and in some respects Mitchell's phrase is peculiarly apt.[9] Yet, given the environment of aesthetic unaccountability that bred much of the most vital, innovative American poetry—that of Whitman, Dickinson, Hart Crane, Pound, Langston Hughes, cummings, William Carlos Williams, and others, none of whom toiled within the academy, won ready acceptance from the literature professoriat, or worried overmuch about it—the danger of poetry's diminishment to a competent, static exercise could be real. If this is indeed, as it seems to be, an era without poetic masters, the danger may already be recognized. High originality and the willingness to take chances with one's talent and risk ridicule while staking out new literary territory characterized all of the writers named above and are requisites for the poetic pioneer. College and university English departments, which are, on the whole, usually committed to the redefinition, preservation, and transmission of more or less accepted literary values, would not seem to offer the most fertile environment for rebellion. Questions raised by poet-editor Peter Davison at the end of the period studied were profoundly unsettling:

> Could our society possibly have poisoned poetry by transforming it from a calling into a profession? . . . Could it be . . . that we have relegated poets to a role like that of housewives gossiping across the back fence? And that we've done so by the same means we've kept housewives at home, by putting them down and buying them off?[10]

However, it may be that the age does not lack masters, or at least true originals, but that the domination of contemporary poetry by academic critics and writers prevents wide recognition of those who work outside their beam unless, like Bly and Ginsberg, they are excellent self-promoters. Examples of impressively gifted, idiosyncratic poets who work in the shadows of everyday life with little or no university support are many and include the independent small-businessman William Bronk, who just a few years ago began to attract plaudits after decades of obscurity; the late George Oppen, a classic Objectivist poet who was independently wealthy and published sporadically; Hilda Morley, once of the Black Mountain clique; and the working-class lesbian feminist writer Judy Grahn. Even if one assumes the harmful influence of the academy, it may threaten the quality and range of what is *appreciated* more than what is *written*. There is a connection, of course; lack of appreciation can discourage writing altogether. Still, the cause-and-effect are neither direct nor inevitable. That any talented poet of original vision, let alone the rare genius, can be levelled to safe mediocrity through contact with a university is impossible to prove or disprove but seems implausible. There have always been very few brilliant, original poets, and they usually have had to struggle for the praise given freely to many of their more pedestrian cohorts.

What made the end of the 1950–80 period different from preceding eras may have been merely the *number* of conventional poets published, making the avant-gardists seem unusually scarce by contrast. Probably the new willingness of higher education to nurture and sustain large numbers of poets contributed to this situation—but, given that publication of some sort was available to nearly everyone, allowing even underappreciated work to find print and await its natural audience, the long-range effect on literature may have been slight. That conclusion does not, however, take into account the often-expressed fear, discussed in the previous chapter, that this very accessibility of print and resultant mushrooming of publications may cause good work to be overlooked. Nor can the hope of discovery at some unspecified future date do much to allay the daily suffering of wrongly neglected individuals.

The Poet in the Academy

When not appealing to the quality of the poetry itself, defenders of academic affiliation circle the inescapable practical problem of economic survival. The poet must live but cannot live off his poetry, must write but cannot write on the job if employed in a filling station, taxicab, or teller's booth. Isn't it absurd, they ask, to deplore the existence of a comparatively nonintrusive patron offering numerous poets regular paychecks, congenial work, and writing time—even though the time afforded is not as plentiful as outsiders usually think it to be.

Poets on university or (especially) college faculties find much time and energy consumed by work with students. However, many poet-academicians consider institutions of higher education unusually tolerant of their needs and on balance rather easy places to earn their livelihoods. They derive some intrinsic benefits from teaching. Frequent conversations with intelligent people who share their interests offset the loneliness of writing itself and structure opportunities to gain the stimulation of others' ideas. Teaching literature not only allows but forces poets to read their great forebears closely, discuss their meaning and value with students, and clarify ideas about poetry. Neoclassical poet-critic Yvor Winters once declared: "Had it not been for my academic career, it is quite possible that I should still be a minor disciple of W. C. Williams doing little impressionistic notes on landscapes."[11] Four and a half decades later, the intensely contemporary young Cleopatra Mathis of Dartmouth College said that her very different work was benefiting similarly from the teaching of the master poets.[12]

The most common defense of teaching, however, rests on the simple fact that most poets must earn more money more dependably than is to be had from writing. Winters suspected that other careers would have left him fewer hours to write and "directed most of my energy away from the matters which most interest me instead of toward them," and poet Roger Mitchell noted that while hardship may provide some poets with interesting subject matter, "most people are simply beaten down by it."[13]

The practical advantages of academic life are often irresistible even to poets who are deeply ambivalent or negative about its other aspects. Robert Frost saw no good solution to the problem of physical survival. He thought college teaching was probably "the lesser of two evils"—farming, for instance, being "too hard work" and publishers' offices "deadening" workplaces—but warned that "the act of correcting papers is weakening, deadening . . . a young poet can be buried and never recover."[14] W. D. Snodgrass, who was never fond of teaching ("It keeps me out of jail") and was glad to have spent some of his earlier years at unskilled labor, would have quit working if he could, but admitted ruefully that with unlimited free time, he might not write at all.[15] Having reduced his teaching as much as possible, longtime academician Philip Levine claimed to have "no respect for academia, none," and had found there little substance to enrich his poetry, but remained because "It beats working" and afforded several mornings a week for writing.[16] In other interviews he discussed with pleasure his experiences of teaching talented young writers, but never rejoiced in the academic environment itself.

One of the most praised American writers, and the person named second most often by respondents to this study as the "best or most interesting" living American poet, was Galway Kinnell, who has been treated generously by universities and has had much to say about their attractions and pitfalls. Having avoided faculty appointments for a number of years, Kinnell began accepting them at last because he enjoyed teaching, and: "When one gets older and no longer has unlimited energy, it is hard to know what kind of job other than teaching would give him the necessary laziness he's got to have in order to write."[17] However, Kinnell worried that university life was inauthentic, too easy, dangerously lacking in identifiable products and hard demands. Furthermore, he found personal relationships formed within the university lacking in variety and intellectual nourishment: "Many of the people you are talking to are too much like yourself: it's too much like a conversation going on inside your own head."[18]

For some, then, the academic life was an evil—necessary if poetry was to be written without fearsome privation, but an evil nonetheless. Some of these critics seem essentially distrustful of comfort and of any incentive to conform. In this they resemble (and overlap with) the detractors of the academic press, who worry that its publications exclude poetry of the "outlaws," the unsettled and (especially) the unsettling. Work that breaks with literary rules and traditions, they charge, logically enough, will seem inexplicable and indefensible to people who spend their lives assessing literature's quality by how it measures up to old models. In light of the data uncovered by this study, the quality and biases of the academic press are centrally important.

POETS' PUBLISHING THROUGH THE ACADEMIC PRESS

As mentioned earlier, academic publishing—once important to poets principally for its literary journals and the poetry series of two or three university presses—had throughout the 1970s become more and more a haven for books that might once have been accepted but now were spurned by the trade houses. The previous chapter gave evidence that Newer Prizewinners' first books were at least twice as likely as Older Prizewinners' to have been brought out by university presses, even when Yale Younger Poets were removed from the NP group but not from the OP.

Poets in both newer groups more often won early periodical acceptance from academic journals than was true of their older counterparts; between nonprizewinning groups, the difference was almost negligible, but Newer Prizewinners' proportion of early appearances in academic journals exceeded Older Prizewinners' by almost 28 percentage points. College- and university-sponsored journals accounted for about 43 percent of Newer Prizewinners' earliest publications, ranking them second in importance to independent little magazines, which accounted for 53 percent. As Newer Prizewinners' careers progressed, the academic press was less significant as a publishing outlet, the commercial press correspondingly more significant. Older Prizewinners were similar in that fewer of their latest than their first books, by 14 percentage points, were published by university presses—fewer by almost 21 percentage points when chapbooks were discounted. At the same time, Older Prizewinners became *more* likely by about 7.5 percentage points to bring new work to the public through academic journals. In the most recent period examined, Newer Prizewinners' proportion of periodical appearances in university and college journals fell from about 43 percent to 38 percent, while Older Prizewinners' rose from about 15 percent to 22.5 percent.

By contrast, Older Nonprizewinners came to rely on the academy somewhat more heavily for both book and magazine publication. Newer Nonprizewinners saw about as many last as first books, but fewer periodical publications by 4.5 percentage points, ushered into print through academia.

Perhaps most striking and most significant was the magnified importance of the academic sector as earliest supporter of authors who went on to win the most prestigious prizes available to new poets. While this could reflect academicians' aesthetic acuteness or literary-political prescience, an at least equally reasonable speculation—in light of the educational and professional data presented earlier—is that the academic literary world had become, if not a closed system, at least one that turned in and fed on itself. That is, universities and colleges trained writers in certain stylistic preferences and norms, rewarded them by creating many of their first publishing opportunities, employed them as poet-teachers, and continued to publish a good deal of their work (though a declining percentage) as their careers progressed—careers spent, in large part, training the next generation of serious poets so that the cycle would repeat. This is, of course, a simplified scenario, but it is interesting as conjecture and has been implied, in one way or another, by both critics and supporters of the academy as poets' patron.

In any case, the involvement of academic publishing in poets' careers, and especially in the early careers of poets who would go on to win accolades and the chance to wield influence, increased between the early and late periods spotlighted in this study. To estimate what this means, it will help to build on the previous chapter's brief consideration of academic publishing. In the following section, discussion of periodicals will be emphasized because until the 1970s, at least, they were more prominent poetry publishers than university book presses and generated the most commentary. Many of the same strengths and weaknesses characterize academic poetry books.

EDITORS' VULNERABILITY TO CONTROL

In most cases, critics charge, the predictability of academic periodicals offsets their occasional excellence. A force for caution often mentioned is the everpresent possibility of university control. This *has* happened, most famously at the University of Chicago, where in 1955 the administration enjoined student-run *Chicago Review* from publishing a group of manuscripts accepted for a special issue featuring San Francisco writers. This led to mass editorial resignations and the founding of an independent journal, *Big Table* (a now-legendary publication that survived for four issues), to accommodate the proscribed pieces. To the university's chagrin, one suspects, these were written by men who would soon emerge as the seminal voices of the Beat movement and the most influential writers of the decade: Ginsberg, William Burroughs, and Jack Kerouac. Another famous fifties' case of direct academic censorship involved the *Beloit Poetry Journal*, which broke with Beloit College as a result and has been independent for thirty years.

Others of the few academic journals that actually have been censored directly by university powers-that-be include *The Purple Sage* (University of Wyoming), *Northwest Review* (University of Oregon), and *New Mexico Quarterly* (University of New Mexico). Nearly one-quarter of forty-one academic literary journals surveyed by the National Endowment for the Arts in 1975 were subject to the approval of faculty review boards.[19] Of course, such boards did not necessarily interfere with editorial processes, but they provided a mechanism through which interference could quite naturally and easily occur.

Still, overt suppression by university or college officials was rare; the greater danger might lie in the possibility of self-censorship—that is, the selection of manuscripts with only one eye on their quality, the other on potential reactions to them. In 1953 Paul Stewart described self-censorship imposed by *Prairie Schooner*'s founding editor:

> Wimberly is not blind to the fact that much good and legitimate modern literature not only contains but depends heavily on a frank treatment of sex. When confronted with such a piece of writing, Wimberly's editorial decision is a matter of practical judgment rather than of literary taste. His own sensibilities are not easily offended. But the existence of the *Schooner* depends upon continued support from its two chief sources of income—the subscribers and the University of Nebraska. Anything which would raise questions of morality serious enough to endanger the continued support from these two sources, Wimberly has declined to publish regardless of its literary quality. Homosexuality and other perversions fall under the general taboo. The act of love may of course be suggested but may not be described. Nor may the story contain intimate anatomical detail or reference to the bodily functions.

Accordingly, in 1934, Wimberly had decided to reject one of the best-written stories ever received by *Prairie Schooner*.[20] While specific biases may have been fewer and quite different by the end of the period studied here (and probably related as often to style as content), undoubtedly they were felt by many academic editors to exist. One can only speculate about examples of this, since by their nature they are invisible. It is, however, hard to imagine politically extreme content in an academic magazine, especially reflecting far-right attitudes. Consistently end-rhymed poetry and other poems written in conventional form or in dialect would probably be unacceptable to most editors regardless of quality, as would strongly religious verse or graphically gay/lesbian content. While poetry of other types might encounter resistance, the above are so totally absent that one suspects them of being taboos. Some may be imposed by the host university, others by prevailing literary tastes or, more specifically, the preferences of subscribers or college English departments. The rarity of overt censorship suggests either a high incidence of self-censorship, a lax review process, a convergence of editorial and external attitudes, or, most likely, a combination of these factors.

ACADEMIC JOURNALS' STRENGTHS AND CONTRIBUTIONS

Yet academic journals persist and are read. They are often handsomely produced, attract famous contributors, win grants, and quite frequently publish works that win prizes and are reprinted in anthologies. All of these rewards may be reaped because of good editorial taste, but more surely because of reliable financial support—a condition regarded by some readers (especially impoverished little-magazine editors) as not only compromising them aesthetically but draining any passion they might otherwise have, any motivation to assert an identity, spark interest in their aims, and build readership. Yet economic stability (which has been the condition of academic journals only in relative terms) does offer a sort of freedom: a measure of comfort and externally perceived legitimacy that can lead to influence and psychological space for planning, development, and growth.

In light of the strident criticisms hurled by some poets at academic magazines, it is striking that in questionnaire responses offered for the present study, these outlets fared very well. Of course, anyone who was intensely hostile to academia would not be likely to cooperate in the study. For all their institutional constraints and alleged commitment to convention, these journals had far more fans than critics among the responding poets, who, as a group, valued publication through all academically sponsored sources. Although academic journals were accused on occasion of cliquishness and undue entrancement with writers of impressive reputation, they evidently remained much more open to new poets than did the more commercial magazines. The main reason for this was probably practical: that is, the much larger numbers of academic-journal pages to be filled with literature each year.

College and university magazine editors are fond of commencing their maiden issues with statements of intent. While a very few—usually those located in areas remote from other publishing activity—favor contributors identified with their own regions, virtually none can be described as regionally exclusive.

Bias in favor of the sponsoring institution's authors might also be expected in academic publishing, but there is little evidence of it. The aforementioned 1975 NEA survey turned up only four (out of forty-one) college- and university-affiliated journals that strongly favored their own students and faculty when selecting manuscripts, one that had a policy *prohibiting* their publication, and thirty-six that were more or less neutral.[21]

Purposes

The following statements typified the academic journals' senses of mission:

We of *Poet And Critic* believe that little magazines such as ours must exist to stimulate and publish the work of creative talents that our commercial world neglects.[22]

Poet and Critic
Iowa State University (1964)

Although published at The University of Kansas, the staff will consider materials from anywhere about anything and in any form imaginable. Its sole purpose is to provide an outlet for creative talent.[23]

Cottonwood Review
University of Kansas (1966)

We read [talented new writers'] work, we offer constructive criticisms, we suggest other places the authors might submit, and whenever they meet our standards, we publish their work. . . . whenever we get a submission that seems to have some value, we try to say at least something.[24]

Sou'wester
Southern Illinois University (1980)

Honest efforts are made to realize these intentions. Stanley Koehler, a poet-participant in this study and a past editor of *Massachusetts Review*, claimed that all unsolicited *MR* submissions were read, despite their "impressive" volume, in order to "keep free of the regional and the established." And many other knowledgeable readers defend the quality, individuality, and overall contributions of college- and university-supported journals.

As has been pointed out, until the late 1970s almost all academic literary publishing—with a few glittering exceptions—was handled by journals. By the end of that decade, however, university book presses had attracted attention by adding many more poets to their lists. Helping them bear the burden of poetry publication was the Associated Writing Programs series, which lifted the extremely time-consuming and sensitive editorial screening task from the presses' staffs and placed it with well-respected authors. The program was exploited by a number of presses—among them the University Presses of Virginia and Florida, the Universities of Alabama and Illinois, Texas Tech University, and Hardin Simmons College—and facilitated the publication of books by such poets as Leon Stokesbury, Gibbons Ruark, Phyllis Janowitz, Janet Kauffman, Sandra Gilbert, and, from this study, Carole Oles and James Applewhite.

While the number of academic press books put out annually was not large, in 1983 still numbering only thirty-seven titles from fourteen university presses, they tended to be well-regarded, and the simple fact of their existence undercut a longstanding assumption about the proper role of the academic press.[25] This development was bracing for poets and aroused new hopes.

POETS' VALUATION OF ACADEMIC PUBLISHING

Several of the poets in this study were emphatic in their preference for academic-press over small-press publication, although, interestingly, they tended to rank trade publication as at least equally desirable, or nearly so—for example, Donald Junkins, Kenneth Rosen, Shelley Neiderbach, Dorothy Lee Richardson, and John Gill, himself copublisher of Crossing Press, an important small house. Yale Younger Poet Maura Stanton preferred university presses "because they keep books *in print for a long time*," and ranked commercial presses second because they did not, but still desirable "because they pay advances."

Poets were asked whether they had tried unsuccessfully to win acceptance in any particular markets—that is, any particular publishing houses or periodicals, types of house or periodical, or sectors of publishing—and if so, to identify the market(s). Of the 135 poets responding, ninety-four (69 percent) identified at least one such market. Prizewinners had experienced the problem of attempting futilely to place their work in specific desired markets less often than had nonprizewinners; less than half the Newer Prizewinning respondents and one-quarter of the Older Prizewinners answered in the affirmative, while over three-quarters of both Newer and Older Nonprizewinners did. This suggests, of course, that even poets who remain relatively obscure after years of writing do not necessarily resign themselves to publication through obscure sources, but make the attempt to travel more prestigious (or otherwise more desirable) avenues and may continue to do so over decades-long careers as published authors. In a number of cases, a written comment accompanying an answer indicated that the poet had tried and failed to win acceptance in the desired market several times over a long period.

Of the sixty-six outlets where poets said they had tried unsuccessfully to publish, twenty-two were academic. None of those, however, was among the five outlets cited most often. Ranked sixth was the "university press" as a general category and eighth was Oberlin College's *Field* magazine, which, incidentally, was one of only two organs named by any Older Prizewinning poet in response to this query. In total numbers of citations (as distinguished from number of separate markets cited), the independent sector outdistanced the academic by 7.5 percentage points, and the commercial sector, which overwhelmingly dominated responses, outdistanced the academic by 33 percentage points.

When poets gave their opinions about which were the "best or most significant" poetry-book publishers, nearly every academic press putting out any poetry at all was named by at least one person (which was also true of commercial publishers of poetry). Two of the ten most respected houses were academic: Pittsburgh (ranked second, after the trade press Atheneum) and Wesleyan (fourth). Of the twenty-one houses cited most often as "best or most significant," six (29 percent) were academic: the two above, plus Yale (ranked thirteenth), Princeton and Georgia (tied for fourteenth), and Illinois (seventeenth). This was a strong showing, considering the comparatively small number of university presses issuing poetry, their modest output, and the recency of some of these presses' entry into the field.

Three of the ten most-read journals printing poetry were academic: the University of Georgia's *Georgia Review* (ranked fifth), *Field* (sixth), and the University of Washington's *Poetry Northwest* (ninth). There was marked generational divergence in responses to the question of which poetry-publishing journals were read regularly. *American Poetry Review* (*APR*) was the journal most read by both groups of newer poets, while both older groups were most likely to read the much longer established *Poetry*. Older Prizewinners cited *Field* more often than *APR* and *Georgia Review* just as often.

The choices of "best" journals followed those of "most read" fairly closely, as would be expected. The widely distributed independent *APR*, however, seemed somewhat more read than respected, receiving fourteen fewer citations as "best or most significant" and ranking third on this list instead of first. Also among the top eleven were the college- or university-sponsored titles *Field* (ranked fourth), *Georgia Review* (sixth), *Iowa Review* (seventh), and *Poetry Northwest* (ninth). Thirty-six percent of this top group of periodicals, then, originated in academe. Nine academic titles appeared among the most-cited twenty-one, those above being joined by *Ohio Review* (ranked eleventh), *Missouri Review* (thirteenth), *Kenyon Review* (fourteenth), and *Prairie Schooner* and *Virginia Quarterly Review* (tied for sixteenth rank).[26]

Whether for good or ill, by 1980 much of American poetry, including the most noticed, seemed to have been absorbed, institutionalized, and professionalized in a manner and to a degree without precedent. That this led to larger numbers of poetry magazines and poets, hence to much more published poetry, resulted from the various forms of academic and government support and presentation. Much evidence suggests that the overall result was more printed poetry both good and bad, spread among enough new magazines to make distinguishing the best poems and poets a difficult chore. While it may have been difficult ever since the 1920s or 1930s, it has become more so over the past three decades and especially since the late sixties to mid-seventies.

5

The Small Press and Poetry

A second major disclosure that invites discussion was the overwhelming importance for all poet groups at all career periods of little magazines and small presses unaffiliated with colleges or universities.

POETS' SMALL PUBLISHING

As explained earlier, the independent noncommercial publishing sector, comprising nonacademic small presses and little magazines, emerged repeatedly as the most significant source of exposure for all poet groups, older and younger, prizewinning and not, at early, mid, and late career. So dominant was it that it seems worthy of remark only when *not* dominant.

The small press was not the most active publisher of prizewinners' first books, bringing out just over one-quarter of both Older and Newer Prizewinners' initial volumes. This contrasted with the role played by trade houses in OPs' early careers, which published just over 41 percent of their first books, and by university presses in NPs' early careers, which brought out just under half. Of seven publishers whose imprints appeared on two or more first books of Older Prizewinners, only one, Stone Wall, could be described as a small press. Of eight publishers holding similar records with regard to Newer Prizewinners, again only one, Swallow Press, was small. Small presses were, however, immensely useful to nonprizewinners in early career, accounting for about 71 percent of Older Nonprizewinners' first books and 85 percent of Newer Nonprizewinners'. (Although some of these books were self-published, especially in the case of the newer poets, a great many were not.) In early *periodical* publication of *all* poets, however, little magazines were clearly the most active.

Interestingly, with the passage of time, small presses became somewhat more prominent in Newer Prizewinners' bibliographies, accounting for about 38 percent of their latest books—the same proportion handled by commercial houses, more than were published by university presses, and an increase over the proportion of first books handled by small presses.

While over two-thirds of Older Prizewinners' most recent full-length books were issued by trade publishers, both groups of lesser-known poets continued to depend heavily upon small presses: almost 94 percent of Newer Nonprizewinners' last books and two-thirds of Older Nonprizewinners' full-length volumes were produced by small presses.

Again in the realm of periodicals, where new poetry usually debuted, every poet group was most reliant by far in the recent period on independent little magazines. Group proportions of appearances in these ranged from one-half for Newer Prizewinners to almost three-quarters for Newer Nonprizewinners. While NPs' and OPs' rates of publication in little magazines declined slightly between the earliest and latest points in their publishing histories, both generations of nonprizewinners came to use them slightly *more* in the later period.

The basic point to be made here is that small literary presses and little magazines, fragile, uneven, and poorly funded as they usually were, contributed enormously by giving voice not only to the lesser-known poets of the period but also to the most celebrated.

However, the findings suggest that poets often turned to these sources more out of need than choice.

POETS' VALUATION OF SMALL PRESSES AND LITTLE MAGAZINES

As noted in the preceding chapter, poets were asked in which market(s), if any, they had tried and failed to win acceptance. Rather than listing every place that had rejected their work, respondents invariably listed one or a few periodicals, book presses, or whole categories of publishing that to them represented important goals.

Some respondents named publishing *sectors* where they aspired to win acceptance (for example, "commercial publishers" or "the New York press"—meaning the trade press), while many more cited specific journals or houses. Most often cited by every group was *The New Yorker*, and among Newer Prizewinners it was an especially significant goal. Eighty-two percent of those answering "yes" to the question listed it among the publications where they had been hoping and trying to appear. *The Atlantic*, the only other mass marketed magazine that publishes a substantial amount of poetry, was cited second most often by poets overall. Again, it was most important to Newer Prizewinners, who were less likely than their older counterparts to have appeared in it and likelier than nonprizewinners to view it as a feasible goal. Cited third most often, along with that most atypical of little periodicals, *American Poetry Review*, was trade book publishers as a general category. The category of trade magazines was also mentioned frequently.

Again, there was sometimes marked ambivalence. One young poet whose sole book had attracted some favorable notice, though it was brought out by a very small press, believed that "commercial publishing today has little to do with talent," yet asserted that her second book would "*NOT* [go] to a small press, *that's* for sure—will go for . . . Atheneum, Pitt, etc.—but no little stuff." Later, listing poetry-book publishers whom she admired, she named four big New York houses plus New Directions, which was perhaps too large to call really small, but resembled small presses in its tight focus on serious literature. Donald Junkins, a better-known poet whose single collection had been issued by the University of Pittsburgh, told where he would prefer to place his manuscripts: "The best place. I'd love Farrar Straus. Then almost any N.Y. house. Then the university presses. I wouldn't go lower." Answering another question, Junkins singled out his third *New Yorker* acceptance as the "most gratifying" poetry-related event of his career.

Presumably, poets longed for the money and prestige that accompany large-press publication, and several survey respondents frankly acknowledged this. "*They pay*," said William Harmon, explaining the attractions of *The New Yorker* and *The Atlantic*. Kathryn Stripling, on the other hand, said that she believed acceptance in the most selective journals, whether commercial or not, to be necessary for career development: "The attempt to get one's poems into the 'right' magazine is often a desperate one. To be taken seriously one must have had work in the *New Yorker*, or *Antaeus*, or *American P. R. [Poetry Review]*—so the theory goes. To some extent, I'm sure that's correct."

However, the motivation might be less specifically definable though equally as strong. To be accepted over hundreds of the rejected, by editors who surely had their choice of famous poets and access to large reading audiences, was intrinsically irresistible to many authors, regardless of their attitudes toward these editors' products. Marilyn Hacker, a feminist in this study with politically left views, was drawn to commercial outlets right along with her more conservative colleagues. "I confess to a perverse desire to publish in *The New Yorker* and *The*

Atlantic," she wrote. Small-press poet Alice Cabaniss said that she held *New Yorker* publication as a "personal lifetime aim," and took pride in the fact that "once they said I got close."

The high incidence of trade-press answers to the question probably reflected the unusual difficulty of winning acceptance in this sector (as well, of course, as the hope of more money than noncommercial publishers usually offer). The exact wording of the question should be kept in mind when answers are interpreted: "Is there any *particular* market or publication that you have tried to break into without success? (E.g., a specific magazine or publishing house—or a particular *sector* of publishing, such as the academic press or commercial press, etc.) . . . If 'yes,' please identify the market(s)/publication(s)." A poet-respondent who greatly valued publication through a given source and had achieved it at least once would probably not list it in a response to this question, nor would a respondent who desired publication in certain sources or sectors, but thinking them beyond reach, had never approached them.

While poets might cherish highest hopes for trade publication, small presses and little magazines were cited with surprising frequency and accounted for four of the ten most mentioned sources: *American Poetry Review* (ranked third), *Poetry* (fourth), *Paris Review* (eighth), and *Antaeus,* which is associated with the highly esteemed small press Ecco (tenth). None of these, it may be noted, fit the classic little-magazine image, whether drawn in the muted colors of struggle and bare survival or in garish hues of fiery dissent. The same was true of journals named by poets in this study as unusually good or heavily read.

An impressive six of the eleven periodicals most read by poets were independent literary journals, although of these only *Ironwood* fit the aforementioned classic little-magazine profile, at age thirteen being relatively young and with a modest circulation of 1,120.[1] The others were *APR,* founded only in 1975, but with 24,000 circulation; the venerable *Poetry,* cited second most often, which at age seventy-five claimed a circulation of 6,700; *Antaeus* (founded 1970, circulation 5,000); *Ploughshares* (1971, 4,500); and *Paris Review,* a slick thirty-five-year-old journal with a circulation of 10,000 and decidedly commercial bearing. Of the twenty-one most read journals, ten (48 percent) were independent. Added to those above were the tabloid format *Poetry Now* (1973, 2,500), poet Sydney Lea's *New England Review* (1978, 2,000), *Hudson Review* (1948, 3,500), and *kayak* (1964, 1,400).[2]

Poetry, the progenitor of twentieth-century little magazines, and originally, at least, the warm receiver of new voices and styles and maker of reputations, had survived decades of criticism, editorial changes, and the competition of thousands of new journals to emerge as still the best periodical publishing poetry, in the opinion of this study's respondents. Fifty-six (39 percent) of the 141 respondents to this question mentioned it. Next most admired was *The New Yorker*, mentioned by forty-six. The most read periodical, *American Poetry Review*, was listed only forty-one times as "best." The same six independent periodicals named among the eleven most read also showed up among the eleven best.

Interestingly, little magazines were valued most highly by the most established group of poets: Older Prizewinners. Over 70 percent of the thirty-seven poetry-publishing periodicals cited by OPs as "read regularly" were littles. This contrasts with a 46 to 55 percent citation of littles from each of the other three groups. Responding to the question asking for "best" periodicals, Older Prizewinners named twenty-nine different titles, of which twenty, or 69 percent, were little magazines. Other poet groups' answers ranged from 40 percent to 65 percent littles. However, when *all* of the Older Prizewinners' answers—that is, including repetitions—were totalled, only 59 percent referred to little magazines, reflecting the fact that several very obscure publications were mentioned by Allen Ginsberg alone.

Interestingly, *Poetry* was held in highest esteem by Newer Nonprizewinners, thirty-two of whom judged it best. The periodical ranked second by this group was *APR*, mentioned by twenty-three people. That the youngest and least recognized poet group should value so highly the oldest small literary magazine in the country suggests that it must have retained at least a share of its early vitality and receptiveness to the new and still had a remarkable ability to attract and hold young readers.

The small-book press probably has received less attention over the years than the little magazine. It has been discussed and memorialized in print less often and is seldom as passionately and sentimentally defended. For one thing, whatever the limitations of the trade press, it is much more visible as a publisher of poetry in book than in magazine form. More individual trade book publishing outlets exist, each contributing more to printed poetry in volume than, say, *The New Yorker* or *The Atlantic*, with their two or three poems per month buried in surrounding pages of prose.

This may help account for the fact that Ecco, Graywolf, and New Directions were the only small-book presses on the list of the eleven most often cited by respondents as best. (New Directions, a literary publisher that in a sense bridged the commercial and noncommercial sectors and might more properly be called mid-sized than small, was here assigned to the latter category because of its single-minded concentration on serious literature, little apparent concern with commercial values, and list of modest length.) Copper Canyon, Black Sparrow, North Point, and Godine appeared among the following ten, for a total of seven small presses, one-third of the most mentioned twenty-one.

All data confirm the enormous importance of independent publishing to all poet groups. Yet in the early eighties it was engulfed in a controversy having to do with quantity and quality of output and the related issue of grant funding. In order to understand why this was so and how and why the independent sector was playing so prominent a role in publishing the least saleable type of writing, it is useful to consider characteristics of this sector, its unique purposes and contributions, and its problems.

DEFINITIONS OF "SMALL" AND "LITTLE"

"Attitude," wrote editor Charles Angoff in 1966, was the key to defining small magazines and publishers: "A little magazine should always be raffish."[3] In the late seventies, Felix Pollak and Peter Michelson, both poets long experienced with little magazines, spoke of a profoundly irreverent "littlemag spirit." To Pollak this was "the spirit of the loner, the rambunctious, intransigent, irascible, all loving, asocial, rugged, individualist, who is so nonconformist that he refuses to conform even to other nonconformists."[4] This could have served as a personality profile of that famous little-magger Ezra Pound, the Ferlinghetti of the fifties (City Lights Books and *Journal*), or any of their many spiritual descendants. "We're feisty and persistent, like Snopeses," Michelson warned. "We'd as soon grind a shoeful of *Horse shit* on your new white carpet as anywhere else."[5]

Certainly, combative irreverence and self-assertiveness have characterized hundreds of both the best and the worst small publishing ventures and virtually all of those remembered most fondly: for example, among book presses, Harry and Caresse Crosby's Black Sun, Jonathan Williams's Jargon Books, John Martin's Black Sparrow, James L. Weil's Elizabeth, Douglas Messerli's Sun & Moon, and Lyn Hejinian's Tuumba. Magazines possessed of "the spirit" have been even more numerous but might be said to include early volumes of *Poetry* (1912+), *Partisan Review* (1934+), Robert Bly's *The Fifties/Sixties/Seventies* (1958–72), and *Evergreen Review* (1957–73); *The Little Review* (1914–29); *Hound and Horn* (1927–34); Curt Johnson's *December* (1958+); Clayton Eshleman's *Caterpillar* (1967–73); and *Amazon Quarterly* (1972–74). Poet George Hitchcock named his mimeographed journal *kayak* as a statement of independence. On each of its issues was emblazoned the following definition:

> A kayak is not a galleon, ark, coracle, or speedboat. It is a small, watertight, vessel operated by a single oarsman. It is submersible, has sharply pointed ends, and is constructed from light poles and the skins of furry animals. It has never yet been employed as a means of mass transport.

Despite (or because of) its headstrong individualism, *kayak* developed into one of the most warmly regarded littles and when Hitchcock ceased publishing it after sixty-four issues, he did so not from necessity but by design. Reminiscent of *kayak* in some respects was *Wormwood Review*, edited by Marvin Malone, who disapproved of editorial "team-work" and boasted that *Wormwood* was "non-local, non-sewing circle, non-political, and non-profit."[6]

During the 1970s, however, a change came over the scruffy universe of little magazines. Once, the appearance of an independent journal signalled passion if nothing else, passion strong enough to inspire its founder(s) to part with time and money for which there was no hope of tangible recompense. Given that those editors were only rarely rich and leisured, such sacrifice added up to a powerful statement and virtually guaranteed liveliness in the little mag, if not always high quality.

One of the most honored poets in the Newer Prizewinners' group deplored the changes wrought when the National Endowment for the Arts' (NEA's) grant money began to pour into the Coordinating Council of Literary Magazines (CCLM) for distribution to literary periodicals. The quality of motivation for founding and continuing these magazines (both academic and independent) was altered, this poet suggested: "Dozens and dozens of magazines had sprung up. Most of them, the poetry magazines especially, seemed featureless. They existed in order to exist. There was no sense of common endeavor and I thought my poems sat in them among other poems as a suitcase sits among other suitcases on a Greyhound rack at the bus station."

Of course, the presence of money alone will not stimulate creative activity. The type of magazine described by this poet must owe its being to money *plus* increased numbers of poets and story writers, mostly veterans of writing workshops or classes, or holders of fine arts degrees, who desired publication for self-gratification or to build personal bibliographies that might spark or advance careers. An additional factor, then, was the flourishing of degree programs, workshops, and reading series that proffered career opportunities.

Rather than describe the little magazine hazily as the bearer of a certain motivation or spirit, this study employed a more concrete working definition: a periodical that appears to select its material with minimal or no attention to its commercial possibilities and receives no regular support from, nor claims an affiliation with, a college or university. This definition does not convey any sense of the philosophies and operative policies of little magazines. These are usually articulated in print soon after a journal's founding and arrange themselves into types.

PURPOSES AND PRINCIPLES

Editors' statements heralding the arrival of new magazines have never made much sense to me, precisely because most never seem able to say what is really on their minds. These statements always seem to promise to do what is never really deliverable—at least by them—and they rant and rave about what other magazines have failed to do, which is mainly the bottom line for why they are now going into the godforsaken business of magazine publishing in the first place. Then they babble on about how unique and vital and necessary their own publication is going to be. This statement will be no different from its predecessors, except that we do intend to deliver.

Quincy Troupe, founding editor, *The American Rag*[7]

Searching for the Best: Eclecticism

Little magazines are most often consciously eclectic, leaving themselves open to a variety of literary styles, dedicated simply to publishing the best. This is perhaps somewhat less true of small-book presses, each of whose acquisition decisions requires a major investment of time and usually money. However, poet David Lunde's Basilisk Press was begun " 'without a manifesto and with no axes to grind,' just a desire to publish good writing," and went on to issue books that were quite diverse.[8] Similarly, New Rivers Press, which eventually built an excellent reputation, commenced in 1968 with no aim other than to publish good poetry and stay open to surprise.[9]

America's first notable little magazine of poetry shared this aim, of course. Harriet Monroe wanted, simply, "the best . . . English [-language] verse," and, as very nearly the only discriminating poetry editor in practice, she got it. In this as in so many other ways, *Poetry* may have set the stage for its successors, for many demonstrate a similar breadth of taste, hospitality to new authors, and strangely buoyant sense of serving something precious that transcends verse. Margaret Anderson's *Little Review* eschewed literary policymaking, claiming only to print "the good things that the best magazines reject."[10] Richard Johns' *Pagany*, which came in with the thirties and intended to "publish vital writing, articulate and important," was regarded by some as "aimless," a criticism that has plagued such magazines since, though without noticeable dampening effect.[11]

Almost thirty years later, two journals began just months apart, very different in most respects, yet with the same expressed goal. *Contact*, named after William Carlos Williams's little magazine of the thirties and dedicated to his spirit, was founded in San Francisco and announced the intention of "publishing work by anybody from anywhere as long as it meets our standards and is written approximately in the English language." *Contact* refused to take sides on any issue; though it did confess to being on the side of "Humanity," it would "publish an inhuman author should he present us with a magnificent work of inhumanity."[12] Twenty-two hundred physical miles and an even greater social distance away, on the south side of Chicago, black writer Clarence Major began his interesting *Coercion Review* for the sole purpose of printing the best material he was sent. Though he did not expressly hold a brief for "magnificent . . . inhumanity," Major did cherish the naive hope of achieving wide circulation "without any changes in policy."[13] (Seven years and four issues later, *Coercion Review* had sputtered into a semi-legible six-page mimeo authored entirely by Major himself.)

Throughout the period investigated here, numerous littles espousing eclecticism were born every year, and their opening statements, whether combative or idealistic, were earnest and essentially alike:

> Though the editor is an inveterate romanticist anti-intellectual, anti-denotative in poetry, GRYPHON will . . . accept other kinds of poetry. The wild horse's eye is our first choice but if a poem about nuts and bolts or about *The Fifth Ennead of Plotinus* is excitingly written we will use it.
>
> *Gryphon*, 1950[14]

> We will print any poetry deemed good, whether it be conventional or experimental, in slang or "high" English, serious or humorous, regardless of authorship.
>
> *Poetry Newsletter*, 1964[15]

> Capture the universal in the particular. That's all. Let the rhythm of style express the mood. Don't be restricted to one style. Don't strive to be current. I won't curse you if you write like Keats. Or Bukowski. Or somewhere in between. It doesn't matter.
>
> *Proteus*, 1973[16]

> We begin our adventure as editors with no particular causes to uphold, no crusades to carry on, no broad theories of literature to proclaim. . . . We solicit, we respect, we are interested in the work of all living poets.
>
> *Nomad*, 1979[17]

Like *Poetry* and *Pagany*, determinedly unbiased publications such as these have come under attack for lacking unique identities. Poet David Curry, founding editor of the now defunct *Apple*, said that to be representative was the task of "little magazines in the aggregate," not of any single title."[18] Veteran observer Felix Pollak described the "inchoate mass" of magazines that made a virtue of "directionless eclecticism." Yet Pollak believed also that a few possessed of "vigor and zeal" were still managing to emerge.[19]

Searching for the New: Experimentation

A second intention typically declared by small-press and little-magazine editors has already been noted and unequivocally substantiated by the poets' publishing data: the emphasizing of both new and insufficiently recognized older poets and of literary experimentation. The latter interest tends, of course, to dictate the former, and editors most committed to experimental work also show special hospitality to untried writers. Such editors have included Curt Johnson of December Press; D. r. Wagner of *Moonstones*, which was designed to reflect "change, youth, experimentation, and love"; experimental poet and relentless gadfly Richard Kostelanetz of *Assembling*; and Sun & Moon's Douglas Messerli, an experimental poet who wished to help "our most exciting young writers who have been left high and dry by the conglomerate publishers and are unable to find a publisher."[20] All of these editors and many more have promoted experimentation in ways that range from preference for original literary departures to insistence upon the most avant-garde. Sometimes they are affiliated with poetic movements, though often their conscientious progressiveness is vaguer as regards ultimate goals.

The Beat movement, for instance, spawned City Lights; *Fuck You*, edited by poet and rock performer (The Fugs) Ed Sanders; *Yugen* and *Floating Bear*, both coedited by LeRoi Jones (later Amiri Baraka), in the latter case with poet Diane di Prima; poet Harold Norse's *Bastard Angel*; and scores of other publishing efforts, either directly or along a tortuous path of inspiration. The present-day "language" movement is promoted through Tuumba Press and *L=A=N=G=U=A=G=E* magazine. The list could be extended, but many experiment-oriented enterprises are less particular in their attachments. The compilers of *Assembling*, for example, furthered their desire to "get rid of dummy intermediaries" between writer and reader by simply collating and distributing whatever people wished to reproduce a thousand times and send to them.[21] While many of these works were highly eccentric and thus, quality aside, would have been difficult to publish almost anywhere else, a large number would have faced the same problem simply because they were bad. Probably no periodical has equalled *Assembling* in innovativeness or inconsistency of style and quality—making it, paradoxically, at once the most revolutionary, most tolerant, and most eclectic of the little magazines. The more typical experimentalist insists upon selecting and imposes fairly rigid, philosophically based criteria when judging manuscripts received. Because of this rigidity, which Pollak termed little-magazine "elitism," a coterie quite naturally tends to develop of poets who pop up in issue after issue of a given title.[22] These are likely to be either the most exciting or the worst of the literary magazines, the difference depending on the quality of the editor's judgment, the aesthetic and intellectual soundness of the magazine's or press's literary ideas, and the talents of the contributor coterie.

Alan Swallow once listed as one of small pressmen's main functions the sponsorship of experiment and controversy; it is a function which, their increasing establishmentarianism notwithstanding, they did not fail to fulfill in the thirty years studied here.[23]

Opposing Commercialism, Conventionalism, and the Academy

Conjoined with the purpose articulated by Swallow—and basic to the motivation of many small publishers though not, as some assume, implied by their very existence—is an anti-commercial stance, sometimes ideological, at other times channelled into antagonism toward specific publishers, magazines, or industry sectors (for example, publishing enterprises embedded in multi-interest conglomerates). Often coexisting with anti-commercialism, sometimes emphasized above it, and, indeed, in some ways inherent in it, is anti-academicism. Again, this can be ideological—a rebellion against general academic conservatism and obeisance to established writers—or it can be reified in hostility toward specific institutions, schools of criticism, poets, prize competitions, or some combination of these. Because academically trained editors, reviewers, and critics, as well as college classroom teachers themselves, are perceived as having undue influence over which poems are published, anthologized, and sold by the trade, negative attitudes toward commerce and the academy tend to be linked—as witness Pound's remark, quoted earlier, that publication decisions would never be rationalized until all college presidents were disposed of.

Making up in passion what they lacked in resources during 1950–1980, little magazines and small-press editors lashed out through both direct statements and the example of their choices, providing a vociferous and, in toto, influential alternative to the conventional. Pollak called their enterprises "rivulets off the mainstream."[24] Thus, *Umbra*, unhindered by "monetary or prestige considerations," offered "a platform to writers who are . . . *too hard* on society"; *Premiere* sought "especially those young voices crying out in an academic wilderness"; and the long-running *Smith* (later *Pulpsmith*) declared itself "the enemy of civilization itself, combatting the repressive institutions and the petty specialties."[25] Kirby Congdon, rebel poet, publisher of Interim Books and its subsidiary Crank Books, and of the mimeoed *Magazine*—deplored the "academic fear of betting on the wrong horse," while David C. Yates used his journal, *Cedar Rock*, to berate both commerce and academe: "Perhaps . . . the 'learn'd professors,' and the commercial publishers don't need us—the small presses. But what might surprise most of these people is that we don't need them either—in fact, in many cases, don't even want them."[26]

Reminiscing about *Mother*, a short-lived and lively little magazine of the 1960s that inspired a special devotion in its small band of readers, coeditor David Moberg said,

At its best [it] had a dada irreverence. . . . Most of the poets and writers in *MOTHER* considered themselves in rebellion against the poetry and prose produced or glorified in academic circles. Their arsenal of literary devices included (among others) irony, parody, plagiarism, cut-up, fold-in, time-jumble, il'logic, nuttiness, abstraction, distortion, outrageousness, humor, pornography, lying, scatology, hallucination, frivolity, gibberish, and confusion.[27]

It was, in short, a peculiarly pure example of independent literary publishing. Recalling the wave of mimeographing in the 1960s—some literary, some political, some a blend of those interests—Len Fulton, who founded the literary periodical *Dust* at that time and began his series of small-press directories, mused: "It seems to me we considered [small publishing] a last desperate assertion of the individual against the giant machine."[28] The clenched fist of individual assertion is perceptible behind many independent publications, often, but not necessarily, in support of what would normally be called experimentalism.

Various other poetic interests have motivated small pressmen—among them, formalism and the writing of women or minorities or foreigners. A final important example is what might be called common-language poetry: easily comprehensible work shorn of compressed figures of speech, sophisticated vocabulary, difficult allusions, and abstracted mental experience. It is exemplified in the rough-and-tumble verse of Charles Bukowski, which Len Fulton considered a major inspiration to post-fifties small publishers and editors.[29] Bukowski, whose deliberately outrageous poetry is better known and respected in several Western European countries than in America, was discovered by the legendary small-press figures Lou and Jon Webb of *The Outsider* magazine. For over thirty years, John Martin, of the now prestigious though profoundly counter-cultural Black Sparrow Press, has issued Bukowski's books and earns substantial sums from their domestic and foreign-rights sales. In a way, Bukowski can be considered a classic small-press author.

Calling for a poetry of "reality" rather than "surreality," poetry that "sticks in the throat like a Texas sandstorm or plunges for the heart like a hawk for a rabbit," Paul Foreman of *Hyperion Poetry Journal* spoke for many independent literary publishers who are struck by the direct appeal of such work, its relative ease of comprehension (and in some cases, one suspects, of composition), the democratic purpose it lends itself to fulfilling, or some mixture of all these. "Our poetry is the speech of the common man," Foreman continued, "as natural as the hand that darts the needle through the wool, as sturdy as the single tree that swings above the plow, flecked with the sweat of mules. Truly, we must struggle like mules to make it through the bogs and fens of the contemporary poetry landscape."[30] Putting aside Foreman's unintentionally comic images and the incongruity of this statement with the magazine's Berkeley location, it can be seen that the attitude expressed was anti-experimental *and* anti-traditional, and certainly anti-commercial and anti-academic by implication. e. e. cummings, himself a beneficiary of small publishing, lampooned the reality bias by inventing a small-pressman's diatribe. "To hell with literature," he exclaimed, going on to propose bathroom graffiti as the model for poetry.[31]

The independent small press, while associated with experimentation in writing, is more fundamentally anti- or at least noncommercial, representing a range of work as wide as the range that cannot easily find a publishing home.

STRENGTHS AND CONTRIBUTION

Felix Pollak raised a point that was interesting though not susceptible to research: that if gifted writers who were first printed by little magazines and small presses had lacked these avenues, they would have persevered and "eventually . . . have become just as celebrated as they are now."[32] If this is true, independent editors and publishers can perhaps claim to help writers and speed their ascent, but the ascent itself, if merited, is inevitable. Of course, simply to speed an author may be to open a path of poetic development and permit the creation of specific works that otherwise would not have appeared. It may also spare the writer psychologically ruinous discouragement and bitterness, and even prevent the abandonment of a writing career. There is no reason to believe that every talented author will persist through long periods of disappointment.

Some celebrated poets firmly believed that the support of small pressmen dedicated to the new and the different was necessary for them. Philip Levine, an Older Prizewinner with a long string of honors and longer bibliography of prestigious publications, stated flatly in a 1978 interview:

> Without the little magazine, the small publisher, I never would have survived as a poet. I published my first book at 35 although I'd been writing very seriously for eleven uninterrupted years. It was with a small press [Stone Wall]. I'd been turned down, I'd been lied to, been promised and all that shit by the big publishers. Finally, they didn't print it. But the small press took the chance.[33]

In his questionnaire, Levine named George Hitchcock of the little magazine *kayak* as one of two "marvelous" periodical editors who had encouraged him before he became known. (The other, interestingly enough, was *The New Yorker*'s Howard Moss.) Among many other respondents asserting that the small press was necessary to new writers were Nona Nimnicht and Walt Whitman Award winner Karen Snow.

In addition to publishing them early and over long periods, small presses supported established poets by keeping their work in print, which might have been done less reliably by academic publishers and seldom at all by trade houses. Assuming that a small press itself survives, it is likely to keep its list alive for a long time. It does not, after all, expect quick, high-volume sales and publishes in the first place out of a commitment to authors and styles and an entire genre that, typically, require time to find appreciative readers. Prizewinner Sandra McPherson said that she prized her association with small Ecco Press partly for this reason.

Gradually, through the agency of the small press in giving it public life and keeping it alive even through periods when few have found it worthwhile, a particular school or type of poetry has sometimes entered the body of our generally recognized national literature. Its finest and/or most palatable examples may eventually separate themselves from the rest and become part of a broadly known poetic heritage. Instances include a handful of the once outrageous early Beat works of Ginsberg—which, more than thirty years after their first and shocking appearance, were brought out in a respectfully reviewed Harper & Row collected edition; the militant black feminist poetry of Audre Lorde, who was eventually nominated for major literary awards and came to be widely recognized as an interesting contemporary talent; the harshly realistic "Common Woman" poems of Judy Grahn, a working-class feminist who sometimes writes fairly experimental verse; and a very few of Bukowski's works. All of these came to be perceived as closer to the cultural mainstream than when they were written and were anthologized and studied, although their authors had changed neither their poetic nor their personal styles to conform to mainstream tastes and values, and their new works continued to be ushered into print by small presses and little magazines.

As the earliest hosts of literary experimenters and protesters, the winnowers and (after a tortuous, diffused process) the definers of new literary movements, the more adventuresome small presses and magazines are, inevitably, awash in the mediocre and ephemeral while at the same time offering the possibility and occasionally the reality of reading excitement. Nona Nimnicht said she liked "small presses because they *are* small, experimental, ephemeral, and open to risks, ridicule being one of them." In Ron Overton's opinion, although "good poems" were appearing everywhere, "the most exciting discoveries have been in the small magazines—not in the usually disappointing, predictable and conventionally 'literary' work to be found in the classy, prestigious mags."

The small-book press is also highly valued by authors for the virtually unique opportunity it affords for the involvement of writers in production and design decisions. Nimnicht (who had been published by the small Second Coming Press), McPherson and Robert Hass (Ecco), Steve Benson (Tuumba), and Marie Harris (Alice James Books) were among the many small-press-published poets in this study who mentioned that they treasured this opportunity. One Newer Prizewinning author had refused a $1,500 advance from a trade press in order to accept a $300 offer of a small publisher (even though he "could have used the money") because he believed a close professional relationship with greater long-term rewards might follow the latter offer. (He has stayed with that press.)

A final small press and little-magazine function often singled out for praise is the key role these ventures take in opening avenues of communication and thereby enabling a much-needed sense of community among writers, who, as has been pointed out, always do their essential work in isolation and, in this country, are both numerous and geographically dispersed.

The noncommercial independent press, then, is appreciated for a constellation of characteristics and actions fully possible only for publishing enterprises that are beholden to no one, including their readers, and operate at the cottage industry level: openness to the unknown, the challenging, and occasionally the offensive; individuality and flair; and the gentle, thoughtful handling and nurturance of each work, each author.

Because the small press at its best offers all of this, some onlookers have been unrestrained in its praise, even claiming that the very survival of literature depends upon it. For instance, David Curry declared that: "The small publishers, collectively, are keeping poetry alive in America today." In the 1970s and to a lesser degree since, many government arts agencies apparently shared this belief in the salubrious cultural effects of small publishing, and public monies became so widely available to the enterprise as to challenge the very concept of it as independent.

GRANT DEPENDENCY

The rise in the number of small publishing endeavors, particularly those with substantial life spans and products of polished appearance, coincided roughly with the funnelling of NEA and state arts council funds into little magazine and small press support. (The Coordinating Council of Literary Magazines [CCLM] began dispensing NEA funds and some [much less plentiful] private monies to literary magazines in 1967.) This support, while minuscule when compared to government budget slices for most other purposes, became pervasive. Peter Martin's 1978 selected bibliography of eighty-four significant postwar literary magazines included statements about each title's sources of financial support.[34] (Presumably, he depended on the magazines' self-reporting for this information.) Exactly the same proportion of independent and academic literary journals had received public funding support: 59 percent. Of the sixty-six noncommercial journals begun after or surviving through 1969, 73 percent had received tax money: sixteen (64 percent) of the academic journals and thirty-two (78 percent) of the independents. How large a part of the journals' budgets these grants comprised could not be determined from the bibliography. One assumes that grantwinning journals affiliated with institutions of higher education were less dependent on direct government support, just as they were less likely to receive grants at all. Exactly 50 percent of the 160 literary-magazine respondents to NEA's 1975 survey had received CCLM grants; one-third of the half that had not were ineligible, not yet having produced the three consecutive issues under consistent editorial direction that the Council required.[35]

Far from being greeted with unanimous applause from the writers and small-press staffers who were presumably its beneficiaries, state and federal funding caused discomfort and not a little vociferous dissension, in some cases from awardees themselves. A few other editors and publishers took the difficult step of refusing to apply for these grants. For example, *Samisdat*'s Merritt Clifton, a strident opponent of grant dependency, used a 1974 CCLM grant to resume publication after a discontinuance and then vowed to survive on income from sales.[36] The alternative to grants, Clifton insisted, is "called grit and integrity, working for a buck instead of begging it, then publishing within one's physical and financial means." CCLM and NEA, he charged, were promoting "literary welfare." The lesbian feminist enterprises *Sinister Wisdom* and Daughters, Inc., both eschewed grants. So did John Bennett's rebellious *Vagabond*, which changed from offset to mimeo reproduction as a result; *Sparrow*, run by the determinedly independent poets Felix and Selma Stefanile; and City Lights, which refused both government and corporate moneys ("the price of freedom is eternal indigence"[37]).

Tax-supported funding of publishing enterprises, especially when those that became dependent on the funding, had been, practically since it began, the most controversial issue in the small-press world—especially, but certainly not exclusively, with regard to periodical publishing. A variety of questions was posed in the debate, the most radical being whether the government should take any role at all in supporting artistic efforts. Felix Stefanile, for instance, an intransigent foe of public funding, called "government intrusion into the arts" the most important issue for the little magazine and claimed that he discerned an "Orwellian grants atmosphere."[38] Merritt Clifton deemed the NEA "our single most impregnable, conservative, and outright repressive literary institution," because of its involvement in publishing as "patron."[39]

On more practical grounds, critics worried that accepting government money, like accepting college or university support, laid small-press people open to outright censorship or control or might tempt them to self-censorship. While public agencies had remained almost entirely aloof from involvement with the content of publications they funded, the potential for manipulation obviously existed. For example, in 1975, *Granite* magazine, run by the respected small-pressman Anselm Parlatore (later editor of *Bluefish*), saw his grant rescinded by the New Hampshire Commission on the Arts because two years earlier *Granite* had printed a poem thought offensive by the governor.

Critics were also concerned that grant funding encouraged financial irresponsibility while discouraging the building of a subscriber base, which in the very long run would render little magazines not more but less stable. In 1979 the ubiquitous Clifton voiced his suspicion of a "Big Brother-like plot to force us either into complete subservient dependency on the NEA or total bankruptcy," thus undermining "American press freedom."[40] Three years later, he added,

> Where jail sentences and book-bannings couldn't stop the "mimeo revolution," Big Government money stopped it cold. Where in pre-grant days poet-editor/publishers sold their chapbooks on the sidewalks, directly to any reader they could interest, Big Government grants made selling unnecessary, hence readership unnecessary to publishing, hence expressing vital ideas unnecessary to writing.[41]

Among those sharing his concern were longtime small-press observers Tom Montag and Rich Mangelsdorff.

Finally, opponents of public funding for small presses and little magazines claimed that publications not sustained by sales or editorial passion and sacrifice were apt to be artificial and self-indulgent, even pointless. Phillip Lopate satirized the situation in the second stanza of his poem about little magazines:

> "I want my magazine to be
> a simple collection of poems," says one editor
> fastidiously
> as he asks everyone at a book-party to send him their
> poems

and a year later he is sorry
but he must go to press
because he has a grant
from the Coordinating Council of Literary Magazines![42]

It was true that on the face of it, accepting government money was antithetical to little magazines' most commonly avowed purposes and that this kind of dependency could not but blunt the sharp edge of independence that had historically been their unique merit. Furthermore, by encouraging the foundation of new enterprises and acting as a life support for older ones that have lost their vitality, critics charged, public funds swelled the total number of presses and journals, which led to the ills of general mediocrity and the diffusion and possible burial of good work. Finally, on a more directly practical and often self-interested level, some observers challenged the disbursal of the funds—for example, the qualifications of NEA Literature Panel officials, the choice of CCLM as the major intermediary, the enforcement or nonenforcement of certain standards, the neglect or favoring of some enterprise, person, literary school, or clique, the awarding of large proportions of the available funds (or of any amount of money at all) to academically supported journals, and the variation in amounts granted. Such an environment, some observers believed, would foster coteries, exchange of favors, sycophancy, and even corruption.

Alternatively, public money had helped a great many notable presses and journals become established and had permitted the printing of much excellent but noncommercial literature, though it is conceivable (and in some cases probable) that these enterprises and this literature would have found other supports and emerged nonetheless. Morty Sklar (The Spirit That Moves Us Press) insisted that the editor of integrity could resist being compromised: "Grants do not manipulate people . . . they offer people the opportunity to manipulate themselves. The creative act is influenced by technology and many other things, but ultimately it is the individual *responding* to his/her environment who is boss over all."[43] Dustbooks' Ellen Ferber and Len Fulton argued that small-press people who accepted grants could resist the drift into financial dependency and that, indeed, the best and smartest of them were basically self-supporting or could become so.[44] In a 1982 *Publishers Weekly* survey article on small publishing, Judith Appelbaum declared that "virtually every observer interviewed" agreed with this judgment."[45] While this argument could be used to counter critics concerned about the deleterious effects of grant funding, turned another way it suggested that the best small publishing would survive on its own, thus the public agency's most significant function was to spawn and shore up the superfluous. Yet many people, evidently not interviewed by Appelbaum, would have disagreed with her. For instance, fine-printers and literary publishers Richard Mathews and Barbara Russ of the reputable Konglomerati Press claimed they could not have survived and certainly could not have improved the quality of their books as they did without substantial grant support: "Poetry publishing in America is likely to remain grant-dependent for a long time to come."[46]

In any case, the elimination of grants to small publishers or any major change in the grant-giving machinery would have to be initiated by the agencies themselves. Even as an assertion of independence, few small-press people could have brought themselves to reject grants or seriously question their ultimate value, for small publishing was sorely beset with problems for most of which money was the solution or at least an alleviator.

The words of William Carlos Williams, one of this century's most influential poets and greatest supporters of small publishing, were especially pertinent to the post-sixties' literary funding environment:

> The little magazine is something I have always fostered; for without it, I myself would have been early silenced. To me it is one magazine, not several. It is a continuous magazine, the only one I know with an absolute freedom of editorial policy and a succession of proprietorships that follows a democratic rule. There is absolutely no dominating policy permitting anyone to dictate anything. When it is in any way successful, it is because it fills a need in someone's mind to keep it going. When it dies, someone else takes it up in some other part of the country—quite by accident—out of a desire to get the writing down on paper. I have wanted to see established some central or sectional agency which would recognize, and where possible, support little magazines. I was wrong. It must be a person who does it, a person, a fallible person, subject to devotions and accidents.[47]

In some ways the organization and systematized funding of small publishers by government paralleled chronologically and in potential effect the organization of poets' training and provision of their paychecks by the educational establishment. Of course, many poets stayed outside that establishment and many publishing endeavors remained financially independent through choice, ignorance, or failure to plan ahead. But some data and opinion uncovered by this research, as well as a mass of printed articles, interviews, and editorials, pointed repeatedly to a wide and wandering but ultimately still controlling fence being erected around poetry writing, publishing, and the lives of poets in the 1970s and after. One of its effects had been to create vested economic interests in the sheer survival of literary publishing ventures and of poets *as* poets, regardless of the intensity of their literary drive, the depth of their enjoyment of literary activity, or, most important, their quality. As a result, both the number of published poets and the volume of poetry presses and periodicals had proliferated and probably not faded as readily, or for the same reasons, as would once have been the case.

One might, then, expect recent poetry to be more visible, better integrated into the nation's mass culture, more widely read and enjoyed. If this was true, it was certainly not clearly apparent or easily demonstrable. Two certain and at least superficially positive results *were* clear, however: poets' increased ease of achieving print and finding congenial paid work.

6

How the Poets Published

> This is the book written by the person who was the student of the person who edited the book for the student that got reviewed by the colleague of the teacher who reviewed the book written by the colleague who hired the teacher to teach his students while he took a leave on the grant that was awarded by the panel on which the teacher sat as a replacement for the colleague who edited the anthology that included the work of the student who wrote the book.
>
> Russell Banks[1]

> [After being named a Yale Younger Poet, it] became apparent to me that in addition to the country of art, of which Li Po and Balzac and Cezanne and Virginia Woolf were citizens, there was also an actual society or network of literary people, which was quite another thing and made me feel slightly uneasy.
>
> Newer Prizewinning Poet, questionnaire response

Poets and other writers have long affirmed the importance of connections in getting published. Frequently such affirmations accompany complaints, and it has usually been difficult to distinguish accurate observation from informed guesswork from simple misinterpretation from self-serving rationalization of failure.

Hart Crane, author of some of this century's most original, ambitious, and admired poetry, was encouraged early in his career by Maxwell

Bodenheim, a once-respected writer whose work has not worn well. In 1917, when Crane was eighteen years old and had only recently moved to New York City from Ohio, Bodenheim undertook to help him by showing his poems to the *Seven Arts* magazine editor, a personal acquaintance of Bodenheim's. Crane, who was delighted, wrote his mother:

> Bodenheim is at the top of American poetry today, and he says that after four years of absolute obscurity, he is succeeding only through the adverse channels of flattery, friendship, and "pull." . . . Editors are generally disappointed writers who stifle any genius or originality as soon as it is found. They seldom even trouble to read over the manuscript of a "new man." . . . As soon as *Others* [a well-regarded literary magazine of the time] begins again this winter [Bodenheim] says I shall have an organ for all my melodies, as he is one of the editors.[2]

Two years later Crane became Advertising Manager for Margaret Anderson's *Little Review*, a spectacularly unpromising position financially whose chief attraction was the chance it offered to associate with, in Crane's words, "influential people."[3] In 1920 Crane reported to a friend concerning a particularly prestigious literary magazine, "[Matthew] Josephson writes me that *The Dial* is causing a great stir, but that clique favoritism, the old familiar and usual magazine pattern, is beginning to become evident."[4]

Throughout numerous volumes of letters and biography focused on pre–1950 American poets, the advantages of knowing other writers and editors, of being tied into the literary grapevine, a member of certain literary-social circles, and in a position to return favors of publication are everywhere apparent. Among the most striking examples of this are poet biographies and literary histories of the teens and twenties, with Ezra Pound's role as promoter of promising authors often highlighted. James Atlas's study of Delmore Schwartz, a poet who achieved fame in the thirties, and Allan Seager's of Theodore Roethke, who published his first book in the forties, also teem with anecdotes illustrating the importance of friends and other contacts.[5] Roethke, ambitious in the extreme, cultivated acquaintanceships with influential people who would, he hoped, better his chances for recognition and the awards and fellowships that might come with it. Seager judges very important Roethke's early relationships with his teacher Rolfe Humfries, his lover Louise Bogan, and a third poet, Stanley Kunitz. Roethke's first book of poems, accepted by Knopf in 1940 after rejections elsewhere, was assembled with the help of Kunitz and greeted by favorable reviews from Humfries and Bogan among others.

Four decades later, *Too Bright to See*, the first book of Linda Gregg, would be published by Graywolf, an especially eminent small press, at the behest of her friend Tess Gallagher, who was a well-known poet already on Graywolf's list.[6] The book would be dedicated to Gregg's ex-husband, poet Jack Gilbert, and its back cover festooned with endorsements from prominent literary figures including Gilbert's longtime friend Gerald Stern, an award-winning poet who labelled Gregg "one of the best poets in America."[7] In the year of publication of *Too Bright to See,* Stern's own book, *The Red Coal,* would come out adorned with a cover photograph of Stern and Gilbert walking a Paris Street in 1950.[8] On her questionnaire completed for this study, Gregg would list Gilbert and Stern as "close friends" and as among "the best or most interesting" living American poets. Stern, on his questionnaire, would list Gilbert and Gregg in both categories. In a 1984 *American Poetry Review* interview he discussed his friendship with them.[9] Jack Gilbert, who was not included in the present study, published his acclaimed collection, *Monolithos,* with Graywolf in 1982—one year after Gregg's and Stern's books—and dedicated it to Linda Gregg. Numerous poems within memorialized their relationship.[10]

As it happens, *Too Bright to See* was regarded by many disinterested readers as an extraordinarily fine volume and was favorably reviewed on its own merits. Her gifts were so evident that Linda Gregg's boost from friends was unlikely to be deplored by other poets. Pound's sponsorship of such unknowns as H. D., Frost, and Eliot, and Humfries' and Bogan's support of Roethke are today regarded as great services to literature rather than blameworthy favoritism. Just so, any personal help received by Gregg might be considered vindicated by the quality of her work. For the most part, criticisms are made when the support network is thought to lead to the *closing* of doors against fine authors so unfortunate as to lack personal contacts.

A prime postwar example of literary mutual aid and sometimes unjustified influence wielding is found in that loosely defined group of writers sometimes called the "Beats," but overlapping with the Black Mountain and San Francisco Renaissance poets. The tangled train of personal connections among these people—involving affairs, marriages, and shared homes and drug adventures, as well as simple friendship and professional admiration—can be traced through many books, poems, and articles, among them Philip Whalen's volume of interviews, collections of prose pieces and criticism by Ekbert Faas, Robert Creeley, and Gary Snyder, Ted Morgan's biography of William Burroughs, and virtually anything written about, and much written by, Allen Ginsberg.[11] The existence of a few such prominent cliques, coupled with other poets' needs to understand or excuse their and their friends' publishing rejections, contribute to the widespread belief that personal connections are necessary to publication and often promote the undeserving.

Ironically, the many magazines and presses founded to give print to a particular poet or poetic circle both serve as evidence of the difficulty some writers have in getting published and give the appearance of extending that difficulty through their sheer existence as publishing outlets biased in favor of particular people or styles. While the creation of more outlets, even though biased, does not actually damage the unconnected, unpublished writer's chances, his discouragement increases with the proliferation of outlets that seem closed to him.

Such publishing enterprises also attract criticism from people who see danger to literature in the multiplication of small journals and presses and mediocre published poems, a concern discussed in chapter 3. John Martin, of the small Black Sparrow Press, warned that to be successful, one must "never publish yourself or your friends—only the best."[12] Of course, close friendship can influence one's perception of what is best, and in any case, Martin's dictum imposes a hard test of integrity, especially for a writer-publisher who himself seeks publication under an imprint other than his own. *Field*'s David Young cited as one advantage of shared editorship the easing of tough decisions that might offend acquaintances: "I think it's very difficult if you're an editor and you're solely responsible for what does or does not get printed. Then the pressure on you, through friendships and . . . implied reciprocities . . . gets pretty intense."[13] Poet Clayton Eshleman, who was sole editor of the esteemed, now-defunct little magazine *Caterpillar*, once noted that the magazine's lapses in quality usually occurred when he "allowed [himself] to be influenced by friendship. This latter consideration, as everyone clearly knows, is a big determinant as to what gets in the little magazines and what does not."[14]

That "everyone clearly knows" about the power of friendship in the small-press world is commonly assumed. The only factor believed to be as powerful or more so is reputation. Many little magazines and presses are thought to seek legitimacy by soliciting and publishing work, sometimes even inferior work, from name authors.

While connections and reputations built by the well-connected are believed to influence many independent press decisions, they are rumored to be even more important—in fact, overwhelmingly dominant—in commercial publishing. To have a good agent or know someone with influence in the trade, or to gain the active support of an established trade-press author, is usually believed essential. If only because of the sheer number of poets clamoring for entrance at these doors, a wedge other than the work itself must be available; good poems, even brilliant poems, will not suffice.

Friendship and Editorship

Two survey questions were written to ascertain whether the poets counted people involved in the poetry world among their close friends or continuing professional acquaintances and whether they themselves had been involved in literary publishing as workers, thus having the chance to establish contacts and, possibly, reciprocal publishing arrangements.

It was thought that all prizewinners and the great majority of the other respondents, all of whom had managed to publish a substantial amount of work, would have these relationships and work experiences. The exact wording of the two-part question was:

> (1) Among poetry people (other poets, editors, publishers, reviewers, critics), are there any individuals whom you consider close friends?
>
> If "yes," please identify the individual(s) if you are willing, and, in the case of editors or publishers, the publishing enterprises with which they are affiliated. . . .
>
> (2) Among poetry people, are there any individuals who are particularly close and continuing professional associates—though not close friends?
>
> If "yes," please identify the individual(s) if you are willing, and indicate the nature of your professional association (e.g., "my agent," "my editor").

It cannot be told from the answers whether personal connections generated publishing opportunities, arose as a result of published work that others admired, or whether there was a more complex interplay, in which contacts affected first publication, which then generated more contacts, which aided further publication, and so forth.

These questions seemed particularly vulnerable to nonresponse, but as it turned out, response was strong. Ninety-two percent of questionnaire respondents answered part 1; 95 percent answered part 2. Close friendships were claimed more commonly than ongoing professional associations by poets in all groups except the Newer Prizewinners'. As was expected, all responding Older Prizewinners had friends in the world of poetry, but, surprisingly, both groups of nonprizewinners claimed friendships more often than did Newer Prizewinners, a full 20 percent of whom claimed to have no close friends in poetry. One striking case was that of Karen Snow, winner in her fifties of the prestigious Walt Whitman Award for new poets. Self-described as "a recluse and a loner," Snow had always published under a pseudonym, was living with her husband on a remote island that she rarely left, did not work for pay (writing excepted), and seemed to have absolutely no personal acquaintances in the poetry community, dealing with editors only by mail. That Snow could win a major award might seem to belie the importance of contacts, but she was rare. (On the other hand, Stanley Kunitz, who for many years selected manuscripts for the Yale Younger Poets series, claimed to have chosen an author known to him only once;

and Karl Shapiro recently declared that, except for shaking hands once with Auden: "I had never met a poet in my life before winning the Pulitzer in 1945."[15])

Almost all Newer Nonprizewinners enjoyed close friendships with people in the poetry world. One explanation for this may be the tendency of poets who fail to win prizes or have difficulty achieving publication to found their own magazines and presses and form groups for mutual support and criticism. (Notably, more Newer Nonprizewinners than Newer Prizewinners, by 11 percentage points, had worked for or operated literary periodicals or book presses.) Effectively, people writing poetry had friends writing poetry.

One might speculate that for Newer Nonprizewinners, writing was more often perceived as avocational, dabbled in as a hobby and continued because it was a shared social interest. However, since Newer Nonprizewinners had written nearly as much and over nearly as long a time as Newer Prizewinners and were just as likely to give "writer" or "poet" as their primary occupation, it seems unlikely that their writing was any less serious or more social in nature than NPs'.

Answers to part 2 were much as expected. A large majority of prizewinners had established continuing professional relationships—most often with editors, in a few cases with agents—while only two-thirds of nonprizewinners had managed to cultivate even one such relationship. Still, that six Older Nonprizewinners, or more than one-third of those responding, had over their long publishing careers established no reliable professional connections was rather surprising and suggests the stress and uncertainty of the poet's life. Even a bibliography of many poems spanning many years did not guarantee easy publication or reliable social support.

Several poets elaborated their answers, further confusing any attempts at interpretation of yes-no counts. Several listed numerous acquaintances, but emphasized that none represented, in Kenneth Rosen's words, " 'productive' relationships." Rosen continued: "It makes me feel terribly lonely to identify as 'friends' people with whom I am neither in close nor even regular contact, and also somewhat foolish to realize how little practical career-leverage I enjoy with respect to my professional acquaintances. I don't think my situation is unique." Jack Myers, who like Rosen directed an annual academic writing conference attracting poets, listed names, including some that are very well known, but emphasized: "I have never and would never call upon them to help me publish." Myers added:

> There is a lot of buddyism and nepotism and trading-off that goes on in the publishing and prize-granting world. (I'm happy to report that I did not know, personally, one judge on the N.E.A. panel which awarded me a grant; and that's

exactly how I'd like to make my way—cleanly.) But every other area of human interest has this same socio-political structure, from the local chamber of commerce to world-wide diplomatic affairs.

Another poet, less known than Myers, who had many renowned acquaintances but not a particularly impressive publishing record, lamented her failure to exploit these contacts, musing that she should perhaps try to do so in the future. Like Rosen and unlike Myers, she gave no hint of considering such tactics unclean.

Somewhat surprisingly, two women poets confirmed speculations that are often stated in gossip and occasionally in print. Love affairs that develop between young poets and editors, publishers, or more-established writers may work to the neophytes' advantage. Again, of course, cause and effect are impossible to determine at long range. Personal problems had silenced one of these women for over a decade, causing her abandonment of an active literary career. Before succumbing to her difficulties, she had read in New York's prestigious 92d-Street-Y poetry series and published in a wide range of prestigious periodicals—among them *Harpers, Saturday Review,* and *Shenandoah.* Recalling that early period, she wrote in a letter enclosed with her questionnaire:

> I am awash with memories, just having read your questions, and I tried to answer them, re who my friends were, and the like. . . . No, I was not a groupie; they were good poets but I really loved them, and most of them really loved me, or at least liked me a lot and took me seriously, I think. . . . Without turning this into Shelley Winters' memoirs, I do have a lot more to add about old friends, circles of influence, and such, but I want to think it over a bit . . . (her ellipses).

On the questionnaire, however, while explaining that she had met in social situations people who facilitated her publishing, she noted: "This could cut both ways—sometimes I was eclipsed by . . . friends, sometimes treated well for their sakes, occasionally snubbed for their sakes. (Some people took ME seriously, some saw me just as so-and-so's girlfriend.)" Throughout her questionnaire responses, this writer tangled the problems of being a poet with those of being a woman involved with men, sometimes discussing them as though they were the same. For her, apparently, they often had been. "What the hell went wrong with my life?" she wondered, and enclosed with this letter several new poems. This poet is quoted at such length here because of her unusual candor about experiences that are probably not unique and her discovery that contacts did not afford unmixed or permanent blessings.

Several poets described the poetry community as a "small world" where, as a matter of course, one eventually made many friends. Those who themselves ran presses or magazines had developed especially wide circles of acquaintances. Yet for all this, the poet might remain alone.

Occasionally, the questions asked brought forth wistful ruminations on just how few real friends the respondent actually had after years of publishing. This was true of Kenneth Rosen, quoted above, and of William Stafford, who was among the most honored, prolific respondents and observed that, living in Oregon, he "seldom [crossed] paths" even with those poets he regarded as close friends. Having said this, he reconsidered: "Well, come to think of it, very few literary people *are* close."

To summarize, hardly any of the poets seemed to be writing in complete isolation from other people engaged in literary work, but this did not necessarily mean that they saw these people on a regular basis or counted on their help when seeking publication.

Another question designed to elicit suggestive information about literary circles and contacts asked poets whether they perceived themselves as members of "a poetic group or 'school'." Two-thirds of the 143 respondents to this question gave flat negative answers—several adding, sometimes with underlining and exclamation points for emphasis, that they considered themselves "unique," or that they "do not *want* to be part of a group." A few poets whom critics often associated with a school of writing (e.g., the Beats, the New York Poets) refused to affirm any such association. One prizewinner who was closely linked to the Iowa Workshop marked "no" when asked if he perceived himself "as a member of a poetic group or school," then added: "but others do." "I can't imagine anyone answering yes [to this question]," wrote Michael Ryan, but over one-fifth did, and an additional 10 percent modified their negative replies with notes that they did draw upon, or feel affiliated with, some special group or mode of writing. Three poets, all of them Newer Nonprizewinning women, marked "no," but indicated that they wished the answer were "yes," and several NN respondents suggested that being linked to a group or school might facilitate publishing or award-winning, or offer support of other types. Jared Carter, an Indiana native, was more specific:

> At the present time there is no shortage of aspiring writers who wish to be thought of as "New York school," "Black Mountain," or "Beat," even though those schools are old hat and out of date now, because each of the three named was fiercely partisan in its day and rewarded (and published) followers and adherents not on the basis of quality or excellence, but on the basis of group loyalty and group promotion.

Yet this study turned up very few people seeking identification with those groups.

The explanations offered by poets answering affirmatively showed a great variety of ways of interpreting the question. Very few of the thirty-two people giving unqualified "yes" replies had in mind any clearly defined group. Some found a particular literary tradition inspiring or drew strength, psychologically or aesthetically, from the sheer existence of other writers who shared their interests in poetic content or style, or even politics—though they might not be in contact or even acquainted with one another. Carter himself, for instance, claimed to

> write out of an old tradition loosely identified as "Midwestern," one which stems from the original Chicago Renaissance just before World War I to slightly after, and that includes Dreiser, [Edgar Lee] Masters, [Sherwood] Anderson, Harriet Monroe, and others. But hardly anyone alive today even remembers that tradition and it is certainly no longer a school in the sense that you have defined it. A school must be ongoing, with masters and apprentices, teachers and students.

John Gill, a Chicago native and upstate New York resident (since relocated in California), also thought of himself as a "Mid-West poet."

Other poets with similarly vague affiliations sometimes checked "yes." Several women—among them Maxine Kumin, Ruth Stone, Marie Harris, and Nona Nimnicht—identified in a general way with other feminist poets, though not with specific organizations or segments of the women's movement. (Kumin also saw herself as a "nature" and "anti-nuclear-proliferation" poet.) Interestingly, only one respondent, Elaine Starkman, claimed to think of herself as a "Jewish poet," though she checked "no" to the question and said that she made this association only "sometimes," that is, when using content drawn from her sojourn in Israel.

Also among poets answering this question affirmatively were Randall Ackley, who placed himself in the "oral tradition of storytelling," and Lyle Glazier, a Harvard-educated lifelong academician, who saw his work as derived from a " 'school' of pure poetry, running all the way from the Greek Anthology through William Carlos Williams and on to a magazine like ORIGIN. Poems that make their statement through 'texture' not 'argument'." That this question was subject to a range of interpretations is exemplified by two Older Nonprizewinners' answers: Ann Hayes marked "yes," saying she was a "formalist" writing in "traditional meters," while James Facos marked "no," adding, "I am a maverick, a traditionalist."

The creativity of some poets' descriptions of their schools belied their positive responses. After noting his association, perforce, with the Pacific Northwest, where he had long resided, William Stafford continued: "I am of the available-meaning, content-significant group; social action, yes; open-and-welcoming, yes; wide-commonality-language, yes." Charles Behlen, also regionally identified, extended the character of his harsh region into the character of his poetry: "I consider myself a poet of the northwestern prairies of Texas—that part of Texas known as the Panhandle, the Caprock. Since I hale from a particularly stark and barren neck of Texas, I like, when I am feeling flippant, to describe myself as an advocate of Abject Clarity, as a sentimental populist." James Grabill, who writes an individualistic, demanding poetry, was quite sure he belonged to a "school or group," but: "It has no name . . . maybe, a little 'neo-surrealistic,' a little 'deep imagist,' a little the 'Robert Bly School of Dragon Smoke and the Presence of Trees'??" Gary Snyder (who had often been grouped with the poets of the San Francisco Renaissance) checked "yes" and, possibly with tongue at least partly in cheek, declared himself one with the "Post industrial Bio regional Anarcho-Buddhist Pacific Basin neo-Mythographers."

While there is surely a sense of shared sympathy among some writers and editors, while circles or networks of acquaintances do exist and probably are sometimes mutually beneficial professionally, most poets in this study saw themselves as finally alone, speaking in idiosyncratic voices and self-dependent in finding means of publication. One would assume, then, that their decisions about where to submit work would not be highly structured. If they tend to submit to personal acquaintances, this must be due to the feelings of friendship rather than hard-headed fealty to a shared aesthetic, political, or regional purpose. Preference for outlets run by friends might also, of course, reflect the simple desire to get work into print. As we have seen, most poetry journals and presses were receiving so many manuscripts that authors might have suspected that a hook such as friendship was necessary to assure that their submissions would even be read.

Publishing the First Book

Because poetry is almost surely the least selling literary genre (unless this dubious honor belongs to printed plays), one may wonder how the poets surmounted the commercial obstacles to publication of their first books. Chapter 3 presented evidence that few did; instead, they skirted them by settling for publication of their first books through noncommercial outlets: university houses and, more often, independent small presses. Instances of self-publication were not isolated in those data; however, it is probably the case that publication of many first books of poetry was either handled entirely by their authors, subsidized by them while others contributed labor, expertise, and an imprint, or sponsored by family or friends. While for-profit publishers could not be credited with a majority of any poet group's first books, such publishers were apparently more accessible in the 1950s and early 1960s when the older poets' first books were coming out.

Given poetry's low sales, the recent proliferation of poets seeking publication and of poetry prizes, and the increased ease of self-publication resulting from the past two to three decades' technological advances, it was assumed that most poets won publication of their first books through connections, receipt of a prize, self-publication, or some combination of these. Although many small presses are by policy and nature receptive to unknowns, even here, one guesses, connections might have been useful. The most prestigious small presses, especially, such as Graywolf and Ecco, are almost as swamped with manuscripts as the bigger houses.

To test these assumptions, poets were asked how their first books found print, and their narrative responses were organized into categories. (Table 6.1 displays for each group only those answers given by three or more poets. To facilitate analysis, methods of publication are divided into three categories: "Not through connections," "[Certainly or probably] Through connections," and "Self-Published.")

Like the declarations of membership in schools of poetry, these answers, and especially the way they are categorized, must be accepted cautiously. The most problematical section falls under "Through connections: Requested by editor or publisher." The solicitation of a first book does suggest the strong possibility of some prior contact between publisher and poet; one can surmise that, very often, they were friends. However, in at least a few of these cases, the request was probably preceded only by the publisher's accidental, pleasurable encounter with the poet's work while browsing a little magazine or attending a public reading, or by the publisher's receipt of an earlier, unsolicited manuscript from the poet—either book-length or in the form of a few poems for magazine publication. (Many small presses bring out both books and a journal.) Such events occur independently of connections, unless the publisher picked up the particular magazine or went to the particular reading on the recommendation of someone who was known to the poet and hoped to promote his work.

People who have not perused the completed questionnaires might take exception to the "Not through connections" category, arguing that a poet claiming unbiased selection of his manuscript might simply be unwilling to confess that he knew an editor or prize judge. Given the tone and expansiveness of almost all answers to this question, concealment seems unlikely. Also, to have difficulty in placing a first book is for poets the typical experience, and, as they know from the literary history many of them have studied, it always has been. The majority of respondents answered this question at unusual length and in some detail, describing the first manuscript's history of rejection as well as the events preceding its final appearance in print. One senses that, naturally enough, the first major publication is for most poets an exciting, joyous occasion vividly remembered and offering continued delight in

Table 6.1
How the Poets' First Books Came to be Published[a]

Response	NP (N=30) No.	NP %	OP (N=18) No.	OP %	NN (N=78) No.	NN %	ON (N=18) No.	ON %	Total (N=144) No.	Total %
Not through connections										
Unsolicited submission	5	17	3	17	18	23	3	17	29	20
Direct result of winning open competition	15	50	3	17	1	1	1	5.5	20	14
Totals	20	67	6	34	19	24	4	22.5	49	34
Through connections										
Contact or connection at the press	5	17	3	17	8	10	1	5.5	9	6
Requested by editor or publisher	2	7	5	28	17	22	2	11	26	18
Published by friend	--	--	1	5.5	16	20.5	1	5.5	18	12.5
Recommendation of influential person	1	3	--	--	--	--	--	--	1	.5
Agented	1	3	--	--	1	1	--	--	2	1
Totals	9	30	9	50.5	42	53.5	4	22	56	39
Self-published[b]	--	--	2	11	16	20.5	7	39	25	17
Other	1	3	1	5.5	1	1	3	17	5	3.5

[a]Poets' responses to: "Please describe how your first poetry book came to be published. (I.e: How did you select a publisher? Was the book rejected by any publishers before final acceptance? If you self-published the book, why did you decide to self-publish? Etc.)"

[b]Includes vanity press publication, but *not* publication through nonvanity publisher with poet's subsidy

the retelling. Whatever disappointment follows, that early triumph remains whole and untarnished. To some extent, this is true even in the case of self-published first books, the only exception discovered in this study being James Facos, who explained with frank embarrassment that out of ignorance he allowed the vanity press Dorrance to handle his first volume, thus sacrificing any chance to win the attention of influential reviewers and critics. If the response data are inaccurate, then, they probably err on the side of overemphasizing connections, though only slightly.

Given that the Newer Prizewinning group was selected from lists of people winning 1970s' new-poet prizes, several of which guaranteed publication of a first book, these poets' relatively high incidence of unconnected publication was predictable. As expected, much more than half of all other groups had to publish through friends' or their own efforts. Narrative responses indicated that most of the press contacts and requesting editors were actually the poets' friends, operating small presses. That Older Nonprizewinners relied on self-publishing much more heavily than did Newer Nonprizewinners and correspondingly less on the help of friends is probably attributable to the increased numbers of publication-seeking poets attending poetry clases and workshops in the 1970s where they might meet likeminded people and the proliferation of poet-run presses and journals. All of this led to a mutual-aid as well as self-help publishing ethic. While Newer Nonprizewinners' unsolicited submissions, which accounted for nearly one-quarter of their first book acceptances, may appear surprisingly successful, it should be noted that every one of these was to a small press.

The two older groups have identical records regarding unsolicited submissions. But in an interesting way these groups differ. Those who would become major prizewinners were much less dependent initially on self-publishing than those who did not attract prizes later on. This suggests that whatever factors caused their careers to develop in contrasting ways—whether differences in quality, style, content, ability to make useful personal connections (which aided at least half of OPs' first book appearances, but less than one-quarter of ONs'), or various combinations of these—were present from the start.

The poets' tales of their early publishing accomplishments give detail and color to the widely known fact that ushering a commercially unpromising manuscript into print is usually difficult and stressful, as rejection slips pile up or, worse, as submissions are swallowed by editorial black holes, never to be acknowledged in any way or returned.

Most self-publishing occurred by default, not choice, after constant rejection. "I published it myself," explained one Newer Nonprizewinner of her first volume, a limited-edition chapbook. "I may have to publish my 2 full-length collections myself and if I do, the reason will be that I am sick of trying to convince insensitive, trend-conscious editors that my work is better than most of the work they publish." She had been sending out book manuscripts, she added, for seven years, and she had a long bibliography of literary journal appearances.

At age forty-five, with "neither time nor energy to wait around until [her first book] struck someone's fancy," Anne Hazlewood-Brady had paid a personal visit to Macmillan to pick up her manuscript, which had been held there for three months "without even an acknowledgement of receipt," and published it herself. Elaine Starkman seems not to have made even a first approach to other publishers: "I self-publish [as Sheer Press] for fear of rejection and unwillingness to wait years before acceptance." Susan Hauser endured six rejections before bringing out her own delicate "theme book," *Forager*, in a lovely edition, under her own Raspberry Press imprint: "I wanted to have it to give to friends and family and it seemed the only way to get it was to do it myself." However, she preferred to limit future self-publishing to poetry postcards and broadsides. Clearly, one attraction to Hauser of self-publishing this particular book was the chance to give it the rather elaborate physical appearance it needed to complement and unify the poems. Zack Rogow also mentioned this advantage of self-publishing. After his query letter to small presses yielded "no nibbles," he handled his first book himself, "partly to allow me to move on to my next project, and partly so I could produce the book in the way that I saw it. I did the typesetting and layout myself."

Another self-publishing poet, David Lunde, was running an already-established small press founded to publish his friends' books as well as his own when he brought out his first and his press's third volume. While it had not been submitted elsewhere, his failure to place an earlier book apparently impelled him to publish this one himself.

Quite a few self-publishing poets shared with Lunde the refusal even to try traditional methods first because to do so seemed certainly fruitless. Douglas Messerli, for instance, now a well-respected poet-publisher, considered his poetry "difficult in the sense that it is *new* (arguably 'experimental')." His publisher friends, he thought, were the only people likely to take it on, and as they were "overbooked," he published it himself. But despite the enviable reputation built by his Sun & Moon Press in the years following, Messerli added that he would not self-publish again "unless all presses disappear."

Keith Rahmmings, an unarguably experimental writer, self-published with no apparent second thoughts or regrets and continued to do so, although by the time of this study, after many books and magazine appearances, he was intensely bitter about the entire effort and claimed to have given up poetry: "Poetry publishing as it exists today is some hideous Frankenstein of dead body parts indiscriminately patched together, shambling aimlessly toward a Bethlehem of apocalyptic whocaresness." Of his first publishing venture, he declared, "it worked pretty well," although, "right now there's a couple quadzillion copies sitting in my closet I'm planning to unload the quick way—via the trash compactor because I need the space for more recent insanity."

Another poet, who had never yet self-published, in 1983 described a series of exhausting problems in his dealings with small presses. Such problems could lead even a reluctant poet to bring out his own work:

> I was extremely pleased to have my first book accepted by a publisher. I was *not* pleased when it took four years for the publisher to publish my book and I was *not* pleased to find that the book was crudely illustrated when it finally appeared. Ironically enough, a poet and editor whose book I was in the process of publishing decided, I suppose out of a mixture of gratitude and respect for my work as a poet, to publish my next book. However, he withdrew the manuscript after I failed to bring out his book within two years. After this incident I dropped the subject of his publishing my book. Now, four years later, he has again asked to see my manuscript. . . . In the meantime, the publisher of my first book has made some tentative noises about publishing my next book, which fills me with joy and trepidation: joy that someone has the money and appreciation of my work to publish it, and fear that I will have to wait almost half a decade to see it appear in a crudely illustrated edition. These events have tempted me to consider self-publication—something I would not have dreamed of five years ago.

Usually, it seems, self-publishing was a pragmatic act which, if possible, was not repeated. Despite the encouragement of a slew of how-to-publish manuals and the romantic aura lent by the precedents of such self-publishers as Walt Whitman and Anaïs Nin, most poets wanted the validation and support of an external publisher.

Those who had won such support with the help of connections told greatly varying stories. Some had received so many prior rejections and published through presses so close to them and so small, that, except for their access to other people's resources, their experiences resembled those of self-publishers. Jack Myers, for example, was published by a small-pressman married to one of his classmates after encouraging but, in practical terms, unhelpful responses from well-known poets and rejections from other small presses. William Stafford, whose first book came out more than thirty years ago, had also endured rejections from several presses, "but always for reasons that seemed good to me—schedules, commitments, etc." When a friend starting a new small press solicited the manuscript, "I felt a little wistful for Macmillan or someone, but also liked Greenwood and the idea of a prompt, elegant edition, and so it was (a run of about 300 as I recall)." By the early eighties, Stafford had been published for many years by Harper & Row, bringing out only special editions through the small press.

For a few respondents, unusual help from friends had produced an extraordinarily easy first-publishing process. Jerry Ratch, for example, remembered meeting the eccentric poet-publisher alta of Shameless Hussy Press "at a kitchen table at a very crowded and noisy party in

Berkeley after a poetry reading." Within a week or two, she had read his just completed, never submitted poetry manuscript and offered to publish it herself. Gary Elder's friend and publisher, Len Fulton of Dustbooks, had taken an even more aggressive initiative regarding Elder's long poem *Arnulfsaga*: "I conceived and set to work on it in response to his urging. . . . Fulton was definitely the greatest booster of my early career."

Quite commonly, teachers facilitate the publication of their most promising students' work. In Charles Behlen's case, a creative writing instructor whom he had known in the late sixties began, unknown to the poet, to edit a collection of his poems and letters, eventually obtaining Behlen's permission to publish them. The volume was issued in 1978 by the instructor's Prickly Pear Press. In more traditional style, the acclaimed poet David Wagoner, who was also an English professor, sent the work of his student Sandra McPherson to his own publisher, Indiana University Press, which accepted it. McPherson went on to become a prominent member of the poet generation born in the 1940s and by 1980 was publishing with Ecco, one of the most renowned small presses.

Rarely, however, was support so enthusiastic, so fruitful, and so gladly received. Whether self-publishing or working through friends, poets often settled for less prestigious publication than they had hoped. Gilbert Schedler placed his first book with the reputable small press Wampeter after meeting its founder at a conference, but he had to underwrite the book's expense: "I decided to [do it] because I simply felt I had no chance with a regular publisher. I never did submit a collection to a publisher." Another poet, Phyllis Koestenbaum, was less fatalistic, trying many publishers, although finally she published as Schedler did. Her story is interesting in its catalog of common misfortunes and small triumphs:

> The first poetry book of mine published was *Hunger Food*, two long poems. It was published by Jungle Garden Press after the publisher decided not to publish the book she originally accepted for publication, *That Nakedness*. She felt the book [was] too long for a letterpress like hers limited to certain size books, and the length of the lines in many of its poems and the length of the individual poems in the manuscript made it stylistically unsuitable for her press. So she asked me to give her some other work, and I gave her two poems connected thematically—she agreed to publish them. . . . Our financial arrangement . . . was her customary one: expenses and profits split down the middle (she took half the books, I took the other half). I sent out review copies and sent the books to competitions. She did some distribution. I did some. . . . A year after *Hunger Food*'s publication, after submitting *That Nakedness* over five years time to more than 45 editors, prizes, publishers, etc., I decided and she agreed that she would publish the book using her press name and supervising and designing, but that I would have to pay for it totally and pay her to design and supervise, and I

would receive all profits. A distributor will distribute it. I will send out review copies. [I made the] decision to have small press publication because realistically I thought it was all I could have.

Another Newer Nonprizewinning poet had accepted the publishing offers of a small-pressman lover even though the quality of his books disappointed her: "But . . . his is the offer, and the competition is difficult, and the *effort* to keep submitting all over is overwhelming."

And indeed great effort and patience and steely self-confidence were necessary to sustain unknown poets as they strove to place the first book. Even those who eventually achieved critical recognition and awards had often received multiple rejections early on. For example, Alberta T. Turner sent her manuscript out "several times . . . in different forms" before its acceptance by the University of Pittsburgh Press. Philip Levine recalled being "turned down several times" before his book was requested by the small press Stone Wall, while Margaret Gibson, who finally brought out her first book through the prestigious Louisiana State University Press poetry series and won the Lamont Prize for her second, recalled a long string of early frustrations:

Signs was a finalist in the Walt Whitman Contest, a finalist in The Associated Writers [Program] competition, barely rejected at U. Mass. (Juniper Prize), turned down by Alice James Press [a feminist cooperative] & I forget who else. University of Georgia Press, University of Illinois Press also rejected. I don't think I ever tried (although I queried) New York presses.

Pittsburgh poet David Huddle saw his first book accepted "after having been rejected by approximately a dozen other presses, including Pittsburgh in its previous year of considering manuscripts. My manuscript was a sort of 'bridesmaid,' having been among the finalists in competitions at Yale, Massachusetts, and the Associated Writing Programs."

Robert Pinsky, whose work had received much favorable notice and who, at the time of this study, was poetry editor for *The New Republic* (since replaced by Richard Howard), eventually had his first book accepted by Princeton, but: "It had been rejected by other publishers, definitely, with one or two close calls. One editor nearly published a long poem from the book by itself, but then wrote that though he enjoyed it he finally had decided that it was not a poem. My favorite such memory."

Even the much envied winners of the Yale Younger Poets competition, which is the oldest and probably the most prestigious of the first-book contests, often succeeded partly because of persistence and self-confidence that refused to flag in the face of rejection. Maura Stanton, for example, won the Yale contest after three years of trying, Leslie

Ullman after four years. Bin Ramke's Yale prizewinning manuscript had been rejected "by about 4 other 1st book contests," and another poet won with a book that had been rejected elsewhere a dozen times. (Ramke's second collection, *White Monkeys,* was brought out by the University of Georgia Press in 1981, but two years later, he was seeking a home for his third book; after two acclaimed collections, publishing was still no easy matter.[16])

Peter Klappert warned:

> The greatest mistake an aspiring poet can make is to allow a single editor, publisher, or aesthetic group [to] determine the poet's own evaluation of his or her work—whether that work be a single poem or a collection. My first published poem (in *Epoch*) had been turned down by about 8 magazines before I sent it to *Epoch*; the week it was accepted it also won me a $100 prize in a contest, and the poem was ultimately included in the book that won the Yale Series. Similarly, the year I won the Yale series the same manuscript received only a standard rejection from the Pittsburgh series.

Mark Strand, later among the most respected and decorated of poets, "lost the Yale series . . . twice . . . and decided to begin modestly, via the small press route. My next book, *Reasons for Moving,* was solicited by several publishers and subsequently turned down: Knopf . . . FS & G [Farrar, Straus & Giroux] . . . Harcourt Brace . . . Holt, Rinehart." However, Strand's story had an unusually happy ending: "Atheneum responded in three days saying they'd do the book. In three months the book was out." Similarly, Linda Gregg recalled: "I almost won the Yale Younger Poets award. Ecco Press held it for one year. Farrar, Straus & Giroux looked at it. Tess Gallagher took it to Scott Walker at Graywolf. He said no. She said read it again. He accepted the book. In one week four major houses in New York called, saying they would publish my book right away."

A final memoir of disappointments survived and transcended is Gallagher's own. By 1980 numbered among the more respected American poets, she recalled:

> I had had the manuscript rejected by Daniel Halpern at Ecco Press, Jonathan Galassi at [Random House], Fran McCullough at Harper & Row (she kept it for one year but wrote a very sensitive and encouraging letter with it). I had been teaching a poetry workshop in my hometown—Port Angeles, Wash.—for several summers. A former student . . . said there was someone starting a press he wanted me to meet. He drove me to Pt. Washington an hr. away where Scott Walker of Graywolf Press was working at a bookstore. I met him and saw beautiful copies of a small chapbook by Norman Dubie he had done. "Do you plan to do full length books?" I asked. "Yes," he said. . . . He worked 2 years on a hand press to print it.

The book, her award-winning *Instructions to the Double,* launched the extraordinary careers of both Gallagher and Graywolf.

But even poets who had had such luck tended to regard it as just that, so familiar were they with the tangled world of literary publishing, in which fine authors may remain obscure while poets of comparable or lesser gifts become prestigiously published. "Won a contest," Yale Younger Poet Reg Saner said of his first book. "(1,600 entries. Pure luck.)" Robert Hass, who won the same contest, remembered that he sent Yale his manuscript "at [the] the suggestion of a friend who was doing the same. Was my first submission of mss. (Like winning a lottery. Seemed a fluke.)" The lottery simile was used by several other respondents, both prizewinners and nonwinners. John Ashbery, who is among the most respected and challenging senior poets writing in English, once told an interviewer the story of his own Yale win:

> I submitted the volume to the Yale Younger Poets and it was returned by the Yale University Press, not forwarded to W. H. Auden, the judge. He had decided not to award the prize that year because he didn't like any of the manuscripts that had been sent to him. At that point a mutual friend of ours mentioned that I had submitted mine and he asked to see it directly and accepted it. Though I think somewhat reluctantly, actually, from the preface he wrote. I think he respected something in it but didn't understand it very well. In fact, in later life, I heard that he told a friend that he had never understood a single word I had ever written.
>
> I mention this because getting published is very much a result of chance and connections and all kinds of factors that, in my case, didn't have anything to do with poetry. I didn't know Auden very well but the fact that I knew him at all was how I got a first book published; but, on the other hand, it does happen a great deal for everyone. Chance occurrences and fortuitous events do happen in the life of the poet, very much more than you think.[17]

Once the first-book hurdle was surmounted, poets hoped—might even assume—that later collections would find print easily. But, as Ramke's experience showed, there were no such guarantees. "[My] second book," recalled Barry Goldensohn, "[was] rejected by fifteen commercial publishers, & then accepted by L'Epervier press. In the middle of my arguments with them a new publisher contacted me about whether I had a manuscript to submit (Vermont Crossroads). I did. They liked it. I took it back from L'Epervier and Vermont Crossroads went bankrupt *after* selling out the 1,000 copies of my book." Goldensohn's earlier volume had been published by the historically distinguished small press Cummington after only three rejections elsewhere.

E. G. Burrows told a different but not unusual tale of multiple disappointments:

First published book was submitted "over the transom" after reading publisher's plans for a poetry series. The same manuscript had not been submitted elsewhere previously. An earlier version had been accepted by a small press publisher who folded before collection could [be] printed (and maybe just as well!). The only trouble with the publisher of my first book was that he refused to look at further collections, stating his interest in publishing "first books" only.

Kathleen Norris, whose first manuscript found print relatively easily as a contest winner, noted that because of the considerable number of first-book competitions like the Yale, Walt Whitman, and others at the regional and state levels, finding publishers for first poetry volumes was often easier than publishing succeeding volumes. But for only a very occasional poet in this study was finding a publisher for the first book a simple matter. Karen Snow, who, ironically, was perhaps the least connected respondent, explained that her first work was "published by Viking as a condition of winning the Walt Whitman award. I had not previously submitted it to any publisher." Coleman Barks, a friend of a friend of Harper & Row's famous literary editor Fran McCullough, waited two years for her acceptance and two more years for publication, but never had to send the manuscript anywhere else. A few, mostly older, authors of various styles and subsequent strengths of reputation were invited to submit by trade or university presses before having received many rejections: for example, Donald Justice, solicited by Wesleyan University Press, apparently on a friend's recommendation; and Dorothy Dalton, solicited by a press director who had "read [her] work in various publications."

Yet even easy and triumphantly prestigious attainment of what for most poets is the second major career goal (with first printed poem being the first) might eventually bring as much disappointment as pleasure when the struggle to publish did not subside but continued or even accelerated.

DECIDING WHERE TO SEND MANUSCRIPTS

When this study was begun, it was thought likely that after accumulating substantial numbers of publications, as virtually all the poets examined had done, many or most authors would have built up contacts and would send out work mainly when solicited, circumventing the often frustrating process that involves submitting to a stranger's judgment, perhaps waiting months for any response, and then, very often, receiving only a form rejection slip.

Older Prizewinners were thought likely to place their work almost entirely through connections. Newer Prizewinners and Older Nonprizewinners, it was presumed, also could rely heavily on contacts, while Newer Nonprizewinners would probably have had neither fame enough nor time enough to build up an adequate array of connections and would still mail out the majority of their poems as unsolicited submissions. Among other factors believed to carry some weight with Older Prizewinners was pay, as their work would tend to be more saleable than other poets'. Newer Prizewinners, currently building careers that had begun by showing unusual potential for fame, were expected to be the group most concerned with a magazine's or press's prestige.

Two survey questions were designed to ascertain how poets decided where to send their work, and another pair of questions sought to determine the relative proportions of solicited, unsolicited, and self-published material among the poets' poems in print.

Thirty-two different factors were mentioned by respondents as entering into their decisions about where to send poems for periodical publication, but only a few were mentioned oftener than once or twice by respondents in any one group; these are listed in Table 6.2 and are ranked by their importance overall and for each group.[18] A companion query, which asked how poets settled on potential publishers for their book-length manuscripts, also elicited more than thirty responses, but again, only a few were mentioned frequently; they are listed in Table 6.3.

Some factors taken into account by poets submitting work clearly had to do with connections, or friendship—most obviously, "Friendship with periodical's editor." Others almost certainly had nothing to do with this; for example, "Physical appearance" and "Circulation or distribution." However, many considerations that are neutral on their face may well be affected by friendship—for example, the poet's perception of a journal's or press's quality or prestige, and the likelihood of acceptance of his work. But the impression left by a reading of the questionnaires is that the respondents were quite willing to acknowledge literary friends and in some cases even proud to be part of a circle or network affording publishing-related contacts. Older poets, especially, were so likely to have met or corresponded regularly with poets, editors, and publishers over the years that concealing such relationships would be futile and pointless. And, once they were established, to take them into account when submitting work would be only logical.

In the contexts of the completed questionnaires, answers that sound potentially ambiguous in themselves appear to be straightforward. For example, poets considering quality important and listing what in their opinions were the best or most significant journals when answering the question related to this often described in other parts of the questionnaire their continuing unsuccessful attempts to win acceptance from certain

Table 6.2
Major Factors Influencing the Poets' Periodical Submissions[a]

Rank Overall	Factor	NP Rank (27 Total[b])	OP Rank (16 Total)	NN Rank (39 Total)	ON Rank (15 Total)
1	Quality of the periodical	1	1	2	1
2	Appropriateness of the periodical for the particular poem being submitted	7	5	1	2
3	Invited by the periodical's editor to submit	6	2	5	3
4	Prestige or reputation of periodical	3	11	4	5
5	Payment offered by periodical	4	7	11	6
6	Poet's personal enjoyment of periodical	7	8	9	7
7	Quality of periodical's readership	5	3	13	11
8	Poet's history of publication in periodical	8	9	13	4
9	No specific factors; poet submits in haphazard or random fashion	14	12	18	9
10	Circulation or distribution of periodical	2	4	4	--
11	Friendship with periodical's editor	7	6	3	--
12	Physical appearance of magazine	10	--	6	8
13	Likelihood of acceptance	15	10	7	--
13	Special thematic or political concerns of periodical	15	3	14	--

[a]Poets' responses to: "What are the major factors influencing your decision as to where to send a particular poem for periodical publication?"
[b]That is, total number of ranks encompassed by the responses of the group.

of those journals. Sections of the survey tended to interlock in such a way that the frankness and completeness of the answers were largely affirmed.

Not surprisingly, nonprizewinners seemed to struggle hardest to place their poems. Both the Newer and Older Nonprizewinning groups rated appropriateness of a poem for a periodical much higher on their scales of concern than did prizewinners, and both ranked likelihood of acceptance of a book manuscript as a fairly important consideration, while prizewinning poets mentioned it much less often. Nonprizewinners were, then, more likely to ask, "Who will take this?" Indeed, for Newer Nonprizewinners, who were the most likely to lack both contacts and reputation, the question of appropriateness outweighed that of quality.

Table 6.3
Major Factors Influencing the Poets' Book Submissions[a]

Rank Overall	Factor	NP 19 Total[b]	OP 12 Total	NN 28 Total	ON 14 Total
1	Quality of press	3	1	1	4
2	Distribution, promotion, or sales of press	1	6	2	4
3	Prestige or reputation of press	5	8	4	1
4	Invited by press's editor or owner to submit	11	3	5	6
5	Poet's history of publication with press	9	2	20	2
5	Physical appearance of press's books	2	10	3	8
6	Payment or royalty rate offered by press	11	11	21	9
7	If offering publicaton prize or contest	10	--	9	8
8	Whether poet will have opportunity to participate in production decisions	11	11	12	--
9	Press recommended by friend or literary colleague	12	--	21	7
10	Likelihood of acceptance	--	--	6	5

[a]Poets' responses to: "What are the major factors influencing your decision to place a booklength manuscript with a particular press? (Please list the factors and, if you can, rank them in order of importance.)"
[b]That is, total number of ranks encompassed by the responses of the group.

"Suitability," wrote Shelley Neiderbach, "what the emphasis/bias of the periodical may be. . . . For me, that's the *only* factor." Steve Benson, an NN-group experimentalist in language poetry, listed several well-articulated factors affecting his submission decisions, then bracketed the one ranked first and scribbled a marginal addendum: "To publish *at all*." And Phyllis Koestenbaum noted that early in her writing career, she "used to try more magazines I thought would publish me than I do now; this still would be a consideration if I hadn't published for a long time." Major prizewinners and long-experienced poets who were comparatively confident of being able to publish *somewhere* could be the most discriminating in their choice of outlets.

Interestingly, Older Prizewinners, while much interested in quality of a potential publication source, were the least concerned of any group with either a press's or a periodical's prestige or the physical appearance of its product. Presumably, these matters were most critical when an author was striving to build a reputation, an activity no longer important to most established prizewinners. Another notable deviation of this group from the others was its greater sensitivity to political affiliations and thematic likenesses. While this consideration was of third most importance for Older Prizewinners deciding where to send work for periodical publication, it was rarely mentioned by the newer groups and not at all by Older Nonprizewinners. When choosing a book publisher, OPs took its political concerns into account as the fifth most weighty factor in the decision, while the other poets never mentioned it. Gary Snyder, for instance, ranked second after quality the importance of sending to "workers in the same vineyard: politics, region, religion." And Maxine Kumin listed as third most important her "desire for outreach and to identify with certain groups—women's groups, ground zero groups, etc." Such sensitivities undoubtedly reflected the extra-academic working backgrounds of these poets and their tendency from early career to have formed groups around aesthetic and political ideals and circles around journals and presses designed to promote their ideas. Most obviously exemplifying these tendencies, of course, were the Beat-, Black Mountain-, "deep-image"-, and feminist-identified writers in the Older Prizewinning group. Perhaps important also was the fact that many of them had flourished in the 1960s, were left-affiliated, and participated in the famous anti-Vietnamese-War poetry reading series arranged and promoted principally by Robert Bly. At the time when these poets were winning the awards that qualified them for inclusion in this study, political stance may well have been one characteristic rewarded, consciously or unconsciously, by prize judges.

As expected, book publication histories were very important to older poets, who tended to submit to presses that had handled them in the past. "For seventeen years," Daryl Hine wrote, "I have enjoyed a productive and friendly relationship with Atheneum [which] has published everything I have sent them almost without cavil, and attractively." Philip Levine, another longtime Atheneum author, sometimes brought out chapbooks through small presses and had never forgotten the early struggle for recognition. When placing a book manuscript, he took into account "the qualities of the editor: intelligence, taste, candor, decency, trustfulness, friendliness. This has to do with considerations *now*. Back then, 1963–1970, the consideration was *will they take it*." Answering another question, regarding periodicals, Levine singled out two editors for praise: Howard Moss (*The New Yorker*) and George Hitchcock (*kayak*). "Now almost everyone is nice to me, but they were straight *then*, when it mattered. There've been a lot of inconsiderate jerks." In the early 1980s, when he completed the questionnaire, Levine was agreeing to contribute poems to periodicals partly on the basis of answers to these questions: "Did [the editors] publish me before I was well known," and

"Do they treat me like a person?" It is remarkable that these old experiences remained so alive for a poet who had long since attained success.

History was less important to Newer Prizewinners, who ranked this factor ninth, as contrasted with second-place ranking by both older groups. Not only had they had shorter careers, but many of their first books had been printed as a condition of winning contests, the victors of which were *expected* to find different publishers for their second books.

The history factor carried still less importance for Newer Nonprizewinners, many of whom had published only one or two books and with small presses that were unstable, paid little or nothing or even charged them, and could not award contracts or make promises for the future, hence could not demand their authors' loyalty.

When queried about periodical submission decisions, however, Older Prizewinners laid much less emphasis on their past publishing than did Older Nonprizewinners. While both groups had had time to build contacts with periodical editors, ONs seemed to use them more—very likely because past acceptances suggest that future acceptances may be forthcoming, and many poets in this group still worried about their ability to place their work in any acceptable organ. OPs, on the other hand, worried much less or not at all about this, nor did they feel obligated to favor a past editor with each new submission, as periodical submissions were numerous compared with book submissions and could be used in many ways—to bestow or repay favors, to reconnect with established audiences or to reach out to new ones, to endorse a point of view, to earn fees. OPs were also more likely than any other group to send out work on invitation, presumably because they were invited most often, and this was a simple way of getting work into print. While Older Prizewinners ranked an invitation to submit second as a factor in journal publication and third for books, Older Nonprizewinners ranked it third and sixth, respectively. "I seldom submit unless asked to do so," wrote Hine, who, in addition to a long career in print and the enviable publishing arrangement with Atheneum, had once edited *Poetry*, surely a prime source of contacts. "No point in sending one's work where it will not be appreciated," he added.

One more difference should be noted before moving on to a general discussion of contacts, and that is newer poets' greater concern with presses' and periodicals' circulation or sales, distribution practices, and promotional expertise. While economic reasons could underlie this concern in the case of books for which poets had royalty agreements, large sales for a magazine never result in escalated fees for contributing poets, except, perhaps, eventually and indirectly. Emphasizing this consideration seemed instead to reflect, again, newer poets' need to build reputations. "A major factor," wrote Michael Ryan, "is making the poem available to the largest number of readers I might respect." Perhaps it reflected also some poets' naive, rather poignant hope of making a message heard and acquiring a large readership. (Before many years pass, most poets resign themselves to their genre's minuscule natural public and abandon such hopes.)

Some observers might find surprising (though no serious poet could) the relative unimportance of money on respondents' scales of priority. Only among Newer Prizewinners, and only in relation to periodical publication, did it rank among the top five factors considered. Again, these poets were relatively young, relatively successful, and many were aiming, quite realistically, at acceptance by the few magazines that were offering substantial payment—mainly *The New Yorker* and *Atlantic*.

What should be emphasized here is that the poets needed and desired money, as anyone does, but realized that there was very little chance of making much by publishing their work. Poetry writing and publishing might offer substantial economic rewards, but mostly in teaching appointments and offers to give readings and workshops, not directly through publishers' fees or royalties. The fascinating truth is that people simply did not devote themselves to this most difficult and emotionally involving work for reasons of cash gain and probably not even for indirect benefits, welcome as those were.

One additional interesting disclosure was the rarity with which poets seemed to be responding to the calls for manuscripts published regularly in such papers as *Small Press Review* and *Coda*, or the Dustbooks directory listings, most of which offer guidelines to potential contributors. While the information these offer could have been used to help determine appropriateness of a poem to a source, in fact these sources were almost never mentioned. Probably, poets experienced in publication relied on their own and their literary friends' knowledge and intuitions, so perfectly adapted to the idiosyncrasies of their own work, rather than relying on the reference works that are routinely recommended to new writers and in which small-press and magazine editors usually take pains to list their enterprises.

Unrationalized submissions also seemed rare, although a few poets confessed to making them. This, too, may be more typical of poets inexperienced with publishing. John Stevens Wade, who claimed to have submitted poems "haphazardly for years to hundreds of [periodical] publications," was virtually the only older poet following this practice. He was similarly unusual in his lack of discrimination among book publishers, saying that for him there was "only one factor: to get my poems in book form." Only two other poets, both in the NN group, operated with like casualness. Keith Rahmmings reported: "My primary approach to unsolicited submissions has been the manuscript blitzkrieg: going through a market list such as the Dustbooks directory and sending to any magazine that looks like it might use my stuff." Another NN-group poet, who also was a heavy user of Dustbooks "for many years (1966 to 1980)," chose places to send poems "primarily on the basis of how they appeared in alphabetical order, trying to go from A to Z in one year, from Z to A in the next." This rather cockeyed method, which he had since abandoned because he needed to develop a coherent body of publications for professional reasons, was chosen "because that way, or so I thought, I could minimize the personal impact of rejection by mechanizing the process. By the same token, I could sustain my momentum by knowing where I was going to send a particular batch of poems next." A few poets indulged in unconsidered submissions only now and then. "Lottery—impulse!" one listed as the third most important factor in book submission decisions. But elsewhere she detailed quite thoughtful, well-informed means of deciding where to send work, including heavy reliance on acquaintances.

However, the most striking thing about the factors poets cited was the relatively low importance assigned to friendship. Only for Newer Nonprizewinners, who presumably found it somewhat difficult to place work and were often acquainted with fellow poets running small magazines and presses, was friendship highly important, ranking third as a consideration in periodical submissions, eighth in book submissions. (Of course, the formation of friendships, like contacts and connections, often occurs as a *result* of publishing, rather than vice versa. Gary Allan Kizer, this study's best example, married poet-editor Lynne Savitt after submitting work to her magazine, *Gravida*, at which time they were strangers. He became her coeditor as well as her husband.)

To poets of small repute, invitations were usually issued by acquaintances; more famous poets often have their work solicited by unfamiliar reader-fans who happened to work in publishing. Being invited was important to every group with regard to both types of submission, with the single exception of Newer Prizewinners' book submissions. These poets, working hard to construct the major literary reputations that must have seemed within their grasps, found a press's image and willingness to serve its authors' interests far more important than any more personal matters.

The attraction of responding to invitations corresponded in degree with the pain of having manuscripts rejected. "To date," wrote Stephen Leggett, who enjoyed a number of literary acquaintanceships, "all my books have been requested by the publishers, so I've been spared the agony of deciding what to do with a finished manuscript. I feel if a publisher has shown enough interest in what I do to ask for a book manuscript, then I'm all for it. I just hope my luck holds." Of course, difficulties avoided by responding to requests could entail more problems and even irrecoverable missteps. "Since I've published all my books on invitation from publishers," wrote Peter Michelson, "my decisions have been based on 1) publisher's enthusiasm, 2) promises of handsome production, 3) promises of reasonable promotion & distribution. Promises, promises . . . " (his ellipsis). The prolific and much-published Theodore Enslin was prominent among poets who usually sent out work only when invited. (In his case, "virtually all" submissions to periodicals and 90 percent of book manuscript submissions had been generated by editors' requests.) Yet, he noted, he had often refused editors' invitations, including those from friends, because their "knowledge and competence" fell short of his standards.

Even when work was mishandled by the solicitor, a poet's sense of injury, which is naturally very keen, might be overwhelmed by gratitude for having been published at all. Wrote one Newer Nonprizewinning respondent: "I had work solicited by an editor who published it with some unfortunate errors and he hadn't answered my letter asking about the errors. . . . (I feel grateful he did the soliciting and publishing—don't cite [this anecdote] with my name.)" Another Newer Nonprizewinner, Harvey Hess, was known as a writer of haiku and, in his home state of Hawaii, as a lyricist and librettist. When planning to send out a book manuscript, he demanded *both* certainty and quality, but emphasized the former, submitting only "on sure-fire acceptance by a press the aesthetic standards of which I can 'live with.' " When sending to periodicals, his priorities were essentially the same and colorfully stated, expressing by implication some of the tension, apprehension, and hope that bedevil so many poets seeking acceptance for their work. In ranked order, the factors Hess claimed to consider were:

1. prayer
2. appropriateness to editors' needs and biases
3. likelihood of acceptance
4. prestige of a given publisher/periodical, with its concomitant ratio of influence
5. intuition/whim
6. hope against hope
7. to exercise the virtues of fortitude, patience, and faith.

Hess noted also that because his work was "counter-cultural," he was "*very* careful [about] what [he sent] to whom."

One reason why lesser-known poets might favor requests and stress likelihood of acceptance above almost all else was their belief that the poems they sent out unsolicited were often not read. For instance, Ron Overton cited "a real chance of acceptance" as his second most important consideration when deciding about submission to a periodical and added, "that is, whether or not it will at least be read."

Only for Older Prizewinners, however, were explicit factors of connection especially important to decisions regarding where to send manuscripts, and for every group including OPs, they were overshadowed by concern for the publishing outlet's quality. Only very seldom did a poet state baldly, as one Older Nonprizewinner did, that he decided where to send a book based partly on available contacts (and even he listed contacts second, quality first).

Finally, for a few respondents, the attempt to articulate factors entering into the decision to submit was fruitless: "It's really more a process of divination than consideration," concluded Stephen Leggett, while William Harmon wrote vaguely, "You hear things."

ACHIEVING AND FAILING PUBLICATION

Given the number of rejections most poets receive in early career and often throughout their lives, where work is sent initially may vary sharply from where it is finally published.

Because publication through their own or their friends' efforts was thought to be prevalent among poets, especially those who were little known, two questions were constructed to determine the percentages of poets' work that found print as a result of self-publication or editors' requests; responses are summarized in Tables 6.4–6.5. Again, it cannot be said with complete assurance where evidence of contacts emerges. However, quite certainly large quantities of over-the-transom submissions were not sent to acquaintances, and editor's request submissions often were.

As anticipated, literary agents turned out to be involved very little in placing poetry for publication, undoubtedly because it was extremely hard to place, and there was scarcely any money to be made from it. Nonetheless, given that almost all of the Older Prizewinners sported famous names and many wrote poetry that, for literature of its type, sold quite well, it had been expected that a number of them would submit manuscripts through agents. However, not a single respondent in this group used an agent as intermediary in submitting to periodicals, and only one had his book manuscripts handled by an agent, which is surely a very different situation than would be uncovered by a study of leading American writers in other genres.

Self-publication was more important for book than for periodical publication. This was to be expected, as books should be more difficult to place than individual poems, which require from editors no special risks and for which there were hundreds of outlets. However, the relatively low importance of self-publishing among poets of all groups was distinctly surprising, especially considering that almost two-thirds had had some publishing experience. It was thought that Newer Nonprizewin-

Table 6.4
Means of Submission of Poetry Published in Periodicals

Poets' responses to: "Of the poetry which you published in periodicals during the past 5 years, approximately what percentage was..."

		NP Group N=32	OP Group N=14	NN Group N=83	ON Group N=17
(1) ". . . published in periodicals which you edit or assist in editing"					
	Range:	0–10%	0–10%	0–75%	0–1%
	Mean:	.6%	1%	5%	.06%
	Median:	0	0	0	0
(2) ". . . submitted by you over the transom (i.e., unsolicited)"					
	Range:	0–100%	0–100%	0–100%	0–100%
	Mean:	64.5%	43%	62%	62%
	Median	80%	50%	77.5%	90%
(3) ". . . submitted by you in response to an editor's request"					
	Range:	0–100%	10–100%	0–100%	0–100%
	Mean:	34.5%	56.5%	32%	37%
	Median:	20%	50%	10%	12.5%
(4) ". . . submitted by a literary agent on your behalf"					
	Range:	0–5%	0	0–55%	0
	Mean:	2%	0	8%	0
	Median:	0	0	0	0

ners would self-publish most because they lacked long careers or major awards to enhance their visibility and enable the forming of contacts and also because so many had belonged to the "Mimeo Revolution" generation of poets, who, from early adulthood, had had access to cheap printing technology and might have become accustomed to the idea that self-publishing was no disgrace. This expectation was confirmed: eight NN respondents had self-published all their books; another four had self-published more than half; and nine more had self-published at least

Table 6.5
Means of Submission of Published Poetry Books

Poets' responses to: "Of the books you have published, approximately what percentage was..."	NP Group N=31	OP Group N=12	NN Group N=81	ON Group N=17
(1) ". . . published by a press which you run or with which you have a close day-to-day work relationship."				
Range:	0	0–100%	0–100%	0–100%
Mean:	0	18%	19%	18%
Median:	0	0	0	0
(2) ". . . submitted by you over the transom				
Range:	0–100%	0–100%	0–100%	0–100%
Mean:	61%	21%	37%	26%
Median	50%	0	20%	10%
(3) ". . . submitted by you in response to an editor's or publisher's request"				
Range:	0–100%	0–100%	0–100%	0–100%
Mean:	33%	52.5%	45%	49%
Median:	50%	80%	50%	50%
(4) ". . . submitted by a literary agent on your behalf"				
Range:	0–67%	0–100%	0–100%	0–17%
Mean:	7%	9%	2%	1%
Median:	0	0	0	0

one book, for a total of twenty-one, or 26 percent, who had used self-publishing to some degree. On the other hand, it must be remembered that 42 percent of NN-group poets had brought out only a single book and another 40 percent no more than three, so numbers and percentages can be deceptive.

The fact is that despite the extremely limited market for poetry by unknowns, only about one-quarter of Newer Nonprizewinning poets had ever turned to self-publishing their poetry in either periodical or book format. Older Nonprizewinners were slightly more likely to have self-published their books but even less likely to have appeared in their own periodicals, perhaps because fewer poets in this group were little-magazine editors.

Publication resulting from an editor's overtures was, however, as common as expected. At least one-quarter of poets in every group found homes in this way for a majority of their poems appearing in periodicals, and 40 percent or more of poets in all but the Newer Prizewinners group placed a majority of their books by responding to requests. It is reasonable to assume that many of these requests came from the poets' friends, teachers, students, or other acquaintances. Such initiatives amounted to especially significant means of publication for Older Prizewinners, and the evidence of printed anecdotes and articles about small-press editors and publishers suggests that many solicit work solely on the basis of authorial reputation.

Taken together, self-publishing and solicitation were shown to stand behind a good deal of printed poetry. However, the findings did not support the common assumption that these were the only, or almost only, avenues of exposure for poets, with over-the-transom submissions being rarely read and unavailing. Responses showed that much accepted work was sent out unsolicited. Roughly two-thirds of NP and ON poets and one-half of NNs saw 75 percent or more of their periodical publications generated this way. On the other hand, in no group did as many as half of the poets place 50 percent or more of their *books* via unsolicited submissions, which seemed to be successful only when sent to prize competitions or small independent publishers. The relatively heavy reliance of Newer Prizewinning poets on over-the-transom book submissions, with 42 percent having placed all published books this way, surely reflected their tendency to have won first-book contests and their typically short bibliographies. While simple exposure seems to have been quite readily available, placement of poetry books in prestigious or remunerative places does appear to have depended upon connections or established reputation. No case was turned up of a newer poet who had managed to place a poetry book with a trade press absent influential recommendations or the receipt of a prize guaranteeing commercial publication.

A final question designed to discover how the poets had achieved print asked whether they had tried and failed to break into any particular market or publication, and if so, how they accounted for this failure. This question was discussed earlier in another context, but here the point of interest is how poets explained their disappointments. Of course, their answers could reveal only their own perceptions of reasons for rejection and by implication their beliefs about how decisions are made in poetry publishing generally, especially in those arenas conferring the most prestige upon authors.

While the reasons poets gave for their rejections did not lend themselves to classification and counting, the answer expected to be dominant, lack of connections, was mentioned by several. However, just as many or more respondents suggested other reasons, including two that were related to the problem of connections: being insufficiently known or famous and being isolated geographically. For instance, Dorothy Lee Richardson, who was of the Older Nonprizewinning group and, having been born in 1900, was the oldest poet studied, noted that although she had begun appearing in major periodicals more than half a century before this study was conducted, during her most productive years she had lived with her husband and children in the Philippines, which removed her from all literary circles. "Now," she added poignantly, "I am going blind and growing weaker . . . but I still love poetry and try occasionally to publish some of my (less frequent now) writing." Several NP poets living far from California and the Northeast also cited isolation as a problem. "This country is too big," observed the Georgia poet Bin Ramke.[19] "Even those of us who care have trouble finding out what worthwhile work is being done in Nebraska, Oregon, New Mexico."

Those poets who did mention lack of contacts as a cause of their failure to break into prized markets often noted other possible factors as well (indeed, most respondents listed two or more), but the no-contacts factor was the only one ever to evoke bitterness. While respondents were usually more or less resigned to the limitations they had encountered, John Stevens Wade was, here as elsewhere, atypical. Almost breezily, he explained why, throughout his very long history of writing and translating poetry, no commercial or university press had ever accepted it: "no personal contacts, and politically I'm a disaster." Most such speculations were less cheerful: "I'm not part of the N.Y. poetry buddy-system by choice," wrote another much better known poet, whose regular publisher was a prominent university press, but who had repeatedly tried and failed to placed poems in *The New Yorker* and *The Atlantic*. Another poet explained that "several poet friends in academic circles" had told her the "academic press is hard to enter unless you have an institutional *link* with which to reciprocate." Anne Hazlewood-Brady had also tried unsuccessfully to place a book with a university press and said this about it: "[A well-known poet-editor] told me years ago that I 'didn't know the right people.' I live outside both the literary and academic communities, belong to no school, and choose not to expend my energies in submissions." And still another poet, a woman who was residing in New York City and had a professional link to the New York book-publishing establishment, but not to academe, set forth her belief that: "Acceptance in some journals is often by recommendation of editors' friends or poets in writing programs. This is in the nature of things & accounts for the sameness of tone & style in some journals. The maverick or unaffiliated writer has a harder time." Ellen Marie Bissert, another New York City-based poet and former little-magazine editor, observed that: "Most work seems to be published via a networking system rather than specific attention to the poem on the page." E. G. Burrows agreed:

> There are so many poets writing today and so few overburdened poetry editors, that publication often depends not so much on excellence as on "who you know." Those writers who are the best self-advertisers—through readings, academic contacts, personal correspondence, socializing—seem, in the short run, to fare better that those without such talents. Fortunately, the survivors, in the long run, usually prove to be the best writers.

Charles Haseloff, like Bissert a New York City native and former little-mag editor, recalled that editing *Penumbra* had allowed him to make "an enormous amount of contacts. . . . You know the old proverb: 'One hand washes another.' " But he also noted:

> at one point I just got totally fed up with all the politicking and obvious wheeling and dealing. I cd. do it as long as I cd. "believe" in it, do it sincerely, or naively, you might say. But after a while that was no longer possible and I became quite cynical about it. Now I'm entering into a new stage—the realization that avoiding it all doesn't solve the problem either.

Haseloff raised a point that must immediately occur to outsiders, but, rightly or wrongly, is often not considered by aspiring poets, at least with regard to their own work:

> this is a complex issue. There *is* the problem and issue of innate ability, talent, inspiration, madness, genius, if you will. Some people just don't have it. But oddly enough, many of the latter do get published, a lot even, in books even. "Everyone knows" this. Why? Because they know how to and are willing to hustle.

Yet he admitted, both echoing and differing from Burrows, "I do think/believe/know that quality *does* occasionally make it to the top. But it is rare. Oh, well, perhaps I'm just dominated by a sour-grapes attitude? You must keep that in mind. After all, I too am human, and in no way an exception to the sins of humanity, especially the 'sin' of self-delusion."

"Self-delusion" would certainly seem to be an inviting trap for the creative worker, yet a surprising number of respondents, mostly Newer Nonprizewinners, raised their work's middling quality or need for development as a significant factor in its rejection. While no more than ten poets gave such a response, none at all was expected to. Indeed, one author who had actually been quite successful, publishing in many periodicals and being anthologized by a commercial press at least once, cited the weakness of her work as its only barrier to acceptance by the " 'big' mags, anthologies, university quarterlies, elite journals." She explained:

> Alas! not good enough . . . (too dilettantish), not assertive enough at editing my work, not impeccable at preparing & submitting mss.s. The work is neither brilliant nor graceful enough, neither crystallized nor rendered into its imagist essences, neither unique nor profound nor witty nor touching enough . . . [not] Whitmanesquely "rich/sprawling" enough, neither radical/innovative, nor classical/competent enough. And I don't work at it enough and I don't *read* enough of other poetry & novels, etc., and I don't rewrite enough *or* SEND OUT enough submissions.

Elsewhere on the questionnaire she had noted the problem of finding writing time amid the distractions of breadwinning, family, and friends. Other self-critical respondents were more temperate. James Grabill, for instance, referred to his "still-evolving technique," and Robert Hedin stated his belief that "top-ranked magazines' " rejections of his poems were caused mostly by his need "to develop more as a writer."

More commonly, poets who saw rejections as rooted in the poetry itself blamed its idiosyncratic characteristics and the rigidity or conventionality of editors' tastes. These poets were not necessarily resentful, but they did tend to locate the problem and its solution in the journals and presses rather than themselves. This type of response, along with references to connections, was the most common. David Lunde, for example, noted both the cliquishness of certain popular journals and their editors' "not very wide-ranging" tastes. "My own book," he explained, "is rather off-beat," a statement echoed by several authors who had been frustrated by publishers' rejections—among them Phyllis Koestenbaum, whose "poetry doesn't fit the mold"; Jane Bailey, who considered her "lyrical/rural" poems not within *The New Yorker*'s range of taste; and Sandra McPherson, who suspected the "strange things [she did] with language," her "quirkiness," disqualified many of her poems from serious consideration at most commercial magazines. Karen Snow noted the unusual length and proselike quality of her poems, as well as their dependence on language "some editors find . . . offensive." And Alberta T. Turner, who was associate editor of the prestigious *Field* magazine, described her own difficulties in gaining entry to certain journals: "My poetry tends to be cryptic and is probably not to their taste. Editors tell me it's 'strange,' 'different.' I am not deliberately obscure, but I have never succeeded in being 'trendy.' "

Several respondents joined Turner in pointing out the trendiness of many organs, and the long-experienced poets Daryl Hine and John Gill spoke of literary fashions that might exclude or include certain poems at certain periods. "Like everyone else," Hine explained, "I have had doors closed to me at some times and open at others." (Elsewhere on his questionnaire, Hine wrote that he was "sometimes seen as . . . sort of neo-classical, formalist, and traditional.") Jerry Ratch remarked that he had given up on contests that rewarded winners with university-press publication "because when I read what finally wins and is published I see that they tend to rehash what has already been considered 'acceptable.' " One determinedly eccentric stylist declared, probably only partly facetiously, that his exclusion from magazines that *pay* was the result of a "conspiracy of philistines & idiots, plus unsuitability of my bizarre poetry for a general audience." Curtis Zahn, an ON-group poet, was equally emphatic:

> I think that increasingly, the "prestigious" periodicals are flooded with unsolicited, no-name authors, and if you are not a member of the club it's into the slush-pile. One must have a halo—or agent—or [be an] inside groupie. I also find *my poetry* vastly more stimulating, perceptive, "artistic"—so am probably out-of-step w/the current gurus . . . (his ellipsis).

Yet the desire to be heard is strong, even if fulfilling it means forcing oneself into step. Not all poets can find sufficient solace in self-publication and knowledge of the poetry world's inherent injustices. The saddest, most startling response was given by a serious young woman poet with a self-published book and an M.F.A. from a respected creative writing program:

> My particular writing may not appeal. I rely heavily on nature imagery. Also, my poems tend not to be hard-hitting. I am currently trying to be more aggressive in my writing. (Does this mean I write to please an audience? Not to *please*, so much as to reach. I am not being heard. Perhaps "they" are not listening, but perhaps I am not speaking clearly enough. At any rate, I can change my writing much more easily than I can change "them.")

It was interesting that style, tone, diction, and imagery, more than basic topic or message, were the characteristics most poets suspected of being problematical. Very few spoke of subject, and three of those who did—Ellen Marie Bissert, Lyle Glazier, and Karen Snow—expressed surprising views, as noted in Chapter 2. All three tended to use homosexual themes or characters and remarked the resistance of small-press outlets, especially gay and lesbian/feminist, to their work, which did not follow "politically correct" lines. Another writer charged both commercial and small presses with resisting political themes, and two others guessed that their regional/rural references were foreign and uninteresting to urban editors.

In their answers many poets mentioned, directly or indirectly, the typically weak saleability of poetry. While other questions often drew forth the judgment that this had become self-fulfilling prophecy through publishers' unwillingness to promote books of poems, most poets seemed to assume that no technique could escalate sales substantially, and that commercial houses, especially those owned by conglomerates, could not afford to gamble with poetry—"unless," E. G. Burrows qualified his answer, "you are already well known, praised by outstanding critics, winner of many awards, or have a best-selling novel in your drawer." Peter Michelson spoke also of the importance of a marketing "handle"—that is, of the obvious and natural target market, the saleable "label," associated with certain key feminist and black authors and with poets considered exemplars or leaders of influential literary schools.

Additional, scattered reasons for rejection were suggested, each by fewer than five poets: lack of persistence and fear of rejection on the poet's part; bad timing; bad luck. Several poets could make no sure reply and cast about for reasons. These were among the most interesting, amusing, and in some ways the most revealing answers, underscoring as they did the complexity and extreme uncertainty of poets' struggles to place their work.

William Stafford observed that, "having tried so long," he had gained entry to every market he coveted with a single exception. He guessed the reasons for this "in order of likelihood":

1. They get better work from others.
2. I estimated their taste wrong when I juggled my current work here and there.
3. My poems are somehow relying on elements that do not rate among important elements I am perpetually blind to.
4. Chance.
5. Something else fascinating and Byzantine.

A young poet who wanted to place her books with commercial or university publishers mused: "I don't have 'connections'; I am not part of an academic writing program; I live in the South; my poetry is not 'fashionable'; a lot of the editors are obtuse; a lot of the editors (esp. academic) are hustlers; I'm unlucky; I'm not enough of a hustler myself; and so forth." ("Hustler" was a recurrent term in these answers, as were "incestuous" and "closed shop" or "closed club.")

Mike Finn is an environmentalist and deep-dyed romantic who, after the successful publication of his first book, with his career as a poet underway at last, "fell in love, chased across the country and Europe and sort of disappeared from sight leaving a lot of readings dangling." Most of his problems, he decided, but not all, resided in his own lack of motivation:

Not having tried in any persistent fashion. Absence of contacts. Stubborness. Fear of rejection. Etc. Laboring under the illusion "I have no use for worldly fame; all the squirrels know my name!"—which has since been disspelled. Getting over "Paper is trees"—which has been a difficult obstacle to overcome in terms of even . . . sending out poems.

And Charles Baxter (who has since won major prize recognition for his fiction) at the time of this survey had never had poems accepted by any of several major journals or by any university press and had not sent work to trade presses, assuming they would be closed to him. Half-jokingly, he speculated on the reasons underlying his rejections:

1. The poetry is the wrong style, too idiosyncratic.
2. It's not good enough.
3. The subjects are too abstract.
4. I haven't made enough powerfully influential friends.
5. I'm a bad person and am being punished.

He added:

I never wanted to get mixed up in the poetry "world," but I have found increasingly that about 50 percent of the successes in that world are intensely political. There is much cheap talk about the way the poetry world operates, but it is much like any other activity for which there is much supply and little demand. It takes a good deal of persistence and willpower, and the rewards tend to be very small. One has to be inner-directed.

"My last response from *Poetry*," wrote another quite distinguished younger poet, "was a personal note on the rejection slip, stating, 'I wish we could print these.' What is that supposed to mean?"

Clearly, most serious, experienced poets of all ages and sizes of reputation continued to seek acceptance in the publishing outlets they esteemed most highly, whether or not they had connections at these. While for almost all groups quality of the potential publishing source was one of the two factors weighed most heavily in a submission decision—save for NPs' book submissions, when it was considered third—and while neither friendship nor invitation ever ranked higher than third in importance, both remained extraordinarily weighty considerations.

When the question was explored of which submissions actually led to publication, it became clear that self-publication was much less important than usually supposed, and this held true even in the case of first books. Only in the ON group had more than one-fifth of the poets ushered their own first volumes into print. However, large amounts of work (book manuscripts, especially) were placed after being solicited by an editor, who was in many or most cases known personally to the poet. While over-the-transom (that is, unsolicited) submission was the single most important means of periodical placement for every group save Older Prizewinners, it was responsible for comparatively few book placements, which were intrinsically more difficult to accomplish.

All poets except Older Prizewinners encountered the highest barriers at the for-profit magazines and presses, whose approval (or at least whose money) poets prized despite their frequent criticisms of commercial values. University presses and journals (especially *Field*) and little magazines (especially *Poetry* and *The American Poetry Review*) were also significant goals and significantly difficult to reach.

While poets did not attribute their rejection by those sources to poor connections and literary politics as frequently as was expected, they did cite reasons that, taken together, emphasized their common sense of poetry publishing as a world beyond their understanding or control. This was especially true of the nonprizewinners, who were roughly twice as likely as either prizewinning group to have tried and failed to be accepted by specific journals and presses that they valued highly.

Almost all reasons for rejection hypothesized by the poets were matters about which they could realistically do nothing much: lack of connections or contacts; geographical isolation; apolitical temperament; hostile prevailing literary fashions and editorial tastes; and poetry's poor sales potential. Only weakness of the poetry and lack of persistence, each mentioned very few times, were problems that a poet might reasonably hope to solve.

There was, then, a general sense of powerlessness among the ninety-four respondents who had tried without success to break into certain markets. This, despite the fact that the authors in this study were by definition comparatively successful, though most would not so describe themselves. They had, after all, managed to get into print substantial amounts of poetry with very little reliance upon self-publication, and in almost all cases over a period of a decade or more. The great majority, furthermore, had been able to establish literary friendships, and nearly three-quarters were enjoying "close and continuing professional" associations. These must have minimized the loneliness typical of the writer's life, provided encouragement and advice, and very often facilitated publishing.

Yet throughout the answers on these questionnaires ran remarks that betrayed frustration and profound disillusionment and cynicism. "I've seen weaker collections than mine done by [two large commercial houses]," wrote one nonprizewinning male poet. "You may have to sleep with someone."

One of the study's youngest and least experienced poets, winner of a major prize for his first collection, declared: "I am astonished than an enterprise so barely rewarding in fame or finances should attract so many people, so much ambition, so much mean politicking, as poetry." (Although he neglected to consider the indirect rewards of grants and academic employment, these do not accrue to all and, even if they did, add up to fairly modest sums when compared with other ways in which poetry-writing time might be spent.) Perhaps the kind of politicking he and other poets see is not a contradiction, but actually a partial result of the art's commercial insignificance. Since for the most part it lacks either buyer response or widely understood criteria for excellence, and since little of it is dealt with in major review sources and no one among its living practitioners is generally agreed to be a master whose work exemplifies contemporary greatness, the small prestige poetry can afford and the slim promise of immortality it holds must seem always available and always beyond reach, always threatening to bypass the person not in position to receive them.

"Without the hope of great wealth the poet's ego thrives on distribution, recognition and prestige," observed Roger Aplon. "I'm at a loss to devise a system which would or could alleviate the good-ole-boy network in this society. . . . However, I think we'd see more risk taking by poets if this 'system' vanished." Aplon's speculation recalls an interview statement made by Philip Levine when explaining why he chose to "live in probably greater isolation than any other American poet my age": "When I don't have my eye on the immediate present—things like acceptance, publication, awards—I'm free to move into an area of real seriousness and adventuresomeness in writing."[20] Similarly, William Stafford once warned: "To curry favor by saying what you do not mean, or what you do not feel, is . . . damaging. You can become a lost soul in literature just as surely as you can in any activity when you abandon yourself to the decisions of others."[21]

Yet many poets—especially those struggling for the first, smallest, scrap of recognition—no doubt feel helplessly in thrall to such decisions, upon which the hope of a public life for their work must seem to rest. "Poets get little support," noted Mark Strand. "But then they have enormous egos and generally come off badly as human beings. Petty jealousies, meaningless wars, are what preoccupy them. If they'd earn money from their work, they'd relax and enjoy the fruits of their labor. But they get only the frailest, most minimal fame." Coming as it did from one of America's most famous living poets, that seems a remarkable statement.

The toughest question posed by the incredulous young poet mentioned earlier was not why the poetry community was rife with politics, but why it attracted so many people. Money was only rarely forthcoming; the work was lonely, demanding, and little-valued by the larger society; and the attempt to achieve even unremunerated publication consumed energy, cash, and usually resulted in some experience of rejection, often for unknown reasons, which many poets found deeply unsettling. And the dreamed-of worldly goal of all this effort was the very success that Philip Levine, who had attained it in a measure beyond most poets' highest hopes, seemed to shun and warn against, that the celebrated Mark Strand deemed "frail" and "minimal."

Why, then, did so many people write poetry? And, having written it, why did so many try to publish?

7

Why the Poets Published

> Stevens said of poetry, "It can kill a man." Most people supposed him to be speaking metaphorically.
>
> Reg Saner, questionnaire response, this study

In Eileen Simpson's memoir of her husband, John Berryman, and his friends Robert Lowell and Delmore Schwartz, she recalls the time when the three men were young, hopeful, still-aspiring poets, not yet overtaken by the despair, alcoholism, mental illness, and worldly success that eventually befell them all. Simpson remembers the aftermath of Berryman's first book publication in 1942, which was handled by James Laughlin's New Directions Press:

> Apart from the free copies he had received from Laughlin, there had been no sign that it had [been published]. No reviews, not a single notice of its existence. Even *The Nation,* where John had been poetry editor, had not listed it among the books of verse that had appeared during the year. "What's the point of publishing?" he asked gloomily. "The advance," Delmore said. We all laughed. The advance had been $24.[1]

Laughable as that amount sounded, and was, its 1980 value would have been roughly $140, a sum that would probably have been considered rather generous by a new poet bringing out his first book with a literary publisher. It was generally taken for granted that unknown poets could not expect book advances, especially from noncommercial presses. Even royalty payments were considered rare. While poets deplored this state of affairs, it usually occurred to them to complain only as years passed, their bibliographies lengthened, and their frustration built. Early on, merely to publish a book at someone else's expense seemed a stroke of extraordinary good fortune. For a contemporary poet, as for Berryman, the greatest postpublishing disappointment is likely to be not the lack of sales but the silence.

That few or no serious poets can live on their verse-writing income has long been so widely believed as to be thought axiomatic. In 1973, for example, editor Thomas Parkinson declared that "if you are very brave and love the art of writing, you might by the age of 50 or so be famous and have an income at the peak of the poverty level."[2] A decade later poets cooperating in the present study made similar statements again and again. Nor has the poet's situation ever been much different in this century. As we have seen, even the most gifted, best known, and best connected of the early modernist poets were poor.

Ezra Pound, for example, is said by his biographer to have used an overcoat "as both clothing and blanket," and in 1914, "a year of large and brilliant production for him," to have earned forty-two pounds in all by this writing. Two years later Pound estimated his American royalties at $1.85 per annum.[3] As his renown grew, his earnings did not, and only in his sixth decade did his books begin to bring him significant sums. Though his acquaintance Malcolm Cowley has written that Pound embraced poverty, declaring, " 'If I accept more than I need, I at once become a sponger,' " in fact he seems to have had little chance to earn beyond his needs without changing his way of life.[4]

In a 1917 speech, the comparatively popular poet Amy Lowell, whose family's affluence protected her from want, described poetry as: "Of all the poorly-paid work . . . surely the worst paid." She went on: "One moment I regret that poetry is underpaid; the next I desire that it not be paid at all. . . . To this failure of the golden lure I believe we owe it that poetry is so single-minded, so prone to follow out its dreams unhindered by public opinion."[5] The possibly beneficial literary effect of poetry's distance from profit is interesting to consider and will be taken up again. But authors listening to the obviously well-fed and famously well-supported Miss Lowell may have resented her discovery of a silver lining to the cloud of their destitution.

From the first year of *Poetry*, Harriet Monroe, sometimes joined by Pound, crusaded to enhance poets' economic circumstances, calling by turns for more poetry prizes, grants, gifts, and more generous book contracts. "The true poet . . . *can* be silenced," Monroe warned, "by starvation of body or soul . . . and there's nothing more dangerous, more bitter and perverted perhaps, than a silenced poet."[6] Exemplifying this seemingly extreme statement were dozens of struggling writers, some superbly gifted. One of the most poignant stories concerns Hart Crane, a brilliant poet of the twenties. The poems of the proud, perfectionist Crane were unusually densely textured with layers of interrelated metaphor and were always revised many times with great care before submission to a magazine. In 1925, without work and in desperate need, Crane allowed *The Dial*'s editor, Marianne Moore, to make substantial ill-advised changes in one of his finest poems, "The Wine Menagerie," for the sake of a $20 payment. Afterward, Crane threw himself on a friend's bed and wept himself to sleep.[7]

On through the succeeding decades such stories proliferated. For instance, the sections of Joel Roache's biography of Richard Eberhart that cover the 1930s and 1940s are a chronicle of economic privation and the sometimes mean-spirited acts and words to which it drove the poet.[8] Eileen Simpson's memoir, James Atlas's biography of Delmore Schwartz, and Allan Seager's of Theodore Roethke, along with many other books and articles, recount similar agonies endured by the leading poets of the forties and fifties.[9] Indeed, to one poet in this study, the matter of remuneration seemed not worth investigating: "Poets," he said, "make about the same percent of nothing."

However, a handful of contemporary poets, especially those who are middle-aged or older and have won such prizes as the Pulitzer and Bollingen, are believed by many to earn substantial, if not princely, royalties and hefty fees from magazines. All of the fourteen Older Prizewinners who filled out questionnaires answered the income-related queries, and most of them were likely to be among those poets earning the greatest amounts directly from publishing their poetry: for example, John Ashbery, Allen Ginsberg, Donald Justice, Maxine Kumin, Philip Levine, Gary Snyder, William Stafford, Mark Strand, and May Swenson.

It seemed useful to test what "everyone knows" by ascertaining just how much that "percent of [almost] nothing" *was* and how it varied group by group. Questions were framed to gain specific information about fees earned from book and periodical publication, respectively.

There is a complication, however. As has been pointed out several times, other opportunities to profit from poetry proliferated during the period studied, though how helpful and widespread their effects were is open to question. Galway Kinnell declared in 1977 that "a poet with even a modest reputation can make his living from readings—provided he's willing to spend half the year on the road."[10] Others' opinions, however, seemed to contradict this. For example, Beat poet Gregory Corso, who once had a considerable reputation, wrote in the mid-sixties, just after his peak period of popularity: "The sad thing about respect and honor in America is that it takes money to have them; therefore the American poet who wishes respect and honor is defeated before he starts because money is a very difficult thing to obtain, and for a poet it is almost . . . impossible."[11]

This difference of opinion may be attributable to the ten-to-fifteen-year stretch of time separating Corso's statement from Kinnell's, to contrary experiences or perceptions, or to their very different personalities. Yet both had been in demand for readings. Kinnell was a polished performer with an impressive body of work to draw upon, while Corso, like his friend and promoter, the extremely popular reader Allen Ginsberg, was colorful and outrageous, a legendary character.

Because of the likely importance of income derived from poetry-related activity such as readings and workshops, and in order to determine the relative proportions of support provided by poetry, more conventional jobs, and other money sources, another query was created as well.

WHAT PERCENT OF NOTHING?: POETS' INCOME FROM PUBLISHING

It will be recalled that while the quality of a periodical of press proved to be the factor weighed most heavily by poets when deciding where to send work, payment and royalty rates were not overlooked, ranking fifth in importance in periodical-submission decisions and sixth with regard to book submissions. In addition, when sending manuscripts to book publishers, poets counted as second most important such money-related matters as the houses' distribution and promotion practices and customary sales volume. Therefore, despite the common assumption that most poets do not write for money and cannot realistically hope for much, they did keep its possibility in mind and strove to acquire it through creative work. For one thing, while the dollars themselves were no doubt welcome, payment also has a symbolic significance that may outweigh its practical value. As the Older Prizewinning poet-academician Donald Justice pointed out, payment seems to indicate editors' respect for the work.

Yet most little magazines, however respectful, cannot pay. In keeping with its editors' early insistence on poets' right to compensation for their efforts, *Poetry* has always tried to pay something despite its chronic money shortage. But Harriet Monroe's 1918 lament over the "ridiculous smallness" of her checks for such classic works as Rupert Brooke's war poems and Vachel Lindsay's "General William Booth Enters Heaven" could probably have been echoed by the magazine's editors in 1980 with reference to other authors and other key poems.[12]

One Older Prizewinning poet who nearly always was paid by periodical editors noted wild variation in amounts—from a usual $10–15 fee from *Antaeus*, which was one of the best-known littles, to $300–600 from *The New Yorker*. And when one considers his strong reputation and the many hours of very difficult work often devoted to the perfection of one poem, even the latter sum was meagre. That it was considered uniquely generous underscores the economic dilemma of the serious poet.

As would be expected, almost all Older Prizewinners were receiving payment half the time or oftener from the magazines in which they published. The sole exception was Allen Ginsberg, who chose to send much of his work to periodicals that were published by his friends or the nonprofit Naropa Institute (where he taught as a volunteer), or which were associated with the gay rights movement. Of the U.S. periodicals in which he had published, only four—two newspapers, a mass magazine, and a little magazine—had paid him.

While the proportion of Older Prizewinners always or almost always receiving payment might seem high to people accustomed to little-magazine practices, from another perspective it is astonishing that these best-known living practitioners of a most demanding literary genre should even occasionally have been giving their work away.

It was expected that many poets, especially among Newer Nonprizewinners, would never have received payment from a periodical. This was true, however, for only 13 percent of the NN group; on the other hand, 79 percent had been paid for less than half their periodical contributions. This record is almost the exact reverse of their prizewinning counterparts', the NPs, about three-quarters of whom were paid half the time or oftener. The greatest surprise was in the Older Nonprizewinners' answers. Given their long careers, it was understandable that they would have been paid at least once in the preceding five years and unremarkable that most would have been paid only rarely. But the existence of two very distinct, nearly equal-sized categories of poets—one paid often, one hardly ever—was unexpected, and no ready explanation suggests itself. One poet falling into the rarely paid category boasted a publishing history spanning forty years and could remember the source, amount, and date of every payment. There had been only three. Part of the explanation may lie in the conspicuous heterogeneity of this group, comprising as it does obscure poets as well as some with considerable reputations; for example, Daryl Hine, Theodore Enslin, M. L. Rosenthal, and Richard Frost. The NN group is also diverse, placing many rather well-known names—for example, Ira Sadoff, Linda Gregg, Coleman Barks, and Carole Oles—alongside names completely unknown to most readers of contemporary poetry. The real surprise may not be the bifurcation of the ON-group responses, but the relative uniformity of the NN group.

As significant as the mere fact of payment is the amount, which in many cases was only nominal. Older Prizewinners emerged as best paid by far, with half receiving average payments of over $50. But again, when effort, fame, and career longevity are considered, their typical fee of $50–60 per poem seems paltry. As would be expected, nonprizewinners were paid less than prizewinners, younger poets less than older, with the prizewinning factor counting more than length of career—that is, the ON-group poets were less often paid, and were paid much less, than the Newer Prizewinners, despite their much longer publishing histories.

Once specific amounts of money paid were explored, the original expectation that numerous Newer Nonprizewinning poets would not have been paid at all was shown to be nearly borne out. While only eleven, or 13 percent, had received no payment at all from magazines during the most recent five-year period, three-quarters averaged $5 or less per poem, and 98 percent averaged no more than $25 per poem.

Perhaps most striking of all were the median per-poem payments for older poets receiving payment: $55 for OPs and $17.50 for ONs. After so many years of publishing, for one's price to remain so low must be disheartening. This study makes clear that even for the most prestigious, most tenacious poets, there was little money to be made from magazine appearances. And the financial burdens of literary magazines, whether academic or independent, were virtually certain to remain heavy, permitting no beneficial change in payment policy.

This might not be as disappointing as it sounds, however, since a periodical appearance is usually only a way station on the road to book publication. Most poems in collections saw print first as magazine contributions. Should income from book sales be substantial, the scant support offered by magazines would be of little concern.

Poets were asked whether royalty arrangements had usually been part of their book-publishing agreements, and if so, the approximate royalties promised. They were also asked the amounts actually paid for their two most recent books. Prizewinners tended to have royalty agreements, while fewer than half of Newer Nonprizewinners and just half of their older counterparts had had such agreements for 50 percent or more of their books. To some small extent, this reflected greater reliance by nonprizewinners upon self-publication, but most of the difference could surely be accounted for by nonprizewinners' heavier use of small presses that did not expect to make a profit and, in some cases, knew nothing about common business practice.

The poets were also asked the usual royalties received and on what figure payments were based: actual amounts paid to the publisher or list price, and whether royalties were paid beginning with the first sale or not until production costs were repaid by sales. A great deal of confusion ensued, rendering many answers useless and revealing startling degrees of unfamiliarity and indifference on the part of poets with regard to business matters.

While most poets with royalty arrangements were to receive 10 percent, this obligation seemed often not to be honored by small presses. Repeatedly, poets indicated that royalties due had not been paid, and they were inclined to be understanding about this, showing none of the anger that surfaced when they discussed other publisher sins such as holding manuscripts for too long, losing them, or returning them with insensitively phrased rejection letters. For example, one poet had received a small advance for a book but no royalties "because of [the publisher's] severe personal troubles & heavy medical expenses." She was generously forgiving about this.

Several respondents, including such long-experienced authors as Allen Ginsberg, William Stafford, and William Harmon, could not say for sure on what price their royalty figures were based. Stafford checked "list price, starting from first sale," adding parenthetically, "I *think.*" Harmon, who usually received a 10 percent royalty, had no idea what it was 10 percent *of*. He added a response line of his own and checked it: "Have no head for figures and don't know." Several other poets suggested that their publishers be asked for details, and one said his agent would know. Ginsberg, author of dozens of books published over three decades, did not understand the difference between "actual amounts paid to publisher" and "list price." (The first figure, of course, is less distributors', booksellers', libraries', or other special discounts; royalties figured on "actual amounts paid" will usually be smaller than those paid on "list price.") Most poets who could answer this question ordinarily had royalty agreements stipulating 10 percent of list price, starting from first sale. Quite a few small publishers, however, paid the author only after production expenses had been earned back.

Asked for amounts of royalties earned on their two most recent books, some poets were unable to recall specific figures and others had published only one work or had no royalty arrangement for one or both of their latest volumes. Still others probably failed to answer because, although they were to receive royalties, none had yet been paid. Therefore, response rates for this question were comparatively low, especially among Newer Nonprizewinners with regard to both of their last two books and among both Newer Prizewinners for the next most recent.

It was expected that royalties would not be large, given the notoriously poor market for poetry books and their usually modest cover prices, but these figures are still amazingly low. The largest total royalty reported by any poet in any group for either of his recent books was $5,000 received by an Older Prizewinner. The average per-book earnings for OP poets hovered around $2,000. When one considers the long experience and great repute of these authors, the investment of effort and time and artistry represented by one poetry volume, and the fact that prior periodical publication of the poems had not often attracted larger (or any) fees, the Older Prizewinners' royalties—amounting, as they usually did, to no more than one-tenth or one-fifteenth of a modest professional yearly salary—seem scarcely believable. Yet for those familiar with the difficulty of selling poetry, a few thousand dollars, or even a few hundred, sounds like a princely reward. Gary Elder, a poet in this study and proprietor of Holmgangers Press, said that he promised his authors "10 percent—after recovery [of costs]" and so far had paid royalties on only five titles: "The press has survived (going on ten years now) exactly as I've survived as a poet—we just keep DOING it, damning the cost. . . . It is actually hard to give poetry books away on streetcorners. . . . " Most sales, he added, were "generated by the author[s]." Accordingly, several poets in the study who published through small presses declared themselves satisfied to receive free copies in lieu of royalties. Sometimes the publishers offered a flat number, sometimes 10 percent of the print run.

In an age of highly publicized six- and even seven-figure advances (that is, guaranteed advance payments against anticipated royalties) for writers of novels and topical nonfiction, the incidence and amounts of poets' advances were hardly worth speaking of. Sixty-five percent of all respondents to this study had never received an advance, including 74 percent of the long-publishing Older Nonprizewinners. Just over 26 percent of respondents had been granted advances for half or more of their books.

The paltriness of the number of books favored with advances is underscored by the paltriness of the amounts paid. The highest advance for any title by any poet in any group, $4,500, was, again, attracted by an Older Prizewinner's latest book. Older Prizewinners' median advances, however, were roughly $1,500 for latest book and only $1,000 for next most recent. Other groups' medians were half or less than half of these amounts when they received advances at all. Most of the time, they did not.

Book publications, then, yielded only modest payment for even the best-known poets and negligible amounts for the effort expended, or in comparison with usual income from any comparably time-consuming regular job.

Yet the poets continued to write and to invest large amounts of money, time, and emotion in the search for publishers, although the relatively small number of Older Nonprizewinners turned up by the random sampling for this study suggests that many writers who remained unrecognized had eventually abandoned poetry as a career if not poetry writing. However, the recent burgeoning of career-oriented poets resulting from the growth of higher education and creative writing programs also help explain this imbalance. Only two of the 158 cooperating poets, Keith Rahmmings and Gary Allan Kizer, declared an intention to stop writing or sending out poems, and Kizer has since published poetry.

Rahmmings, an experimentalist so far acceptable only to the small press and little magazines, explained his reasons for turning away from poetry:

> even if you get . . . your stuff published and funding for your craft or sullen art, etc., you're still nowhere BECAUSE NOBODY READS THE MAGS OR BOOKS PUT OUT BY SMALL PRESSDOM. You have virtually no audience. . . . And you're broke unless you make your money otherwise because there's no bucks in being a poet in late twentieth century America. . . . Let's say you luck out and get a mainstream press to put out a book of your stuff. You get paid enough for about a month's groceries, still remain an anonymous nobody because the books are ineptly distributed and because only a zillionth percent of the reading public even knows poetry exists, and unless your name happens to be Rod McKuen or Diane Wakoski, don't count on getting a second book into print.

Although the intrinsic satisfactions of poetry writing and publishing must be great, given their trivial external rewards, poets, like anyone, are mindful of money and not immune to economic frustration as time passes and little money is forthcoming. At the end of the 1970s, the popular poet Robert Creeley wrote: "For years I was terrified of being compromised by any intimation of depending on writing for a living. But now I just want to stand in the street and scream, 'Goddamnit, *pay* me!' "[13]

The problem of finding time to write, given the need to earn money, was discussed in chapter 2. Figure 7.1 compares time spent by poets on various working activities with income derived. Immediately, causes of frustration are apparent. No single poet earned as much as half his money directly from poetry writing. The largest proportion of income earned this way was 45 percent, by one Older Prizewinner. Even when poetry royalties and fees were added to payments for such poetry-related work as giving readings and conducting workshops, the great majority of all poets in every group but the OP were shown to have a major income source outside the realm of poetry. It is interesting to see, however, that for poets in every group there was much more money to be made from discussing poetry and reading it orally than from publishing it. Median income proportions earned indirectly from poetry were two to five times higher than the proportions earned directly from it. And while no poet derived more than half his income directly from poetry, ten poets, including at least one from each group, earned more than half their money indirectly from it.

Figure 7.1
Time Allocations and Income Sources
(Mean percentages of working time devoted to four types of work compared with mean percentages of income derived from those types of work.)

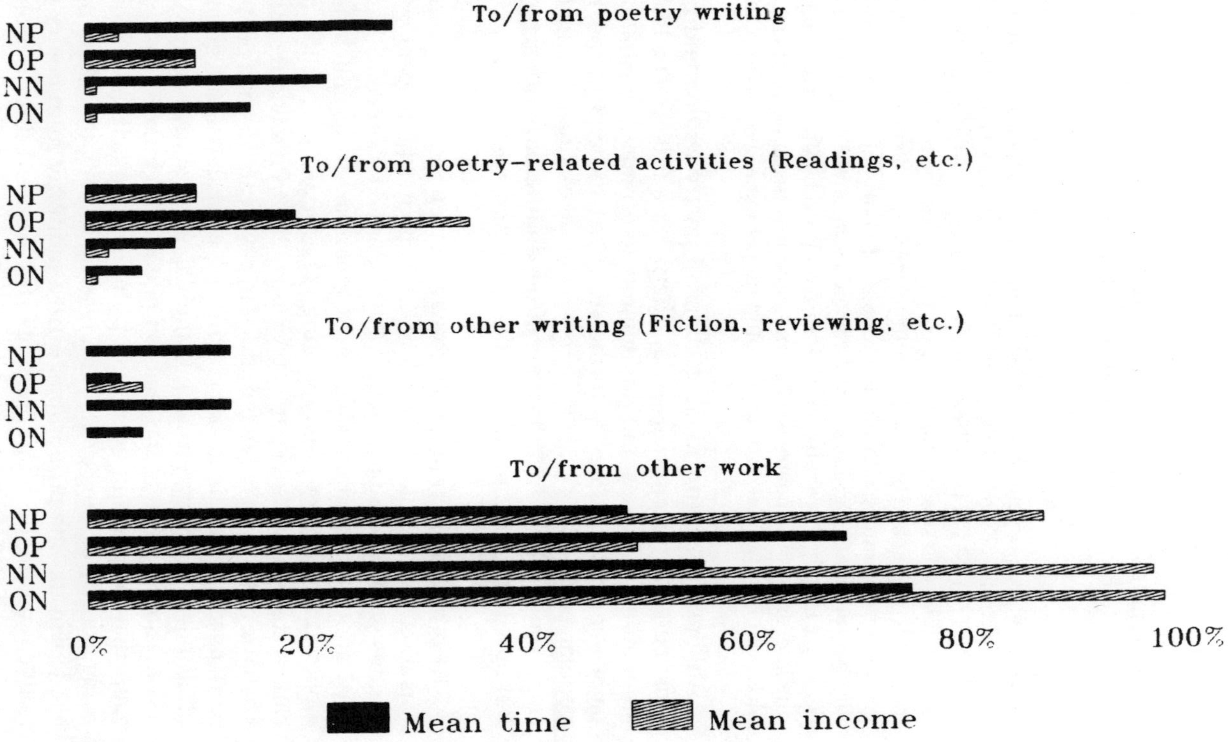

To/from poetry writing

NP
OP
NN
ON

To/from poetry-related activities (Readings, etc.)

NP
OP
NN
ON

To/from other writing (Fiction, reviewing, etc.)

NP
OP
NN
ON

To/from other work

NP
OP
NN
ON

0% 20% 40% 60% 80% 100%

Mean time
Mean income

Perhaps the most important point to be drawn from the income data presented is that being a poet often yielded some money, and for a few people a substantial amount, at least in relation to their total income. At the same time, poetry was for no one a reliable source of all income, not even for the most famous poets, and the discovery that poetry-related income sometimes served as a very substantial supplement should not obscure the fact that the work of earning this income fed on a poet's writing, sometimes offering no nourishment in return. "I do not really like giving readings," Maxine Kumin once told an interviewer, "I have to be honest and say I do it for the money."[14] Several other poets in this study actually enjoyed readings—for instance, Olga Broumas, Gary Elder, Barbara Harr, and Gary Snyder, the last of whom recalled a North San Juan fire-hall reading for local loggers as the single most rewarding event in his life as a poet. This is consistent with many of Snyder's past statements, including one made during a *New York Quarterly* interview: "Giving poetry readings is part of my work, because the poem lives in the voice, and I do it not just for the money, though that certainly is a consideration, but because I feel this is where I try to get my poems out and I get to share a little bit of what my sense of the music of them is with others." (Later in the interview, Snyder remarked that he thought of his audience when he wrote, an unusual admission for a contemporary poet, but envisaged it as "friends, family, community, my face-to-face social network," not a general reading public.[15]) Other poets valued readings and workshops for the escape they offered from the solitude of writing.

Yet however much they were enjoyed or disliked, the fact remained that these activities subtracted time from writing and were lucrative only by comparison with royalties and advances. The very well-known and relatively well-remunerated Kumin, in still another interview, said she "would not recommend poetry as a career. . . . It is impossible in this time and place—in this culture—to make poetry a career. . . . You can, however, make a career out of being a poet by teaching, traveling around and giving lectures. It's a thin living at best."[16] A number of poets without permanent faculty positions were making their livings in just the peripatetic style described by Kumin. Robert Bly, for example, had chosen rural Montana as home not "for romantic reasons, but because I got a free house to live in on a farm of my father's." Having reduced living expenses to a bare minimum, and with his books selling rather well, Bly was still leaving his home for three months each year to earn his and his family's living by teaching "fairy stories and at times Blake" to small groups of adults.[17]

Galway Kinnell, while pointing out the unusual opportunities for fundraising offered by the subsidized creative writing classes, teaching appointments, and "poetry-reading circuits" in America, claimed that readings, like college courses, were attended mostly by young people. The types of prestigious national posts sometimes held by important poets in other countries, he added, were almost never proffered by America to her poets: "Our government assumes a poet is not quite a full adult—that he's a little too dreamy and bewildered for common work. . . . Much as in the old days the eunuchs were put into the service of ladies, so in our day the poets are hired to serve and pamper the young."[18]

From figures presented in this report and detail supplied in poets' narrative replies, it is clear that most respondents, excepting only Older Prizewinners, were deriving three-quarters or more of their income from regular employment, most often teaching. As several indicated, among them Peter Klappert and James McMichael, poets' teaching appointments often depended on their poetry and allowed them some time to write. However, the experience of teacher-poets in this study varied widely. While such renowned authors as Kinnell and Levine had noted in interviews the generous writing time afforded by the academy, younger poets like Yale winners Bin Ramke and Reg Saner were finding that their days stretched very long indeed. Ramke estimated that teaching-related duties consumed most weekdays from 7:30 A.M. through 5:00 P.M., and Saner was frequently devoting fourteen hours a day to his professional duties and writing combined.

Poets without continuing appointments often worked at a succession of brief assignments in different locations, which was probably still more stressful. On her biographical sheet one Yale Younger Poet listed a series of recent teaching jobs, none of more than two years' duration and no two in the same state. Having spent several years in one-year jobs away from her native Northwest, another Newer Prizewinner, Tess Gallagher, told an interviewer in 1979 that she was living "in a state of constant returnings so as to preserve a sense of belonging to my home area."[19]

Most poets seemed to agree, finally, with Michael Ryan, a Yale Younger Poet and academician who concluded: "Writing poetry is a very expensive habit. It is a more-than-full-time job that pays almost nothing. I believe that everything I have to say on the subject [of the life and work of the poet in this culture] is an elaboration of that basic economic fact."

As noted in chapter 2, Older Prizewinners were spending a strikingly low 10 percent average of their working time on poetry-writing—less than the poets of any other group. They undoubtedly tended to receive more invitations to do other kinds of work, such as giving readings and literary lectures, as well as filling faculty slots. Yet while they spent considerably less time, proportionately, writing poems than did poets in other groups, they made much more money through publication, bringing this percentage of income into line with the percentage of time spent writing. Every other group committed much more time writing poetry than the resulting income would justify. When poetry-related work was examined, the differences between Older Prizewinners' experiences and other poets' was even more dramatic. OPs spent an average 18 percent of their time on this work, much more than poets of any other group, but drew 35 percent of their income from it. Newer Prizewinners constituted the only other group that gained as much from poetry-related work in money as they gave to it in time. Nonprizewinners gave only half as much time, but with very little financial return. From this we can infer that, logically enough, they had relatively few opportunities to carry out such tasks and usually received small fees or none.

While all groups spent some time on nonpoetic writing, often literary criticism and reviews, only Older Prizewinners, who spent the least, earned much by it. This probably reflects in part the need of less renowned poets to meet tenure and promotion demands by writing criticism and reviews. Older Prizewinners, on the other hand, were so famous as poets that most needed only to continue writing poetry in order to retain academic credibility. Through commercial print media they might win the chance to write essays and reviews for money. John Ashbery, for instance, was serving as *Newsweek*'s art critic and some of his colleagues' names turned up in the bylines of mass-circulation review sources. Still, such assignments were surprisingly limited, accounting for an average 5 percent of Older Prizewinners' income.

That nonprizewinners were more dependent on income sources aside from poetry was a predictable finding, but somewhat startling was the fairly similar pattern of responding Newer Prizewinners, a group that included such prominent names as Tess Gallagher, Marilyn Hacker, Robert Hass, Robert Pinsky, and Stanley Plumly.

To earn a significant amount, then, from poetry—an amount that might make the investment in it economically rational—necessitated, in most cases, working at writing for many years and winning the kinds of publication opportunities and prizes that bring wide recognition. Even then, however, one could not reasonably hope for a life free of other breadwinning chores. In 1977, the small press Grey Fox published a three-way interview, focused on the subject of economic survival, with Gary Snyder and two fellow poets, Lew Welch and Philip Whalen. Though Whalen and Snyder, at least, were frequently published at this time and widely read, none of the three men held a graduate degree (all are Reed College alumni) or a permanent faculty berth. Welch, who had recently moved to "the woods where things are cheap," earned his livelihood "in any kind of left-handed job . . . that nobody seems to want, and cab-driving. I've gone salmon fishing, worked in the Post Office—usually the rush times like Christmas, and so on."[20] "Get a trade! Get two trades!" Snyder exclaimed a year later when asked by another interviewer for survival advice to young poets. "Or, get a Ph.D.! You got no choice."[21]

That this was true was borne out by an Older Prizewinning poet with a long career distinguished by honors but resulting in less fame than was the norm for poets in this group. Living in a cheap rural area far from a library, the poet could not claim to read any periodical regularly and explained: "I read what comes by—but I have so little money to subscribe." (Few literary magazines cost more than $15 per year; many cost less.)

Jan Clausen, who is known as both poet and fiction writer, in a monograph on links between poetry and contemporary feminism speculated that small remuneration for poetry might eventually discourage its writing by those who can also write publishable fiction or essays: "For once income from writing is seen as a real possibility, it becomes evident that any significant sum is far more likely to come from prose . . . readers are so clear in their preference for prose."[22]

Despite the argument of a Christopher Clausen that postmodernist obscurity alone is responsible for poetry's vanished public, or the assertion of Gary Snyder that public interest in song (and "poetry is really song") proves poetry still commands a public, no one really disbelieves that fundamental reality.[23] People today prefer prose to the writings of serious poets. As Michael Ryan suggested, this "basic economic fact" underlies and in some sense undercuts each poet's commitment. While few American authors today would agree with Robert Frost's view, expressed in 1918, that "Nothing is quite honest that is not commercial," many—especially those with families to support—are somewhat uneasy about devoting their time and strongest creative passion to work that brings little money.[24] As Jan Clausen explained, writing poems comes to feel "like self-indulgence."[25]

Yet for many poets the activity cannot be terminated but goes on unwilled, regardless of other pressures. A number of poets in the study—Robert Pinsky, William Harmon, Theodore Enslin, and others in questionnaire responses, James Dickey in print[26]—mentioned what Michael Ryan perhaps expressed best:

> An interesting thing about being a poet (or probably any artist) is that everything you are, read, do, think, etc., enters the poetry as it must. There's really very little time when I'm not working. But teaching full time perhaps along with other circumstances does not allow me to maintain a daily engagement with my work—I don't know what else to call it but engagement. I don't write every day, though everything I read and do is filtered through that lens; some days I write for 12 or 14 hours.

Notice the surely unconscious statement made by Ryan's choice of words: his "work" was defined as exclusive of his full-time teaching. The work—the "real work," to use Gary Snyder's phrase—was the poetry alone.

THE ISOLATION OF POETS AND POETRY

Time and money strains, not to mention some poets' twenty-four-hour-a-day preoccupation with their art, can be disastrous for personal relationships. Adding to the sense of being lonely and pressured are the intense concentration and long stretches of uninterrupted time required for the writing itself and the travel and brief intervals of work among strangers necessitated by some poets' means of earning a livelihood. Compounding the problem is the fact that much interaction with colleagues occurs by mail as poets submit work or contact fellow writers whose work they find interesting. For some poets there exists no easy, structured mode of daily communication analogous to other professionals' collegial contacts in the workplace.

Relationships with editors and publishers, however distant, do provide some sense of community with likeminded people. Although there are many printed anecdotes recounting the sins of poetry editors, the overwhelming majority of cooperating study poets in every group judged professional relationships with both periodical and book editors generally satisfactory, and a number of poets added that they could not recall a single problem. Newer Nonprizewinners were less satisfied overall than poets in other groups, but even they felt well treated for the most part. Given the reputation of poetry editors for keeping manuscripts over unconscionably long periods of time, evaluating work stupidly, rejecting it frequently, and paying for it rarely, these findings came as a great surprise. Low satisfaction rates and detailed horror stories had been anticipated. Most astonishing was the overall contentment of Older Nonprizewinning poets, all of whom had persisted for many years in the face of many rejections, small remuneration, little or no review attention, and the failure to receive prominent awards.

Considering the pressure of hundreds or thousands of unsolicited manuscripts, understaffing, and money shortages, it was amazing that literary editors were managing to maintain such harmonious relationships with poets. Part of the explanation for this must have lain in authors' patience born of sympathy for those involved in publishing. Poets understood that to publish their work resulted in financial loss, or at best, no real prospect of gain. Hence, they were likely to feel grateful and unwilling to criticize any but the grossest mishandling. The heavy involvement of this study's respondents in publishing probably helps account for their generosity.

Not surprisingly, poets were likeliest to lodge their complaints against commercial houses and mass-marketed magazines which, they believe, have the resources to treat submitted work with consideration. Maxine Kumin, quoted in an earlier chapter, expressed appreciation of the editorial staff at Viking, the publishing house that sought her out and won her away from Harper & Row, which "treated [her] like a charity-ward case," but she was angry about the publisher's failure to promote her work, especially since, in her opinion, "the only reasons for going with a commercial house are promotion & distribution." Marilyn Hacker, another poet of distinguished reputation, had left Viking, publisher of her first full-sized book, *Presentation Piece,* which, in a highly unusual and impressive sweep, had won both the Lamont and National Book Awards. Despite her critical triumph and the publicity she had garnered, Viking offered Hacker a paltry $800 advance for her second book and did not plan to issue it in paper covers until it proved its saleability in hardback. Hacker went on to Knopf and, National Book Award notwithstanding, Viking "let *Presentation Piece* go out of print in three years; they had stopped distributing it (although it had merited a second printing) a year before." Hacker had never been given a chance to buy up remainders and returns, which is a courtesy often extended to authors. Happier with Knopf, Hacker believed nonetheless that "in general, no book of poetry today is advertised or publicized by trade publishers, unless the author is also a novelist. Publishers regard such books as foregone losses: a self-fulfilling prophecy." (Her most recent volume of poetry, *Love, Death, and the Changing of the Seasons,* was published in 1986 by Arbor House.)

Other respondents with trade publishers also remarked the paucity of promotion for their work and one mentioned editorial neglect. Authors with academic- and small-press books were more likely to mention weak editing and less likely to criticize promotion and distribution efforts, but usually, it seemed, because they didn't expect much service in those areas from noncommercial publishers. One notable younger poet, who had published with both a trade and a small literary press, noted that the former was expert in business matters but ignorant of literature, while the latter was knowledgeable about poetry but bungled distribution. Similar complaints were made quite frequently, sometimes with good-humored resignation by respondents who declared themselves generally satisfied with editors and publishers. To encounter business sophistication and adequate capital, in combination with taste and commitment to poetry, seemed to be a rare occurrence.

On questionnaires for this study, as well as in print, the most common sources of poet complaint were manuscript losses and delays in response and publication. Dorothy Lee Richardson, whose career as a published poet extended over five decades, had had positive experiences with editors by and large, but recalled two war poems held for many months by two "very good magazines" that had intended to publish them but then returned them because the war had ended. "They were two of my very best," she lamented, and did not come out until years later, as part of a book. At other times, manuscripts were lost by editors or the post office, a little magazine folded after promising publication, or, as David Lunde mentioned, the manuscript might actually be accepted and published without notification of the poet. Several times, respondents to this study discovered, upon checking their lists of citations to periodical appearances, that a poem submitted long ago and which they had thought was lost, had actually been accepted and published. (That this could have happened reveals communication failure between not only poet and editor but poet and readers, if there *were* readers.) Such problems had been so frequent that in 1979, the American Center of PEN, an international writers' organization, adopted a set of standards to guide periodical editors' treatment of writers and establish a standing committee to review alleged violations.[27] As we have seen, however, poets were pleased overall with the way their work was handled, several respondents mentioning that they had established regular correspondences with editors and even close friendships through the mail.

However, loneliness seemed to remain an essential condition of the poetic life, the most painful kind of isolation being the poet's sense of separation from an audience. "Hey, is Anyone Listening?" Stephen Minot asked in a 1977 *North American Review* article that attracted unusual attention. Reciting a litany of statistics to show that submissions to small magazines dramatically outnumbered sales, Minot concluded that no one *was* listening and urged the National Endowment for the Arts to shift its emphasis from subsidizing magazine production to promoting widened distribution and readership. "The plain fact," he wrote, "is that there's more of us up here on the stage than there are out there in the audience."[28] Or, as Curtis Zahn had written sixteen years earlier and reaffirmed for this study: "If an author is willing to die anonymously, he can choose no better conveyance than lifelong publication in the Little Magazines."[29]

Repeatedly, poets in this study wrote of being haunted by a like conviction. "No one buys poetry except other poets," wrote Karen McKinnon, expressing an often-rehearsed truism. Marilyn Hacker voiced a second truism, which deepens the seriousness of McKinnon's, when she observed that many amateur poets also failed to buy or read poetry:

> Poetry seems to have been eliminated as a literary genre, and installed, instead, as a kind of spiritual aerobic exercise—nobody need *read* it, but anyone can do it. . . . I find it difficult to understand why anyone who doesn't *read* poetry should

want to *write* it. . . . As a "modest proposal"—if everyone enrolled in a poetry workshop at a university, women's center, YM/W C/HA . . . bought one book a month by a living poet, the economics of poetry publishing would be turned right around.

Some poets responded especially warmly to my cover letter explanation that I was neither writer, teacher, nor critic of poetry, but only a poetry-lover. While this would seem a common enough relationship of reader to literary genre, the general impression prevailed that it was rare indeed in the case of poetry. "Were there more such readers [as you]," John Matthias wrote, "you wouldn't—and we wouldn't—need to be concerned about the marketplace."

Serious poets repeatedly say and prove by their actions that they will write what they must, as they must, readership or not. An article and book by Christopher Clausen were described in earlier chapters as laying the blame for poetry's diminished audience on the willful obscurity of the poets themselves. No respondent in a symposium following the Clausen paper disputed his assumption that readers were few, nor was anyone untroubled by this fact, but many made the point also made above: that Clausen's argument lacked practical ramifications because it overlooked the simple truth that serious poets must, in Linda Pastan's words, "go back to their desks and write whatever poems they were going to write anyway—audience be damned."[30]

While poets accepted these circumstances, they regretted them nonetheless and dreamed of solutions. Harriet Monroe's desire for "great audiences" lived on, though not her early belief that they were essential to the development of "great poets."

It is worth noting that only very seldom did poets concerned about audiences vilify television, perhaps because the problem for poets is not an absolute decline in reading but an apparent decline in the reading of good poetry, which, as we have seen, long predates TV.

Several poets admitted a wish to attract a broad audience: extra-literary, extra-academic. "I would like ordinary people to read, enjoy, and value my work," wrote the young Brooklyn (now San Francisco) poet Zack Rogow. Similarly, Charles Haseloff spoke of wanting to write a "universal poetry": "But who would publish it? *Life? Time? Newsweek? Cosmopolitan? The Reader's Digest?*" In the same paragraph, however, he castigated the mass reading public for wanting "*easy* escapism": "Intellectuals," he declared, "at least want difficult escapism." In just five sentences, Haseloff veered among positions of blaming editors for assuming that readers resist serious poetry, blaming readers for perusing only slick magazines, and blaming the same readers for, after all, wishing to read exactly what the editors thought they did. An argument could be constructed to weave together these variegated threads, but Haseloff's single vacillating paragraph represented well the tensions and confusions characteristic of attempts to interpret the problem of audience. That there might be no imaginable solution was hard for some to admit. "I can see why some [poet] aspirants would longingly contemplate playwriting, prose, propaganda, pornography—something immediately useful, and publishable," wrote Mindy Aloff. As Jan Clausen warned may happen, some poets do indeed desert their poetry—fully or partially, out of need or frustration—for more saleable writing. Clausen's own name turned up in this study's sample but was rejected because her prose was at least as well known as her poems. Since the sample was drawn, she has published two novels, but no new collection of poetry. And Mindy Aloff was a professional dance critic when the study was conducted, a position she still holds. However, as the data already presented indicate, prose writing occupied a small percentge of most poets' work schedules and budgets, even though many were academicians and perhaps encouraged to write scholarly prose. Mostly, poets desiring wider readership continued to hope, against all reason, that the "ordinary people," to use Rogow's phrase, could somehow be reached through verse. Nor was this the hope exclusively of young or naive writers. In 1983 Robert Creeley praised the "poetry-in-the-buses" programs, recalling a dinner with a lawyer who had delighted him by reciting a William Carlos Williams poem memorized from a bus wall.[31] Morty Sklar, since 1975 very active as poet, publisher, sponsor of readings and other poetry events and programs (including Poetry-in-the-Buses in Iowa City), and survivor of extremely low sales for his generally well-reviewed books and magazines, recalled with special pleasure a building janitor who had attended a reading and later told Sklar that "he enjoyed my poetry very much because he could understand what I expressed in it. He said that he wasn't a reader of poetry and hadn't really thought he could appreciate it."[32]

Just so, Mary Oliver declared, in her contribution to the Clausen symposium, that she wrote "for the man cutting the grass. . . . For the man . . . who is not primarily or even at all a literary person," but who, she believed, would "fall headlong" into poetry relevant to his life and "be refreshed and begin listening for more."[33] Gary Snyder found *his* "men cutting the grass" in the loggers at the aforementioned fire-hall reading, which he identified on his questionnaire as the "single most gratifying event" of his life as a poet and had also mentioned in a published essay.[34] A. R. Ammons, a much-decorated poet and a Cornell University professor of English, once told interviewer Cynthia Haythe: "I would like for the people who are like the people I was raised with, many of whom could barely read or could not read at all, and who were not very well educated . . . those are the people I would like to speak to. . . . Yes, I would like to speak to the common man."[35] The young poet Susan Hauser showed a certain Snyderesque spirit by suggesting that poetry should be taken to the public wherever it is: "I've thought of poems on cereal boxes."

Yet all such plans, hopes, and isolated episodes linking "common" people to elite poetry rendered poetry no less elite. All evidence indicates that they added up to very little culturally and nothing economically. Sklar's janitor-fan almost surely remained a nonreader of verse; nothing suggests that Oliver's symbolic grass-cutter would really take a break with a volume of her very clear, accessible poetry; it seems unlikely that Snyder's loggers or the Williams-reciting lawyer went beyond their taste of poetry to buy a book, even one by the poets in question; and Ammons would probably be as amazed as anyone to learn that significant numbers of "common men" were buying up his books. The goal of building great audiences seemed as far out of reach as it had been decades before, when Monroe and Pound debated its importance or when Don Marquis, who died in 1939 after creating the popular, witty, and easily understandable series of poems called "archy and mehitabel," said: "Publishing a volume of verse is like dropping a rose petal down the Grand Canyon and waiting for the echo."[36] If Marquis never found a sizeable audience for his printed verse, it is likely that only the rarest poet, perhaps only the most sensational or cannily self-promotional poet, ever can. "If one is a famous poet," John Ashbery once said, "one still isn't famous."[37]

Why, then, when publishing vouchsafed not even the hope of modest sums of money or the chance to touch large numbers of readers, did the poets continue to publish?

The simple answer is that intellectual or creative work undertaken seriously, propelled by ideas thought to be significant, is naturally believed to require public exposure. Poets who write for recreation or therapy, and they probably number in the thousands, either do not seek to build bibliographies through serious literary outlets or in any case do not persist against the usual tide of rejections. While respondents' attitudes toward poetry varied greatly, they held in common a sense of poetic vocation, and nearly all gave evidence of having read a great deal of poetry and meditated long and deeply about the genre. Most had poetic friends, and two-thirds had edited, and often published, others' poems. Theirs were, for the most part, lives lived *in* poetry, whatever their other obligations.

If we accept, then, that virtually all of the poets were so serious about their writing, its vision, and message that they could not bear to contain it in the private domain, the question becomes not Why did poets publish? but, Why did they *write,* and why in this form?

The poets were not asked the impossibly ambiguous question, Why do you write?—though a very few volunteered the information, usually in vague terms. They were, however, asked to identify the most satisfying event of their lives as poets, and what, if anything, they were working toward. Responses to the questions were roughly classifiable into public occurrences—such as publication of a particular book or poem, receipt of a prize, praise from a reader—and the intensely private rewards of the writing process itself, of knowing that an especially good poem had been completed, of forming important personal relationships through poetry.

Taken together, the events ranked third and fourth—"Acceptance or publication of first book" and "Acceptance or publication of a subsequent book"—were mentioned by thirty respondents as the most gratifying events of their poetic careers, making book publication the event cited second most commonly, though almost always by nonprizewinners.

One hundred one, or 78 percent, of respondents to the query about what they were working toward, or looking forward to or hoping for, mentioned a "*single* poetic accomplishment or recognition," and all but ten of these described their goals. Here, book publication was mentioned most frequently, with twenty-two (24 percent) looking ahead to "Publication of next book," "Publication with trade press," or "Publication of a 'Selected' or 'Collected' volume of poems."

It was expected that bringing out a book would loom large, given the occasional and milestone nature of such a happening for many poets, and the difficulty for some of finding a publisher and for all of polishing a book manuscript into printable form. The surprise was that fewer than one-quarter of respondents to each query mentioned book publication. In particular, it had seemed predictable that a substantial number of poets, especially among the nonprizewinning groups, would recall the advent of their first books as their most gratifying poetry-related experience (that is, "event"). While this occurrence was mentioned, mostly by the two groups of nonprizewinners (and never at all by the Older Prizewinners), it did not dominate the answers of any group, even though all poets in the study had by definition seen at least one book reach print. (Sone, though, did treasure the memory: "After years of anticipation," reminisced Dorothy Dalton, "the publication of my first book.") Some poets recalled first acceptance by a periodical editor as the most gratifying event. "That first acceptance note," Timothy Cohrs wrote, "and then that first payment check (a whopping $5 from another magazine a few years later)."

Other writers remembered first acceptance or publication by an especially respected source. For instance, David Huddle mentioned the publication of four poems in *Field*, Barry Goldensohn his first *Poetry* acceptance, Dorothy Lee Richardson her first appearance in the *Atlantic*, toi derricotte acceptance of her second book by Crossing Press, and Coleman Barks acceptance of his book by Harper & Row.

Several people were working, naturally enough, toward publication of their next book or first acceptance by a major trade or university publisher. This was sometimes a nearly mechanical process: "I just work book to book," explained Stephen Leggett, "the new one always being the one that matters." But other poets valued the attendant opportunities as much as the physical fact of a new volume. "It is not an 'ultimate,' " said Peter Klappert, "but for some time the publication of *The Idiot Princess [of the Last Dynasty*] has loomed as a 'single' event, mainly because it will free me psychologically and financially (through possible grants, reading fees and salary increases) to give more time to writing."[38]

Marina LaPalma, who had published with the successful Kelsey Street Press cooperative, sought "publication by a major publisher, with the accompanying publicity budget and chance to read in other countries and be translated into other languages." A few answers—surprisingly few, given the market for poetry—seemed underlain with frustration. "I've had a collection of poems, *The Myth of Heaven,* in circulation for about three years," wrote Charles Baxter. "I want some press to accept and publish it." Isabel Glaser explained that she was trying to place a volume of children's poetry: "All I have to do is get someone to agree to *look* at it." Ron Overton, who had already finished enough poems for two new books, found it "hard to find the time to aggressively pursue book publishing possibilities."

One poet, Karen Snow, was looking far ahead: to "my 'collected poems' when I'm 80," while the indomitable Dorothy Lee Richardson, already past eighty and with failing eyesight, was anticipating "publication of my next book, 'The Invisible Giant' (and two or three other collections if I live long enough)."

Mentioned as "most gratifying" by only a small number of poets, but remembered by these with particular poignance, were poetry readings or performances. "I gave a poetry reading at my 10th reunion at Wellesley College," Judith Steinbergh wrote, "where a whole audience of women (100 or so) & some husbands burst into tears. I was suddenly aware of the incredible power of poetry to bring people together & break down defenses." Ida Fasel fondly recalled "reading . . . to a group of people whose faces gave me great pleasure when I looked up." Most gratifying for Steve Benson was an "improvised poetry performance" in San Francisco several years earlier; for Gary Elder a reading "one spring evening in the Sierra foothills outdoors"; for Alice Cabaniss a benefit reading at Wake Forest University that netted not only a profit but "the *involvement of the audience*"; for Barbara Harr a "reading at the 92nd St. Y [in New York City] . . . as winner of the 'Discovery' contest, where my man-at-the-time sent roses, my mother came and was proud of me." Yale Younger Poet Bin Ramke cited the attendant reading at Yale ("with R. P. Warren, Richard Hugo, and Holly Stevens in the audience"). More generally, Olga Broumas explained the importance to her of public readings, "where the real voice of the poem acts upon tangible people—it is one of my favorite activities (performing my work), through which I am nourished and necessarily am given the deep satisfaction of knowing I have touched and pleased other human hearts."

Here the line between public and private satisfactions blurs, as it does for poets who have taken special delight in readers' reactions to their work, the source of gratification listed sixth most often. Mark Strand, whose career had been studded with honors, singled out as most gratifying "Elizabeth Bishop's praise." A much younger poet recounted in great detail, taking leisurely pleasure in telling the story, her poetry reading at an arts and crafts festival in a small town. The day had ended with praise from a distinguished senior poet, who was also in attendance as reader, preceding her on the program, and, though about to leave, chose to remain after hearing this younger poet begin to read. "It was like being knighted," she wrote, "it was like slipping the sword from the stone." Similarly, Dorothy Lee Richardson remembered Robert Frost's lauding her work after "virulently criticizing" other poets at a workshop, and Theodore Enslin his acceptance by Cid Corman into the inner group of *Origin* authors (*Origin* being an especially fine little magazine edited by Corman), as well as "recognition by George Oppen," the recently deceased Objectivist poet. Robert Pinsky had taken especial pleasure in receiving "certain personal letters; one or two from senior poets, in particular."

Sometimes, for what seemed to be a very lucky few, praise had come in the form of published book reviews. Three authors mentioned these, Charles Behlen adding, "It is incredible to me that someone would care enough about something I had written to write about it."

Other writers found their rewards in the reactions of friends. Kenneth Rosen, a teacher and conference organizer acquainted with many poets, derived his "principal support" from other poets' "respect and friendship." Similarly, Nona Nimnicht's greatest poetic pleasure had been found in "Confirmation. . . . Reading and writing poems with other women for a workshop." Three respondents had had unusual experiences of reader approbation. David Curry took satisfaction in a university freshman's paper written about Curry's first book, *Here,* and forwarded by the young man's English instructor: "The paper . . . is more meaningful to me than any published review or award I have subsequently received," wrote Curry. "The student must have been only 18 or 19 years old. I was left feeling the book had been an actual pleasure and help to him."

Siv Cedering, who had enjoyed "too many" gratifying events to list comprehensively or choose among, nonetheless recalled learning that a

144-word poem of hers had been found chiseled into the walls of a "solitary confinement cell in a maximum security prison." A very prolific and quite popular poet both here and in her native Sweden, Cedering had had strangers name a baby after her, had received "presents, flowers, letters, poems" from readers, and remembered "meeting a man on the street who recites my poems" Most gratifying for Charles Baxter was the discovery, on a trip to the University of Kansas, that a stranger had memorized one of his poems. "Occasionally something like this happens," wrote Baxter. "It's gratifying because it means that someone loved a poem. . . . That means more than publication or other kinds of worldly success." Baxter's comment brings to mind the observation of one very widely published, known, and praised Newer Prizewinner: "External recognitions are always pleasant but they don't prove anything and no one of them is glorious, currently. I sometimes think the most glorious thing would be to write lines that people memorize for pleasure."

Robert Bly once wrote to his friend, the poet Donald Hall, when the latter had become discouraged: "That the poems are useful to other people, that they are bread, that they can be eaten, and strengthen strangers, that is precisely our goal, our reward, and our vocation."[39]

Winning a poetry prize, fellowship, or grant was the single accomplishment listed by respondents most frequently as "gratifying" in the past, and second most frequently as the goal for which they were working or hoping. Yet less than 25 percent overall, and no more than 43 percent of any group, mentioned such accomplishments when answering the question about "most gratifying" experience to date or the one about future goals.

Research expectations concerning the degree of importance respondents would attach to receiving prizes and grants were uncertain. Printed criticisms of prize-giving procedures were quite common (though more radical criticism of the *idea* of such ranking is rare), and numerous participants in this study regarded them as haphazard, dominated by politics, connections, or chance, or reflecting purely traditional tastes. All of this would suggest that respondents might neither value the prizes they had won (or, at least, might be reluctant to express such an evaluation) nor strive for those they hadn't.

However, the very amount of negative attention paid to prizes and the severity of the objections lodged against them underscored the importance they were perceived as having. Certainly, poets almost invariably accepted them when won, usually with express gratitude; publishers of all types noted them in advertising copy; and acquiring them could only enhance opportunities to publish and earn extra income through teaching, readings, and so forth.

Logically, then, a majority of prizewinning poets—especially in the newer group, given their comparatively short histories of recognition—were expected to rate receiving a prize as overwhelmingly their most gratifying experience, while it was thought that a majority of nonprizewinners would be hoping for a prestigious win and working toward it. Both expectations were defeated.

While thirteen Newer Prizewinners viewed winning an award, usually the one that had led to their inclusion in the NP group, as their "most gratifying" experience, seventeen others did not mention award winning when replying to this question. Older Prizewinning poets, all of whom had won at least two major prizes, mentioned them even less frequently; only five did. However, prizewinners did mention prizes and grant winning markedly more than did nonwinners. One might think that this would be predictable. How could a nonprizewinner mention a past prizewinning experience? But two Older and thirteen Newer Nonprizewinners *were* "most gratified" by the winning of an award. This was not a contradiction in terms; some local or regional awards and awards given by particular publications or small associations are excluded from *Literary and Library Prizes,* the authority used when constructing the four poet groups. Among awards mentioned by nonprizewinning poets were the "Who's Who in Poetry International $1,000 Poetry Contest of London," the *Mademoiselle* college poetry contest, the Devins Award, the Academy of American Poets (AAP) prize, the Citation of the Maine Association for Women in the Fine and Performing Arts, the Winthrop College Excellence in Writing Award, selection for the University of Michigan Society of Fellows, and a National Endowment for the Arts grant. The proliferation of awards at all levels, for poets of all types, led Yale Younger Poet John Bensko to wonder whether their "non-monetary value" (presumably, their value in prestige) was being diminished. "When everyone wins a prize—what's a prize?"

Yet for some poets, prizes offered crucial reinforcement of what had been essentially an impractical and lonely decision. David Lunde's AAP prize lent "concrete encouragement at an important point" in his career and led to the publication of his verse in Northwestern University's prestigious literary journal, *TriQuarterly,* and in an anthology of work by writers under thirty. Leslie Ullman, who would soon be designated a Yale Younger Poet, was most gratified by winning an NEA fellowship in 1976, when she was "very unknown and uncertain." And Miriam Sagan believed that *Mademoiselle*'s recognition had led her to begin taking her writing seriously. Awards could also be of more solidly practical use. NEA fellowships typically carried sums of several thousand dollars, and Joyce Peseroff's University of Michigan fellowship supported her for three years, requiring "no duties except to write poems."

The most prestigious awards available for poetry—the Bollingen, the Pulitzer, the old National Book Award, the Academy of American Poets'

Award of Merit Medal, and presumably the Nobel (which has been won by American fiction writers but no American poets)—can wreak important changes in poets' lives and might be valued for this alone.[40] Winners of the major prizes were asked whether winning had resulted in increased interest on the part of publishers and editors; all agreed that it had. Bollingen awardee Richard Eberhart once told an interviewer that immediately following the announcement, sales of his most recent book leaped and continued to be strong for months.[41] Alan Dugan has described in at least two published interviews the dramatic effect of winning, all within a few months, the 1961 Yale Younger Poets contest, the National Book Award, the Pulitzer, and the Prix de Rome for his first book.[42] The financial fallout allowed Dugan to leave his job as model maker in a plastics shop, travel to Europe, and give his best time to writing: "I haven't done an honest day's work since."[43]

Edward Field has written of the despair he felt in his middle thirties, working at a dreary job, faced with "about twenty-five rejections" of his first book manuscript, *Stand Up, Friend, With Me*: "Would it go on like this forever into old age with its ailments, losing my hair, sitting at the office typewriter, sealed off from life?" Winning the Lamont, which guaranteed publication of the book, changed his life "very much," Field found.[44]

To the question regarding future goals or hopes, Allen Ginsberg replied: "Epic money. MacArthur Fund! or Nobel money."

To summarize, there were found in this study many traces of the contempt and suspicion with which poets are thought to view prizes. Yet because poets almost invariably accept the prizes they win and routinely list them among their credentials; and because, in the absence of large readerships and financial benefits, prizes are among the few concrete signs of recognition available to poets, it was expected that most prizewinners would cite prizewinning as their "most gratifying" experiences, and that many or most nonprizewinners would hold prizewinning as their most cherished goal. Neither of these expectations was fulfilled.

Altogether, experiences and goals with a public dimension were mentioned more often than those without—but the wording of the query, which specified most gratifying poetry-related "event," may have directed respondents' thinking about both this question and the one immediately following.

While most respondents seemed to answer the question without difficulty, about a dozen insisted upon listing both a private and a public happening. "This is a very difficult question which I'm sure you're going to have trouble with," warned Jack Myers, who gave three answers. In any case, the boundary between "public" and "private" is not easily drawn. As we have seen, prizes and publications can be valued for the profoundly private benefits they entail: encouragement; vindication of the author's decision to work at an unpaid activity; and the possibility of gaining more free time for writing (although, as shown earlier, this may not result). Many poets, however, did articulate purely private rewards that, taken literally, could exist independent of print publication. Yet for the most part, they imply the validation of editorial acceptance and require, or at least are enhanced by, the feedback facilitated by publication and distribution.

While only two people mentioned the formation of friendships in response to the questions about sources of gratification, perhaps because it was hard to see this as either an "event" or "accomplishment," other replies showed that meeting and loving likeminded people could be a significant motive for continuing to write, if not for beginning.

Ginsberg listed these "most gratifying" experiences: "Continuous publication [with] City Lights, Working with musicians, [and] Association with Burroughs, Kerouac, Corso, Orlovsky, Snyder, Whalen, [Michael] McClure."[45] Since the 1950s Ginsberg had known and conducted readings with those fellow writers, and some of them he had promoted and praised in the face of public indifference or critical scorn. In 1968 he had incorporated his Committee on Poetry to aid problem-ridden artists and had since poured his extra money into this highly personal charity. Given his decades-long residence in the same New York Lower-East-Side apartment, his needs had probably been fairly modest, rendering a high proportion "extra." A *Publishers Weekly* interviewer pointed out the obvious when she wrote in 1977 that he "enjoys being guru to the flock, mentor to a current generation of poets, just as he was to the Beats and the Hippies."[46]

For other poets, also, poetry-generated associations were important, and in a personal way. Karen McKinnon, for example, indicated that she placed great value on her friendship with a fellow New Mexico poet—a relationship founded on, but clearly transcending, his role as her teacher and facilitator of her first publications. Affectionate, admiring references to literary people in an eastern New Jersey poet's questionnaire responses and accompanying letter suggested that she took great personal pleasure in her familiarity with New York-based poetic circles. Maxine Kumin once told an interviewer who asked her "particularly memorable moment as a poet," that "the seventeen years [during which] Anne Sexton and I shared the joys and excitement of being poets constitute a major memory."[47] Philip Levine, also, has discussed in print the fact that being a poet "put [him] in touch with a lot of marvelous people," including "a lot of terrific young people" whom he had met at readings and as his students.[48] And Ruth Stone, an Older Prizewinner with feminist sympathies, wrote on her questionnaire: "Since the 70s—the women I have read to—worked with and for—have made my creative life meaningful."

But to cultivate personal associations for tangible gain or to pursue emblems of success like prizes or particular publishing credits have become increasingly tempting activities now that building a writing-related career of sorts is possible for more people. Many writers warn or fear that a poet can be entrapped by such efforts, letting them become important for their own sake and at the expense of the integrity of one's poetry and sense of freedom in writing.

Vachel Lindsay, who won sudden fame and much trouble with his poem, "General William Booth Enters Heaven," warned in a famous letter to the young, still obscure Langston Hughes: "Do not let any lionizers stampede you. Hide and write and study and think. I know what factions do. Beware of them. I know what flatterers do. Beware of them. I know what lionizers do. Beware of them."[49] Lindsay's coeval, the poet-recluse Robinson Jeffers, who, fortified by inherited money, removed to a lonely cliffside house, issued a plea to the "lionizers" in his poem, "Let Them Alone." Warning that recognition and prizes destroy a poet, Jeffers asserted: "He can shake off his enemies but not his friends."[50]

Allen Seager's biography of the extraordinary Theodore Roethke, who died in 1963, details that poet's painful and, for the reader, embarrassing obsession with prizewinning, and Eileen Simpson recalls that John Berryman, always pressed for money in the early days of his career, "sharpened his pencils and stared at the blank sheet of paper before him. Would he get a Guggenheim? That was what he thought about, not poetry."[51]

As opportunities proliferated for the famous to teach and perform, and as the search for prestigious publishers became ever more frantic and more often futile, the lure of worldly goals could be both more difficult to resist and more dangerous for those who succumbed.

Alberta T. Turner was directing the Cleveland State University Poetry Center Responding to a question, she argued that the poet, if a teacher, should teach something besides creative writing or else seek "a job of an entirely different sort—mechanic, baker, housewife, engineer—just so long as it doesn't use *all* his time and energy." She believes that if writing becomes a "survival tool . . . the poems will suffer. They should be both a release and a temptation." Or, to quote Jack Myers, "If you begin to make a business out of poetry writing, then you're cursed with the business of poetry, and it loses its joy and satisfactions." Anthony Piccione, who claimed not to have a poetry-related goal in mind, believed that "asking for public attention" was "a detriment to writing," and Yuki Hartman, who also checked "no" in response to this question and identified as "most gratifying" the "day to day experience" of writing, wondered whether "so much emphasis on recognition & reward might not have done damage to good poets and poetry." Wrote the comparatively successful younger poet Margaret Gibson: "I'm wary of ambition, [being] susceptible to it & having seen its ill effects on the work and psyches of other poets." Confessing that only by "forcing" herself was she able to participate in poetry's " 'public' life," Gibson explained, "The well I draw from is in another landscape."

Those who had achieved the extraordinary recognition that had so far eluded the poets quoted above repeatedly warned of its negative effects and told of the sometimes immense struggle, the terrific effort of will, needed in order to go on as before, following their own creative impulses wherever they led.

For the extremely rare few who attained celebrity, the crush of attention could be overwhelming. Adrienne Rich, center of feminist adulation that at times seemed almost cultlike and turned her public readings into crowd scenes, responded to the request that she complete a questionnaire for this study with a form letter saying she no longer gave "interviews." Ginsberg, who was even more celebrated, complained to visiting poet Andrei Vosnesensky in 1978: "I've been getting headaches lately. Too much work. Too many hours over the desk, too many hours on the telephone, too many hours answering mail, running around to the Chelsea Hotel in taxi-cabs."[52] When one reads descriptions of Ginsberg's life or attends one of his readings, it is hard to see how he finds time, energy, and mental space for any work requiring concentration.

Most poets face much less strenuous demands, but those who win well-publicized awards usually discover that these triumphs bring new stresses. As has been said, all respondents who had won a major award found their work suddenly more sought after. But other changes can occur as well.

Soon after winning the Pulitzer Prize for poetry, Louis Simpson said that it had changed others' attitudes toward him: "I notice a certain awe setting in among people I know, even friends, and this is very upsetting. . . . I have just had to try for the last couple of months to forget I won that prize so I could start writing again."[53] Numerous other poets have found the recognition attendant upon prizewinning even more disturbing: "It had a muddied effect on my life that lasted over several years," said James Tate of becoming, in 1966, the youngest ever of the Yale Younger Poets.[54]

Maxine Kumin, who for this study identified winning the Pulitzer as her "most gratifying event," nonetheless found that the prize carried with it severe pressures:

> I took the Pulitzer and ran. I really couldn't get out of Boston fast enough. . . . To be catapulted from the relative obscurity and safety of being a poet, who is

the smallest frog in the whole literary pond, to being a Pulitzer Prize winner is incredible. The phone rings every minute. People want to interview you, or they want something from you.[55]

W. D. Snodgrass won the Pulitzer and other honors for his first book, *Heart's Needle,* in 1960, and found this kind of success "terrifying and stultifying." "It is to everyone," he insisted in one interview. "I've never met anyone who wasn't affected that way. You simply become unable to write. . . . it threw me right into [psycho]analysis." While Simpson encountered an unnerving "awe" in his friends, Snodgrass claimed that people he "loved" suddenly exhibited "hate and envy."[56] With perspective perhaps distorted by his own experiences, Snodgrass had observed in an earlier interview: "Poet after poet has given us a *brilliant* first book, maybe even two if he didn't get recognition, but recognition and fame and money hve been absolutely destructive to our poets."[57] (None of Snodgrass's subsequent books received anything like the admiration lavished on *Heart's Needle.*)

William Stafford, winner of the National Book Award and other honors, though at this writing not the Pulitzer or the supremely prestigious Bollingen, noted, immediately post-NBA, "a mild enhancement of interest" among publishers and journals, though apparently not the level of reaction endured by Kumin and Snodgrass. "One had to take the trouble to avoid letting the 'recognition' affect the writing or its destination," he recalled when filling out his questionnaire.

Stafford's point about "destination" is interesting. Poets praised for a certain kind of accomplishment may be reluctant to change style or content, to take new, uncharacteristic directions that may meet with readers' incomprehension or disappointment. James Dickey, a poet who *had* dared to change and had managed to survive the negative effects mentioned above, linked the fear of experimenting suffered by some honored poets to the drastic elusiveness of poetic fame and fortune. As a result: "If they get any recognition at all . . . they're afraid to change that little thing that they painfully acquired. And if they don't change, they just repeat themselves . . . and they never write anything memorable."[58]

Philip Levine, who had, many times, deplored the self-satisfied conservatism of the "successful," once told an interviewer that only when he lost sight of "the immediate present—things like acceptance, publication, awards"—was he "free to move into an area of real seriousness and adventuresomeness in writing."[59] "Now I publish what I want," Levine added in a letter enclosed with his questionnaire. "And I've gotten the awards & I know that . . . is fun, useful, & says nothing—or next to nothing—about the value of the work. I don't think it hurt me to work in obscurity longer than poets who aren't nearly as good as I, but that's very likely because I finally 'arrived.' If I hadn't I could be one bitter man." From one perspective, then, prizes and other external signs of success may function as much in their absence as in their presence, by instilling bitterness and possibly stifling future efforts.

A number of observers, perhaps most vocally (in this as in so many other things) Robert Bly, worried that awards had become such a focus of attention, given that they had little to do with excellence—a proposition believed by Bly as by Levine. A reader of Poets & Writers, Inc.'s news journal, *Coda,* would have to conclude, Bly wrote in a 1981 *Coda* issue, that the American poet was thinking of nothing but how to win a prize or grant and which new presses and magazines might be interested in?" Bly demanded. (If his premise was correct, the answer would be "yes"; in this regard, *Coda* hasn't changed.)

However, for a great many poets, the intrinsic rewards of writing were the ones that finally mattered, and this held true for those who did acquire the trappings of worldly recognition as for those who did not. Some even celebrated the freedom offered by obscurity—as Amy Lowell had done when she hypothesized that absence of "the golden lure" allowed poets to work in freedom, disregarding "public opinion."[60]

Kathleen Norris was a younger author in this study who had published with the University of Pittsburgh Press and lived with her husband David Dwyer, a University of Massachusetts Press poet, in a small town in the nearly deserted northwest quarter of South Dakota where "no one is much interested in poetry." Their friends, Norris said, considered their writing "a hobby like stamp collecting." Although she and Dwyer were isolated from other writers, from readings, even from readers, their invisibility as poets gave them "a certain freedom, which we value."[61]

Just so, said Jerry Ratch, agreeing with Amy Lowell's speculation, the poet has "a great measure of freedom . . . since there is no market for poetry, the marketplace cannot determine the nature of what is written." His feelings about this were mixed. A few sentences later in the questionnaire, he added, "It would be superb if we were paid for what we do, but there is an odd joy in being so completely ignored." An "odd joy," or at least a peculiar pleasure available to very few people, following rough challenges *faced* by very few, constituted a major reason why poets continued writing.

Despite the use of the term "event" in the questionnaire, the source of gratification mentioned second most often had to do with the very process of writing good poems.

"Finishing a poem I like," wrote Michael Ryan, "is far and away the most gratifying event." "Always," said Daniel Mark Fogel, "the writing of my most recent poem"; and, "Finishing a new poem (each time)," agreed Shelley Neiderbach. Robert Hass was most gratified by "writing one of my poems, I'm not sure which." Some poets reminisced about the excitement of writing that first poem many years ago. Jack Barry, who had been "writing poems seriously" for fifteen years and produced "many, many, many" during that time, recalled "rereading the first poem I had written and having it accepted in America and realizing that the poem was part of me and the beginning [of a process] that is still going on."

Other poets named a particularly fine work whose completion stood as a milestone. For instance, Donald Justice remembered "writing the first poem I really liked ('Ladies by Their Windows') "; and for William Stafford the most gratifying event had been "finishing a poem—'A Walk in the Country'—by the fire in my study, reading it over, and knowing that, for me, for what I could do, this came very close."

Daryl Hine, who, like Ryan, Justice, and Stafford, had been favored with prizes and other distinctions, noted, as they did, that although those things had pleased him, they could not "compare with the profound satisfaction of finishing a poem and knowing it is good." May Swenson agreed: "There is no single [event]. And none more gratifying than finding a poem *done.* And feeling sure for a moment that it is *good.*" Mona Van Duyn, laconic in her questionnaire responses, once told an interviewer: "When I'm into a poem and it's coming through, it takes precedence over everything, and there's a fine feeling of satisfaction after it's done."[62]

Other respondents who emphasized the intrinsic rewards of writing spoke in terms of overall process; phrases used included "development of style" (for example, Jack Myers); "personal growth" (Elaine Starkman); "evolution of one's work" (Christopher Fahy); "achievement of mastery" (Harvey Hess); and, from Sandra McPherson, "peace of mind that I have done my best and written some good poems."

The boundaries of one's "best" are never definitively drawn, however, and this fact is both the eternal frustration and the temptation of creative work. Moving to the question that asked about the "poetic accomplishment of reward" for which the poet was working or hoping, McPherson wrote: "Beauty of language & line & wholeness of person behind them—I still think I have a long way to go to attain this level of skill."

Thirty-eight poets, or 42 percent responding to this question, listed one of three private accomplishments: more writing; better, or additional good, writing; or completion of a particular work. Prizewinners, especially in the older group, were substantially more likely to give this kind of answer.

Although the number of responding prizewinners was small, their answers were interesting. It had been thought that most Newer Prizewinners, their expectations raised by having won recognition as neophyte poets, would identify the Pulitzer or another major prize as the most desired future accomplishment. However, nine Newer Prizewinning poets, or 53 percent of those naming a desired accomplishment, gave answers that fell into the three categories of private reward, as did—more predictably—eight Older Prizewinners. Over one-third of Newer Prizewinners, a proportion 17 percentage points higher than that of any other group, were not working or longing for any specific accomplishment. Furthermore, the use of the word "event" in the preceding question probably constrained responses to some extent; it is likely that broader terminology would have called forth more "yes" checks and even more answers dealing with writing's inherent satisfactions.

Nonprizewinners were expected to place heavy emphasis on public rewards hoped for in the future. As it turned out, 72 percent of the Newer Nonprizewinning group did articulate goals dependent upon public recognition, as did 69 percent of Older Nonprizewinners. That *any* of the poets in these groups cited intrinsic rewards, given their career histories and the context provided by the questionnaire, is remarkable. Also, several of those poets specifying a prize or publishing credit when answering the relevant questions made statements elsewhere on the questionnaire or in an accompanying letter that implied the quality of their writing was actually an overriding preoccupation.

"All that counts is the work," wrote Elaine Starkman, and Jack Myers said simply: "It all comes down to doing your work for the original reason(s) you began writing," eschewing the incentives to careerism. Jack Barry hoped only "to find the right words for the blank pages"; Madeline Tiger Bass was looking forward to "working & studying & turning out more refined, better crafted poems"; Carole Oles wanted to "try the (for me) untried"; and Robert Hedin wished to be "able to say, finally, that I have accumulated a body of work that shows integrity and a serious, mature vision." Some poets joined Hedin in looking farther than usual into the future: Jitu Tambuzi hoped to be known as "an important black poet of the 21st century," full-blooded Indian Minerva Allen as a poetic "historian of [her] two tribes"—adding, "Even one would be OK," and several others dreamed rather vaguely of their work's "survival," or of creating "memorable" poems. Douglas Messerli—publisher, editor, teacher, and experimental poet—combined the missions of all those roles in his aims for the future: "I want to be 'recognized' as a poet . . . but I think just as important I want to be recognized for changing—or at least helping to change—the nature of what we understand as poetry. I want to reshape our thinking of what poetry is as a process and as an object." Mike Finn, the romantic environmentalist mentioned earlier, chose to describe his "primary occupation" as "looking (outward & inward, forward & back, here & hereafter)," and gave a similarly half-jocular response: "To write the poetry, to heal the world. . . . Impossible? well then, to be a new voice in Poetry (NBA . . . Yale Younger Poet, Pulitzer). Presumptuous? well really then, to be poet laureate of a little space in time."

The rather cosmically framed responses in Tambuzi, Allen, Messerli, Finn, and a few other poets implied a desire for worldly recognition, of course, but not a yen for immediate worldly benefits. Their focus was really on the work, not the possibility of tangible rewards. These poets seemed to assume that the larger aspirations would be fulfilled through the poetry itself if it were good, and that it was to the poetry that their energies must be devoted. Jack Myers, for example, was looking forward to "writing the kind of poetry that I think I may eventually be capable of. Recognition should or will come naturally after this."

Two poets gave peculiar and especially interesting answers. Both evinced an urgent desire to shed worries about publication, prestige, anything external to the writing itself. John Stevens Wade, an Older Nonprizewinner with a long and varied career, wrote that he was looking ahead to the time "when I can write a poem for the sheer pleasure of writing it without thought of publishing it." Mindy Aloff wished "to be able to work on a poem with the pleasure and stamina of a kid assembling a complicated plastic model. I'd like to know the goal in advance, too," she continued, "all set out, an illustration on a box lid. To wake up with a full blueprint. Is there any other accomplishment?"

Prizewinning poets, like Sandra McPherson, often described goals molded by the perception that, despite the praise of the "lionizers," they had not achieved as much poetically as they had aspired to. May Swenson, for example, anticipated writing "at least one more book—the best," while Ruth Stone hoped "to write the poems that I will be pleased with—that accomplishment always ahead, never quite reached." Reg Saner answered similarly, if more specifically: "I'd like to write a poem I admire without reservation. One that impresses me each time I read it. I think this must be impossible."

While publication in certain places and the winning of prizes occupied many of the poets' minds, the narrow careerism feared by Bly and other observers was not clearly evident in this study. Even those writers who fixed on external signs of success when identifying their goals often discussed elsewhere the larger matter of literary excellence and aspirations to achieve it.

Nearly all the poets were persevering in their writing and many had done so for years with very little concrete recognition. Many responses showed some disillusionment and cynicism; a number, the aspiration for a poetry-related career and public notice; and a few, some bitterness. Yet the choice to write seemed grounded, almost always, in the attractions of the activity itself. As Charles Martin remarked, anyone motivated by desire for prizes and attention would do better to spend his time in a bowling league.

Basically, the poets seemed to publish, or at least to continue publishing, because they wrote so seriously, with a message or vision they considered so importrant, that to keep the work private was out of the question. No more an avocation than a true occupation, poetry is in a classic sense a vocation requiring extraordinary dedication. They were writing for intrinsic satisfactions and in response to fundamental creative drives that finally could not be ignored, although, for many, they never counteracted the attendant isolation, rejection, and threat of failure. One of this century's few almost undisputedly great poets, T. S. Eliot, claimed that the pain much outweighed the joy: "The compensations for being a poet are grossly exaggerated," he lamented in 1933, "and they dwindle as one becomes older, and the shadows lengthen and the solitude becomes harder to endure."[63] But he did not give up poetry.

Pleasure may no more be the rationale for continuing to write and publish than fame or money is. Clearly, most poets, happy or not, do love poetry. Despite the many published observations that few poets read poetry, the great majority of respondents to this study seemed to be widely read, thoughtful, genuinely committed students, as well as practitioners, of the form. James Dickey, a poet who turned his back on two lucrative careers, as advertising man and best-selling novelist, once said: "I've given my life to poetry simply for one reason: I love it . . . If you love it, there's just no substitute for it."[64] Mary Oliver declared in an article that: "Poetry isn't a profession, it's a way of life. It's an empty basket: you put your life into it and make something out of that."[65]

The *inevitability* of poetry was emphasized by many poets participating in the study. "I'm a writer who just has to write," explained Ida Fasel; and Irene Dayton, who had written for a long time with minimal recognition, said similarly: "It is the Poem, not where it is finally published or not published . . . the poet works at his writing whether he is published or not."

Marvin Bell, a poet not in this study, has achieved a great deal of success as measured by publication, awards, degrees, and influential placement in literary networks. In a 1980 essay he offered an eloquent statement of poetic motivation: "The act of writing transcends everything for those of us who need to write. They can take away from you everything but this: the poems you have written, the poems you are writing."[66]

What we come to, at last, is the simple conclusion that in the very long run, the details of publishing may not matter. The real work may always get done, the real poets always persist. Pure opportunists, shallow careerists, and poetry hacks yearning only to see their names in print, meet important people, impress their friends, or inject "meaning" into aimless lives, and naive workshop veterans dreaming of fame probably fall away from poetry very soon. While they irritate some poets, editors, and scholars, the danger they are presumed to pose seems minimal. Nothing in the returned questionnaires suggested that a single such person had turned up in the study.

On the other hand, certain trends developed over the period stretching from 1950 to 1980 that may not have been salutary for the evaluation and dissemination of poetry. Among the ones identified here are the drastically reduced interest of commercial presses in adding new poets to their lists; the increased tendency of promising young poets to lodge in the academy; the enhanced potential of poetry to earn for its practitioners a sort of living through readings and teaching, resulting in increased emphases on connections and the accumulating of publication credits; and the proliferation of, and grant support for, poets and literary journals and presses.

What very strikingly did *not* develop was a poetry market, a broadened readership for serious poetry among people who were not themselves poetry writers, teachers, or critics. Even proliferating public readings, workshops, and classes, some of them well attended, did not seem to generate poetry sales and independent reading for pleasure. Poetry-writing appeared to increase, but poetry-loving did not.

Finally, though, it seemed unarguably true that these matters were of trivial import in the very long run, poignant as they might be in the life of a particular author or a particular work. Serious poetry is a thing apart from publication and worldly rewards, not so much transcendant as ultimately, in its profound nature, unrelated.

8

From the End of the Eighties

Early in 1989 editor Marion Stocking of the *Beloit Poetry Journal* was asked about changes in the poetry world over the preceding decade. She paused, then laughed in some bewilderment. "I'm about to start my fortieth year on the same magazine, so I tend to think in terms of forty years," she explained. "The similarities between when I started and now seem more distinct than the differences."[1]

As I read and talked with writers, editors, and publishers of poetry shortly before sending this book to press, it became clear that the major trends apparent in the 1970s and before had proven resilient, deepened, in the years since. The sole exception pertained to government grants, which had been pervasive, if not truly plentiful, before 1980 and have apparently diminished somewhat since.

TRADE PUBLISHERS AND POETRY

Perhaps most dramatic was the continued decline of trade-press interest in poetry, especially when written by unheralded living poets. Despite the notable contributions of a few houses, the commercial press seemed to be no longer an important force in the contemporary poetry world. Dozens of poets' anecdotes illustrate this point. For instance, the well-known poet Carolyn Kizer endured rejection of her manuscript *Yin* "by about every major New York house" before agreeing reluctantly to the publishing offer of tiny BOA Editions. *Yin* won the 1985 Pulitzer, and Kizer eventually moved on to yet another small press, Copper Canyon of Port Townsend, Washington.[2] Years later, multiple prizewinner Marilyn Hacker recalled Kizer's story because "you comfort yourself by remembering other people this has happened to." Although she was the author of four well-received books published by two prestigious trade houses, Hacker had been forced to seek a small publisher for her new manuscript.[3] A somewhat different, but telling, experience was recounted by Diana Ó Hehir, who, after seeing her first two books brought out as winners in publishers' competitions, had difficulty placing her third. "Then I published a novel, *I Wish This War Were Over*," she recalled, "and it was very successful, more successful than I expected it to be. That changed everything, and [the novel's publisher] agreed to publish the poems." She pointed out, however, that her contract covered future fiction books only, not poetry. "They will go along with [a book of poetry] every so often," she speculated, but grudgingly.[4]

Even those poets in the presumably enviable position of being well established with commercial publishers were unenthusiastic about the industry's contribution and did not always think themselves enviable. Gerald Stern, satisfied with Harper & Row, was nonetheless negative about the future. "The trade presses bought up by conglomerates that aren't interested in publishing have neglected in a radical way activities that aren't commercial," he asserted. "Finally, we'll be better off with the small presses and university presses that will promote the books and keep them in print."[5] Another poet, long published by a respected commercial press, recited a litany of recent dissatisfactions and concluded: "It's hard not to feel that you're a stepchild of the house if you're in poetry." She admitted that she "used to think having a big publisher was really important," but was coming around to a different view.[6] And a major poet who had switched from one trade house to another, following his editor, was even more forthright: "I don't care about those people," he said of both presses. "I don't think they know about about books. I don't think they care about books. I don't trust them. I would have gone anywhere [my editor] went. If he had gone to [a university or small press], I'd have gone there." It is not surprising, then, that university- and small-press editors told me of poets propelled their way by trade-publisher mishandling and neglect.

Some observers have worried as big houses closed their doors to poets. Others note that those doors were never more than ajar, and that, as they closed, literary presses grew up that were truly devoted to poetry and knowledgeable about it. Although it remains impossible to calculate the numbers of poetry books published each year, either by type of publisher or overall, perusal of the 1980s' Dustbooks directories suggests that the number of small presses and little magazines is not shrinking. In the 1987–88 edition, I counted 246 small American poetry-book publishers commencing between 1980 and 1987, inclusive. The most fruitful year, 1980, had seen the founding of forty-eight still-active presses. Assuming that some that started so long ago would already have ceased, this may imply sharply declining activity throughout the decade. The number of presses begun in 1981, for instance, was only thirty-five, a 27 percent decline. In 1982 there were thirty-two, in 1983 twenty-nine—but in 1984, there was a 41 percent jump to forty-one. Though 18 percent began in California and 10 percent in New York, the remaining 177 presses were strewn across forty-six states and the District of Columbia. Their purposes ranged from the revival of rhyme and meter and celebration of Christianity to the encouragement of experimentation and challenging of the political order. On the other hand, though the number of new publishers was impressive, their actual publishing programs were often insubstantial. Twenty-eight percent had published only one title in 1986 and 21 percent anticipated publishing only one in 1987, though in all likelihood the percentage was higher, since publishers' reach may exceed their grasp.[7] It has always been true, however, that many small presses' output is minute in volume and may even cease completely for years at a time. In the somewhat more limited listing of the Coordinating Council of Literary Magazines' 1988–89 membership directory, I counted 105 poetry-publishing little magazines founded in the 1980s—84 percent independent, the remainder academic. Again, the most new publications emanated from New York and California, homes of 24 percent and 22 percent, respectively. And again, the rest were widely dispersed: fifty-seven journals in thirty-three states and the District of Columbia. Circulations were low but by no means negligible—ranging from 90 to 6,000, with a median circulation of 600, a mean of 960. And magazine editors like book publishers represented all conceivable motives: from *Agada*'s Reuven Goldfarb, dedicated to spiritual Jewish viewpoints; to Stephen-Paul Martin of *Central Park*, experimental and aggressively political; to Andrei Codrescu who in *Exquisite Corpse* hoped to create a "print cafe"[8]: "We are violent partisans of fresh air. Material should be opinionated, passionate, occasionally vicious and terminally beautiful."[9]

An intriguing question is what will happen as some small presses, presumably the most ambitious and best able to draw attention to their books, become bigger. John Gill, himself a poet in this study, explained that his Crossing Press, once publisher of several well-regarded poetry titles, had been withdrawing from that field. Crossing was developing into a commercial house, Gill explained, and: "As you get more and more into commercial publishing, unless you have grants to offset the costs, or you're big enough to publish it for prestige and can absorb the losses, you can't afford to publish poetry. It's just a matter of economics: we have eight employees; they need salaries." On poetry, "we'd be lucky to break even."[10]

Usually better subsidized and arguably more resistant to the bottom-line imperative are the university presses—which, increasingly involved with poetry throughout the seventies, have deepened their involvement since. Among the twenty-one publishers most highly esteemed by poets in this study were six academics: Pittsburgh, Wesleyan, Yale, Princeton, Georgia, and Illinois. Since the early eighties, several other university presses' poetry series have flourished and might appear on poets' lists of the best, including those at the University of Chicago, the University of Alabama, Carnegie-Mellon University, and, almost certainly, Louisiana State.

Cited repeatedly by authors and editors undisturbed by trade publishers' snubs to poetry was the success of the small but sophisticated Graywolf Press; mentioned also were Copper Canyon and North Point. One highly regarded poet declared:

> I think there was a time when you could pick up a Borzoi Book by Alfred A. Knopf and expect a certain quality. I'm now with Knopf and I can't read half the people they publish. . . . I'm impressed by Graywolf, Copper Canyon. . . . I think New York and American poetry are not *it* anymore. There will always be a few people like [James] Laughlin and [Harry] Ford who care about poetry, but when I see what Graywolf can do—how many copies they can sell and keep the book in print, which is something New York hasn't been able to do—I don't see a problem at all.

Indeed, no recent writer on the subject, and no poet who spoke with me, argued that the withdrawal from poetry of trade presses would result in lower quality of manuscript selection, of editing, of general commitment, or even of physical production. Most concern was practical. Could the university presses and, especially, the small presses distribute their books as efficiently as the trade publishers? And would the books be as widely reviewed? Ó Hehir attributed to its trade imprint the fact that for her latest book, "I received many more reviews than I *ever* did for poetry before." The fact that she had recently become recognized as a novelist may actually have been more important. But although even in the best case, books of poems are not as widely displayed, reviewed, or sold as prose volumes, many believe that big-house muscle offers a boost. The Pitt Poetry Series' Ed Ochester, who has had numerous talks with poets, discussed literary presses' distribution problems. "Small publishers do really interesting work," he said. "It's no more difficult or easy to get published [now than it used to be].

The difficulty is in getting the books around. Poets' major gripe is, 'You could never find the book. They couldn't get the damn thing out.' . . . They don't have travellers, don't have bookmen." He noted that small presses were beginning to depend more heavily upon direct-mail promotion and special distributors. "But," he added, "most of the biggies won't represent poets very well either."[11]

The evidence, in any case, is not strong and varies house by house, poet by poet. For example, both Stern and Linda Pastan, who is published by Norton, said that although they had become better known over time, and despite their prestigious imprints, their latest books had received fewer reviews than their earlier, a difference they attributed to review sources' diminished interest in poetry. Some poets, in the eighties as in the sixties and seventies, actually preferred small publishers. Robert Hass, who had remained by choice with Daniel Halpern's Ecco Press, said: "My inclination is to maintain that relationship throughout my writing life. I haven't yet gotten in a situation where he hasn't wanted to publish a book of mine. If that happened, I suppose I would publish it with another press and go back to him with everything else."[12] And Theodore Enslin, author of dozens of small-press books, mused, "It seems to me I've spent my whole life away from major publishers. . . . I prefer to stay with small publishers who really care. I don't think the trade publishers *can* care."[13] Both Enslin and Hass, as well as many other observers, questioned the importance of being reviewed. "It doesn't seem to make a difference commercially," said Hass, citing examples of widely reviewed books that sold poorly and vice versa. And Enslin pointed out philosophically: "We do have a limited audience at best."

Poets, then, continued to be *printed* despite trends in the New York publishing industry that conspicuously disfavored poetry. Whether their work reached its potential *public* as effectively was, however, open to question. And beyond such practical matters are the poignant implications of the trade's vanishing interest in poetry. Poems have never reaped large sales, but for a long time publishers continued to bring them out through house tradition, heartfelt loyalty to literature, a sense of cultural obligation, the desire to build prestige, or some combination of the four. That these factors no longer suffice is revealing of the publishing industry's changed priorities and casts doubt on the vitality of its connection to serious contemporary literature. It is striking that so many people in the poetry world now take the industry's irrelevancy for granted.

POETRY AND THE ACADEMY

Increasingly often the publisher of poetry, the academy had also, in the three decades studied here, become employer, educator, and credentialing agent of poets. This trend, too, extended through the eighties, with some results obvious, some still unclear. In 1989 poets and their partisans continued to laud the still-flourishing opportunities for livings to be earned by writing poetry and teaching its writing. As Robert Hass pointed out, "A country usually does arrive at some sort of sinecure arrangement for its poets. It's hard to think of a country where this hasn't happened."

But almost to a person, they had reservations as well. These centered on the proliferating competent but uninspired "workshop poems" born of creative writing programs; on the sameness of work experience settling like a pall over whole generations of American poets; and, most essentially, on the growing perception of poetry writing as a mechanical skill to be acquired, of the poetic vocation as a career prepared for by earning the right degrees. Herself the "bored" recipient of hundreds of "self-indulgent" MFA poems submitted to *Beloit Poetry Journal*, Marion Stocking observed that the "flaming imagination that transforms experience into poetry can't be taught, can't be acquired." On the other hand, she commended creative writing programs as "basically healthy . . . a good moral force" because they were training people "to use language properly, to examine experience." Picking up a theme raised repeatedly by commentators on the subject, she added, "That doesn't mean we're going to have many more, or *any* more, good poets"—as distinct from merely competent technicians. Douglas Messerli, poet and proprietor of Sun & Moon Press, declared recently: "There are good writers in universities, but universities don't produce good writers. Good writers happen."[14] New Directions' James Laughlin was even more emphatic when interviewed by Robert Dana:

> I think one of the worst things in the country are these courses in creative writing in colleges, because I think that they encourage students who have an emotional desire to write, but who have really no talent, to try to become writers. I see this from the manuscripts that come in to our office. You can tell that this person has learned a certain amount of technical competence and fluency, but he really has nothing to say. . . . The real writer, the born writer, the real genius, is going to write whether there are courses in creative writing or not.[15]

What seemed to disturb many people who inveighed against the programs was not that a talentless student might write a poem but that students might be encouraged in futile aspirations, might painfully grind out (and send out) work that contributed nothing, might be attracted more by the pleasant academic career of poetry than driven by passion for language and the need to write. "I don't see anything wrong with people writing a little poetry, anymore than there's anything wrong with people painting a little or playing the piano a little," explained

Marilyn Hacker. "But people who play the piano a little usually don't think they're Rudolph Serkin." Contrasting his own poetic "training," which consisted of voracious independent reading, with academic writing programs, Iowa professor Gerald Stern confessed to having a "mixed attitude . . . It's all right as long as people do not think that by achieving a degree, you become a poet—because there's no connection between the two."[16]

It would cause more harm to constrain the gifted than to unleash the mediocre, and some people continued to worry that academic workshops might do just this. "The university circuit is a closed circuit," wrote Fielding Dawson in 1988. "Very little that is new walks through those doors, and everybody involved becomes accustomed. . . ."[17] Beyond, though related, to the threat of contagious conservatism was the level ease of poetry teachers' lives. Though pointing out that not all campuses resemble ivory towers, Philip Levine, who teaches writing at Fresno State, exclaimed, "I know poets who have never left school! . . . They're really out of touch with American life. There are still a lot of poets not in the academy, and there is a kind of passion and a knowledge of the world that seems vaster in these people."[18] Or, as Roger Aplon remarked, "The streets . . . still seem to produce the most vigorous writing."[19] Presumably many would quarrel with this view, for some of the best-known, best-loved postwar poets hold MFAs—Levine himself, for example, and Robert Bly, James Wright, Carolyn Forché, many others—but it is a view that may have some validity, depending, of course, on one's definition and valuation of "vigorous."

Creative writing programs were also criticized, in the eighties as they had been earlier, for encouraging premature publication, for "democratizing, demystifying" poetry, and for being the prime cause of a bewildering storm of publication in which even the hardiest reader could get lost.[20]

The programs' most apparent virtue, aside from the bread they put in poets' mouths, was their provision of community, or, as James Grabill put it, a place "where concentrated energy is being shared."[21] "There never has been a real alternative to it," opined Bin Ramke, writing teacher at the University of Colorado. "Any poet I can think of—with some exceptions—has been part of an intellectual community. . . . There are fewer possibilities of setting up those communities; publishing doesn't provide them anymore. . . . This is more important even than the financial benefits."[22] As for the students, toi derricotte observed that they, too, needed "community . . . intimacy," and, still more, the special demands that poetry makes: "Poetry asks people to have values, form opinions, care about some other part of experience besides making money and being successful on a job. Many young people hunger for these values," an opinion confirmed by the impressive enrollments in creative writing programs—enrollments all the more startling at a time when traditional English programs had lost majors.[23]

Indeed, the only new issue raised in the late 1980s concerned the increasingly troubled relationship between creative writing programs and mainstream literary programs at some universities. A beginning movement to separate the two, aligning poets with dancers, musicians, and actors rather than scholars of literature, was causing alarm.[24] It raised profound questions about not only how academic administrators perceived poets, but how literary scholars regarded the creative achievements to whose interpretation they were giving their lives, and how successfully writing programs had blended the study of literature with instruction in its creation.

READERS AND SALES OF POETRY

"Everyone wants to be a poet," Jed Rasula wrote recently. "No one wants to own up to being a reader."[25] Some people exposed to creative-writing students, including editors to whom their products were submitted and visiting professors, find them—and often their instructors—deficient in their knowledge of literary masterworks, of principles of prosody, even of major contemporary poets.[26] Others assert that while the programs may not necessarily turn out good writers, they do—better yet—turn out readers. In fact, no one knows just how many poetry books and journals are sold, let alone how many are read. In 1986 the average edition at John Martin's twenty-year-old Black Sparrow Press was 3,000–4,000 copies, a rate that kept him constantly balanced on the edge of insolvency despite his good fortune in being the longtime publisher of Charles Bukowski, whose books sold many times more. "I'm hurt by inflation, I'm hurt by recession, I'm hurt by having to pay decent wages," Martin told an interviewer. "There's no margin anywhere, really, to pick up the slack for anything unexpected." Asked what he did when postage rates increased, he said, "I just close my eyes and pretend it never happened."[27] Three years later Scott Walker said that minimum sales at his exceptionally successful Graywolf Press were 1,300–1,500 per title, with occasional books selling as many as 10,000–12,000 copies. He surmised that these were fairly high figures because a sales representative for twelve literary presses had recently told him that their books averaged sales of only 800. "It's more and more difficult to publish poetry," said Walker. "Sales of poetry books are declining. . . . Libraries aren't buying as much. Trade sales are going down. It's hardly worth putting poetry books in your catalog because there are so few sales."[28] Meanwhile, at the Pitt Poetry Series, sales of 500 in cloth and 1,500–2,500 in paper were considered acceptable, and the series' blockbuster had sold 15,000. Ed Ochester declared: "Poetry sales are improving as small presses and university presses begin to distribute better. It's not reasonable to take a position of despair. It's not true that people don't read poetry." Perceptions of reading volume varied according to which writing programs, students, and presses people knew, what experiences they had had, and how elevated were their expectations. Philip Levine, whose most recent book had come out in an edition of 15,000, was convinced that poetry had reasonable numbers of readers, an opinion shared by observers as different as Thom Gunn, William Everson, Allen Ginsberg, Michael Palmer, Marion Stocking, Robert Hass, Linda Pastan, Ed Ochester, poet Paul Zimmer of the University of Iowa Press, and critic Robert von Hallberg.[29] Others—for example, publishers Gill, Walker, Jack Shoemaker of North Point Press, and Jonathan Williams of Jargon Books; poets Diane Wakoski and Brad Leithauser; and critic Joseph Epstein—perceived a distressingly small readership for printed poetry, though perhaps a larger one for poetry readings.[30] "I sometimes think I know all 500 people who read poetry by their first names," Shoemaker agonized. "The poetry audience has steadily declined since the 1970s. It seems almost parallel with the advent of master of fine arts programs in poetry." Even those who speculated that poetry's readership had increased in the eighties tended to the view that most, if not all, of these readers were poets, that poetry had failed to extend its influence to a broader public. Asked who read poems, *Poetry* magazine's editor Joseph Parisi snapped, "Other poets." He went on to note that a few writers could attract a second type of reader, the nonpoet and usual nonreader of poetry, through essentially political appeals. Adrienne Rich, for example, was drawing some readers interested primarily in feminism.[31] But Parisi and most others believed that whether or not creative writing programs were encouraging reading, it was mostly the writing of poetry that led to the reading of it, and this would seem both peculiar and regrettable.

But there were those in the poetry world who wondered how much the nature and size of readership really mattered. "I often think of poetry . . . as having something in common with philosophy," explained Bin Ramke. "Philosophers don't write bestsellers, either. They hope for influence of a different kind." Philip Levine insisted: "Probably as many people are reading poetry as ever did. I don't think people's failure to love poetry is any big deal. Some people just can't make it with poetry, and they're bright, wonderful people. They make it with something else." And Robert Hass told the story of visiting his daughter while she babysat for a family he did not know. Struck by the absence of a television set, he browsed the books shelved along the walls. They included volumes about sports and the outdoors, histories, and so forth—and "about fourteen books of poetry," some of which appeared well used. Noting that this was the home of a couple with young children, jobs, and, evidently, active pastimes and broad interests, Hass asked himself:

> What have we been *expecting* all these years? . . . All in all, if you think about what people's lives are like, how the pace of American life is antithetical to any sort of inward life, it seems remarkable that poetry flourishes in the way it does—that some, a volume here and there, finds its way into the lives of people. . . . It seems to me that the place of poetry in American life is about right.

GRANTS

The always thin flow of grant funds, which in the sixties and seventies had nonetheless sufficed to prop up hundreds of small-publishing ventures, seemed to dwindle somewhat in the eighties. Some magazines that had once received state funds found them more elusive, and by 1984 the Coordinating Council of Literary Magazines (CCLM), though still supported by the National Endowment for the Arts, no longer had NEA money to dispense to small presses and little magazines. Although the Endowment continued to support literary ventures, editors and publishers were required to apply directly, and eligibility criteria were tightened, excluding some who might once have been funded.[32] Though many member magazines had told CCLM's Beth O'Rourke that they regretted the passing of its funding program, she saw some virtues in the change. CCLM, she explained, now concentrated on helping literary magazines by offering advice about marketing, promotion, and related business procedures so that the magazines would eventually depend less upon grants. Recalling that in the 1970s many magazines were criticized for printing issues and then, propped up by grant money, doing little to distribute them, she declared, "That has really changed. I see it in the number of magazines now that continue to publish year after year after year. They're more professional in their approach."[33]

Before 1980 poetry publishers' reliance on grants had been severely criticized by some, but Robert Hass's 1989 assessment of grant funding was probably shrewd: "There's a lot to be said against it. When it all dries up, it will seem there was a lot to be said *for* it." Actually, full-scale drought did not seem immediately likely. A spell of light rainfall did—but, as O'Rourke and my new-magazine count suggest, this was not necessarily all bad and certainly not universally devastating. It might, however, cause turmoil and even disaster for individual publications and possibly for entire publication types. In a 1988 article, for example, Joseph Bruchac laid the recent "decline and fall of prison literature" partly at the door of the NEA.[34]

"I don't know why anyone goes into poetry," confided Gerald Stern in 1989. "It's such a thankless life." Why did he? "I just had to do it—

for psychological, personal, and emotional reasons. . . . Poetry as a 'profession' never entered my mind. I thought I'd be a bum all my life and write poetry."

My study of poetry writing and publishing, 1950–80, disclosed dedication on the poets' part, regardless of how long they had been publishing, how well known they had become, whether they had won prizes or contracts with big-name publishers or had found berths in the academy. They began and continued writing because they had to, because they could imagine no other way to live. Crass "careerism" could not be detected at the roots of their motivation. Although whether and where they published certainly mattered to them, it was profoundly irrelevant to whether and what they wrote. As I read poets' published interviews and articles and spoke again with poets from this study, none of this seemed to have changed. Though the trade press struck them as ever less hospitable and grants as increasingly elusive, their reasons for writing were unchanged. To publish was a hoped-for result but not the most significant goal. Echoing what many other poets said and wrote in the 1980s was Bin Ramke, prizewinning poet, Colorado professor, and editor of the University of Georgia's poetry series. "What matters," he said, "is doing the work, being involved in making a poem. I know that I need to do it no matter what, no matter if everything else went away. If I never published another poem, I would still write them. I used to say that, but I wasn't sure I meant it. Now, I know it's true."

Appendix

LITERARY PRIZES USED AS CRITERIA FOR CHOOSING POETS TO STUDY[1]

Prize for Both Newer-Prizewinning (NP) and Older-Prizewinning (OP) Group Poets

John Simon Guggenheim Memorial Fellowships (G), 1926-present.

Prizes for NP-Group Poets Only

Lamont Poetry Selection (L), 1955-present; Swallow Press New Poetry Series Award (S), 1965–73; Walt Whitman Award (W), 1975-present[2]; Yale Series of Younger Poets (Y), 1919-present.

Prizes for OP-Group Poets Only

American Academy and Institute of Arts and Letters Awards in Literature (A), 1941-present; Bollingen Prize in Poetry (B), 1950-present; National Book Award (N), 1950–79 (superseded in 1980 by the American Book Award); Pulitzer Prize (P), 1922-present; Shelley Memorial Award (S), 1929-present.

THE POETS

Categories of Cooperation

Q1 = questionnaire completed, or nearly completed; Q2 = at least two-thirds of questionnaire completed; Q3 = less than two-thirds of questionnaire completed; R = reviewed publication and biographical data; B = a bibliography supplying all or a substantial amount of publication data was available; S = slight cooperation (suggestions or some data provided).[3] Note that RQ1 signifies full cooperation. No notation in the left-hand column signifies no cooperation at all.

Interpreting the Lists

On the following poet lists the letter-number response codes in left margin indicate degree of poets' participation in the study; the first date in parentheses is the year a first poetry book was published; codes and years of prizes won, through 1980, appear to the right of the poets' names.

Newer Prizewinning Poets (NP Group)

Code	Poet
	1. Ai (1973) - G (1975), L (1978)
	2. Michael Anania (1970) - S (1970)
	3. James Applewhite (1975) - G (1976)
RQ1	4. John Balaban (1978) - L (1974)
RQ1	5. John Bensko (1981) - Y (1980)
	6. Frank Bidart (1973) - G (1979)
	7. David Bottoms (1980) - W (1979)
RQ1	8. Olga Broumas (1976) - Y (1976), G (1980)
RQ1	9. Jared Carter (1979) - W (1980)
	10. Michael Casey (1972) - Y (1971)
RQ1	11. William Virgil Davis (1980) - Y (1979)
	12. Stephen Dobyns (1972) - L (1971)
	13. Norman Dubie (1971) - G (1977)
	14. Peter Everwine (1973) - L (1972), G (1975)
RQ1	15. Carolyn Forché (1976) - G (1978)
RQ1	16. Tess Gallagher (1974) - G (1978)
RQ1	17. Marilyn Hacker (1967[4]) - L (1973), National Book Award (1975), G (1980)
RQ1	18. William Harmon (1970) - L (1970)
	19. Michael S. Harper (1970) - A (1972), G (1976)

RQ1	20. Barbara Harr (1970) - S (1970)
RQ1	21. Robert Hass (1973) - Y (1972), G (1979)
RQ1	22. William Heyen (1970) - G (1977)
RQ2	23. William Hunt (1973) - S (1973)
RQ1	24. Peter Klappert (1966[5]) - Y (1970)
	25. Larry Levis (1970) - G (1976)
RQ1	26. John Matthias (1971) - S (1971)
RQ1	27. James McMichael (1971) - G (1977)
RQ1	28. Sandra McPherson (1970) - G (1976)
Q1	29. Peter Michelson (1972) - S (1972)
RQ1	30. John N. Morris (1970) - G (1978), A (1979)
	31. Gregory Orr (1973) - G (1977)
RQ1	32. Linda Pastan (1971) - S (1972)
RQ1	33. Robert Pinsky (1975) - A (1980)
RQ1	34. Stanley Plumly (1970) - G (1973)
RQ1	35. Bin Ramke (1978) - Y (1977)
RQ1	36. Michael Ryan (1974) - Y (1973)
RQ1	37. Reg Saner (1976) - W (1975)
	38. Lauren Shakely (1978) - W (1977)
RQ1	39. Karen Snow (1980) - W (1978)
RQ1	40. Gary Soto (1977) - G (1979)
RQ1	41. Maura Stanton (1975) - Y (1974)
RQ1	42. Gerald Stern (1973) - L (1977), G (1980)
RQ1	43. Leslie Ullman (1979) - Y (1978)
RQ1	44. Michael Van Walleghen (1973) - L (1980)
RQ1	45. Ellen Bryant Voigt (1976) - G (1978)

Older Prizewinning Poets (OP Group)

B	1. A. R. Ammons (1955) - G (1966), N (1973), B (1975), A (1977)
BRQ1	2. John Ashbery (1953) - G (1967), A (1969), S (1973), N (1976), P (1976)
R	3. Robert Bly (1962) - G (1974), A (1965), N (1968), G (1972)
RQ1	4. Philip Booth (1957) - G (1958), A (1967)
	5. Hayden Carruth (1959) - G (1965), S (1978), G (1979)
B	6. Robert Creeley (1952) - G (1964), G (1971)
	7. James Dickey (1960) - G (1961), A (1966), N (1966)

	8. Alan Dugan (1961) - N (1962), P (1962), G (1963), G (1972)
	9. Irving Feldman (1961) - A (1973), G (1973)
S	10. Edward Field (1963) - G (1963), S (1975)
BRQ1	11. Allen Ginsberg (1956) - G (1965), A (1969), N (1974)
RQ2	12. Anthony Hecht (1954) - G (1954), G (1959), P (1968)
	13. Richard Howard (1962) - G (1966), A (1970), P (1970)
RQ1	14. Donald Justice (1960) - A (1974), G (1976)
B	15. Galway Kinnell (1960) - A (1962), G (1962), S (1972), G (1974)
	16. Kenneth Koch (1953) - G (1961), A (1976)
RQ1	17. Maxine Kumin (1961) - P (1973), A (1980)
RQ1	18. Philip Levine (1963) - A (1973), G (1973)
	19. W. S. Merwin (1952) - A (1957), P (1971), G (1973), S (1974), B (1979)
	20. Mary Oliver (1965) - S (1970), G (1980)
	21. Adrienne Rich (1951) - G (1952), A (1960), G (1961), S (1971), N (1974)
RQ1	22. W. D. Snodgrass (1959) - A (1960), P (1960), G (1972)
BQ1	23. Gary Snyder (1959) - A (1966), G (1968), P (1975)
RQ1	24. William Stafford (1954) - N (1963), S (1964), G (1966)
RQ1	25. Ruth Stone (1959) - S (1965), G (1971), G (1975)
RQ1	26. Mark Strand (1964) - G (1974), A (1975)
RQ1	27. May Swenson (1954) - G (1959), A (1960), S (1968)
RQ1	28. Mona Van Duyn (1959) - B (1971), N (1971), G (1972)
	29. David Wagoner (1953) - G (1956), A (1967)

Newer Nonprizewinning Poets (NN Group)

	1. Howard Aaron (1979)
RQ1	2. Randall Ackley (1972)
RQ1	3. Minerva Allen (1974)
RQ1	4. Mindy Aloff (1979)
RQ1	5. Marianne Andrea (1975)
RQ1	6. Roger Aplon (1976)
RQ1	7. Jane Bailey (1976)
RQ1	8. Coleman Barks (1972)
Q1	9. Jack Barry (1974)
RQ1	10. Madeline Tiger Bass (1977)

RQ1	11. Charles Baxter (1970)
RQ1	12. Charles Behlen (1978)
RQ1	13. Steve Benson (1978)
RQ1	14. Ellen Marie Bissert (1977)
	15. Adelaide Bromfield (1974)
RQ1	16. Greg Bowers (1977)
RQ1	17. Alice Cabaniss (1975)
RQ1	18. Naomi Clark (1977)
RQ1	19. Timothy Cohrs (1977)
R	20. Jayne Cortez (1969[6])
RQ1	21. David Curry (1970)
RQ1	22. Irene Dayton (1970)
RQ1	23. toi derricotte (1978)
RQ1	24. Emil Dillard (1974)
RQ1	25. Gary Elder (1970)
RQ1	26. Christopher Fahy (1978)
RQ1	27. Mike Finn (1976)
RQ1	28. Gregory Fitz Gerald (1979)
RQ1	29. Daniel Mark Fogel (1975)
RQ1	30. Siv Cedering (Fox) (1973)
RQ1	31. Margaret Gibson (1972)
RQ1	32. Isabel Glaser (1977)
RQ1	33. Barry Goldensohn (1972)
RQ1	34. James Grabill (1975)
	35. Galen Green (1971)
RQ1	36. Linda Gregg (1981)
RQ1	37. Richard Grossman (1977)
RQ1	38. Marie Harris (1973)
RQ1	39. Yuki Hartman (1970)
RQ1	40. Charles Haseloff (1972)
RQ1	41. Susan Hauser (1976)
RQ1	42. Gerald Hausman (1968)
RQ1	43. Anne Hazlewood-Brady (1970)
RQ1	44. Robert Hedin (1975)
RQ1	45. Harvey Hess (1977)
RQ1	46. David Huddle (1979)
	47. James Humphrey (1970)
RQ1	48. Gary Allan Kizer (1977)

	49. Daniel L. Klauck (1976)
RQ1	50. Phyllis Koestenbaum (1980)
RQ1	51. Alex Kuo (1971)
RQ1	52. Marina LaPalma (1976)
	53. Ross Laursen (1968)
RQ1	54. Ken Lauter (1973)
RQ1	55. Stephen Leggett (1973)
RQ1	56. Miriam Levine (1974)
RQ1	57. Jane Lippe-Fine (1980)
	58. Henry N. Lucas (1975)
RQ1	59. David Lunde (1971)
	60. Abigail Luttinger (1979)
RQ1	61. Charles Martin (1978)
	62. Robert McGovern (1971)
	63. Brian McInerney (1978)
RQ1	64. Alexander (Sandy) McIntosh (1970)
RQ1	65. Karen McKinnon (1975)
	66. Anthony McNeill (1971)
	67. Jesús Papoleto Meléndez (1971)
RQ1	68. Douglas Messerli (1979)
RQ1	69. Jack Myers (1970)
RQ1	70. Shelley Neiderbach (1976)
RQ1	71. Nona Nimnicht (1978)
RQ1	72. Kathleen Norris (1971)
RQ1	73. Diana Ó Hehir (1976)
RQ1	74. Richard O'Keefe (1972)
RQ1	75. Carole Oles (1978)
RQ1	76. Lawrence T. O'Neill (1973)
RQ1	77. Ron Overton (1979)
	78. Pat Parker (1972)
	79. Bill Pearlman (1970)
RQ1	80. Joyce Peseroff (1977)
RQ1	81. Anthony Piccione (1975)
RQ3	82. Eugene Platt (1970)
	83. Judith Platz (1977)
RQ1	84. Keith Rahmmings (1975)
RQ1	85. Jerry Ratch (1973)
RQ1	86. Danny L. Rendleman (1972)

RQ1	87. Zack Rogow (1979)
RQ1	88. Kenneth Rosen (1973)
RQ1	89. Ira Sadoff (1975)
RQ1	90. Miriam Sagan (1976)
Q1	91. Primus St. John (1976)
RQ1	92. Gilbert Schedler (1978)
	93. David Schloss (1973)
RQ1	94. Bennie Lee Sinclair (1971)
	95. Marcia Southwick (1977)
	96. Albert Stainton (1974)
RQ1	97. Will Staple (1977)
RQ1	98. Elaine Starkman (1977)
RQ1	99. Judith Steinbergh (1972)
RQ1	100. Kathryn Stripling (1979)
RQ1	101. Jitu Tambuzi (aka Richard Byrd) (1979)
RQ1	102. Alberta T. Turner (1970)
RQ1	103. Janine Pommy Vega (1968)
	104. Doris Wight (1975)
RQ1	105. William Witherup (1970)

Older Nonprizewinning Poets (ON Group)

	1. Robert Bagg (1957)
RQ1	2. E. G. Burrows (1957)
	3. Gregory Corso (1955)
RQ1	4. Dorothy Dalton (1967)
	5. R.H.W. Dillard (1966)
RQ1	6. Theodore Enslin (1958)
RQ1	7. James Facos (1962)
RQ1	8. Ida Fasel (1954)
RQ1	9. David Ferry (1960)
RQ1	10. Richard Frost (1965)
RQ1	11. John Gill (1967)
RQ1	12. Lyle Glazier (1965)
RQ1	13. Ann Hayes (1963)
RQ1	14. Daryl Hine (1954)
RQ1	15. Barbara Adams Holland (1965)
R	16. Bill Hotchkiss (1966)

RQ1	17. Donald Junkins (1965)
RQ1	18. Stanley Koehler (1962)
	19. Claire McAllister (1964)
RQ1	20. Dorothy Lee Richardson (1961)
RQ3	21. M. L. Rosenthal (1969)
RQ1	22. Stephen Sandy (1960)
RQ1	23. John Stevens Wade (1954)
RQ1	24. Curtis Zahn (1966)

Notes

INTRODUCTION

1. Frederick J. Hoffman, Charles Allen, and Carolyn F. Ulrich, *The Little Magazine: A History and a Bibliography* (Princeton, N.J.: Princeton University Press, 1946), pp. 235–398.

2. Daisy Aldan, in Dennis Barone, "Daisy Aldan: An Interview on *Folder*," in *The Little Magazine in America: A Modern Documentary History*, ed. Elliott Anderson and Mary Kinzie (Yonkers, N.Y.: Pushcart Press, 1978), p. 264.

3. Cited in Felix Pollak, "The World of Little Magazines," *Arts in Society* 2 (Spring/Summer 1962): 52.

4. Len Fulton, ed., *Directory of Little Magazines* (El Cerrito, Cal.: Dustbooks, 1964).

5. Len Fulton, ed., *International Directory of Little Magazines and Small Presses*, 23rd ed. (Paradise, Cal.: Dustbooks, 1987).

6. Conrad Aiken in interview with Richard Hunter Wilbur, in George Plimpton, ed., *Writers at Work: The "Paris Review" Interviews*, 4th series (New York: Viking Press, 1976); Jack Gilbert, "The Landscape of American Poetry in 1964," in *Poets on Poetry*, ed. Howard Nemerov (New York: Basic Books, 1966); and Gerald Stern in an interview with Mark Hillringhouse, *American Poetry Review* 13 (March-April 1984): 29.

7. *TriQuarterly*, no. 43 (Fall 1978). Reprinted as: Anderson, and Kinzie, eds., *The Little Magazine in America.*

8. Diane Kruchkow and Curt Johnson, eds., *Green Isle in the Sea: An Informal History of the Alternative Press, 1960–1985* (Highland Park, Ill.: December Press, 1986).

9. Olga Weber and Stephen J. Calvert, *Literary and Library Prizes* (New York: R. R. Bowker, 1980).

10. *Directory of American Poets and Fiction Writers,* 1980–81 ed. (New York: Poets & Writers, Inc., 1980).

11. A complete description of research methods used, including a copy of the questionnaire and lists of reference sources and libraries consulted and periodical issues examined, can be found in Mary Biggs, "The Publishing of American Poetry, 1950–1980," Ph.D. dissertation, University of Chicago, 1986.

CHAPTER 1

1. Christopher Clausen, *The Place of Poetry: Two Centuries of an Art in Crisis* (Lexington: University Press of Kentucky, 1981).

2. William Charvat, *Literary Publishing in America, 1790–1850* (Philadelphia: University of Pennsylvania Press, 1959), pp. 53, 65.

3. Russel Nye, *The Unembarrassed Muse: The Popular Arts in America* (New York: Dial Press, 1970), pp. 88–137.

4. Ibid., p. 32.

5. Clausen, *The Place of Poetry,* p. 122.

6. H[arriet] M[onroe], "Comment: Fifteen Years," *Poetry* 31 (October 1927): 32.

7. Maxwell Bodenheim, "American Menagerie," *Little Review* 12 (May 1929): 99.

8. Quoted in Edward Connery Lathem, ed., *Interviews with Robert Frost* (New York: Holt, Rinehart & Winston, 1966), p. 244.

9. Quoted in Lawrance Thompson, *Robert Frost: The Early Years, 1874–1915* (New York: Holt, Rinehart & Winston, 1966), pp. 389; 400–401.

10. William Carlos Williams, *I Wanted to Write a Poem: The Autobiography of the Works of a Poet* (Boston: Beacon Press, 1958), p. 10.

11. Frederick J. Hoffman, Charles Allen, and Carolyn F. Ulrich, *The Little Magazine: A History and a Bibliography* (Princeton, N.J.: Princeton University Press, 1946), pp. 235–41.

12. Harriet Monroe, *A Poet's Life: Seventy Years in a Changing World* (New York: Macmillan, 1938).

13. Ezra Pound, in "Vale," *Poetry* 49 (December 1936): 137–38. Note that Pound identified 1911, the year during which Monroe's plans for *Poetry* were laid and support first solicited, as the magazine's founding date. However, the magazine's first issue appeared in 1912, and that year is shown on its masthead and routinely cited in literary histories as its founding date.

14. Quoted in Noel Stock, *The Life of Ezra Pound* (New York: Pantheon, 1970), p. 260.

15. Quoted in Daniel Smythe, *Robert Frost Speaks* (New York: Twayne Publishers, 1964), p. 130.

16. H[arriet] M[onroe], "Our Contemporaries: I," *Poetry* 6 (September 1915): 316–17.

17. [Harriet Monroe], "The Motive of the Magazine," *Poetry* 1 (October 1912): 27.

18. Ezra Pound and H[arriet] M[onroe], "The Audience," *Poetry* 5 (October 1914): 30–31.

19. H[arriet] M[onroe], "Comment: Twenty-one," *Poetry* 43 (October 1933): 35.

20. Ezra Pound, "Editorial," *Little Review* 4 (May 1917): [3].

21. Quoted in Margaret Anderson, *My Thirty Years' War* (New York: Covici Friede, 1930), p. 159.

22. jh [Jane Heap], in "Discussion: 'The Public Taste,' " *Little Review* 7 (July–August 1920): 33.

23. jh [Jane Heap], "What Joyce is Up Against," *Little Review* 5 (June 1918): 54.

24. H[arriet] M[onroe], "Review [of Anderson, *My Thirty Years' War*]: Personality Rampant," *Poetry* 37 (October 1930): 98; idem, "Comment: A Century in Illinois," *Poetry* 13 (November 1918): 92.

25. Hoffman, Allen, and Ulrich, *The Little Magazine,* p. 66.

26. William Carlos Williams, "The Advance Guard Magazine," *Contact: An American Quarterly Review* 1 (February 1932): 88.

27. Williams, *I Wanted to Write a Poem,* pp. 19–20.

28. Paul Mariani, *William Carlos Williams: A New World Naked* (New York: McGraw-Hill, 1981), p. 164.

29. Quoted in Monroe, *A Poet's Life,* p. 312.

30. "The New Dial," *Poetry* 9 (January 1917): 217.

31. William Carlos Williams, Prefatory statement in Stephen Halpert with Richard Johns, *A Return to "Pagany": The History, Correspondence, and Selections from a Little Magazine, 1919–1932* (Boston: Beacon Press, 1969), pp. [vi–vii].

32. Jay B. Hubbell, *Who Are the Major American Writers?* (Durham, N.C.: Duke University Press, 1972), pp. 210–11.

33. Clausen, *The Place of Poetry,* pp. 83–84, 118.

34. Maxwell Bodenheim, "Correspondence: Words from a Departing Poet," *Poetry* 16 (July 1920): 228.

35. Louise Bogan, in *What the Woman Lived: Selected Letters of Louise Bogan, 1920–1970,* ed. Ruth Limmer (New York: Harcourt Brace Jovanovich, 1973), pp. 48, 132.

36. G[eorge] H. D[illon], "Spring Cleaning," *Poetry* 30 (April 1927): 37–39.

37. "The Wasteland" had already appeared in part in Eliot's magazine *The Criterion* and in full in *The Dial.*

38. Edward Dahlberg, letter to Richard Johns, dated February 8, 1931, in Halpert with Johns, *A Return to "Pagany,"* p. 256.

39. H[arriet] M[onroe], "Comment: In These Days," *Poetry* 43 (March 1934): 328.

40. Julian L. Shapiro, undated letter to Richard Johns, received Spring 1933, in Halpert with Johns, *A Return to "Pagany,"* p. 506.

41. Susan Howard and Charles Ruas, "New Directions: An Interview with James Laughlin," in *The Art of Literary Publishing: Editors on Their Craft,* ed. Bill Henderson (Yonkers, N.Y.: Pushcart Press, 1980), pp. 17–18.

42. Elise Robinson, St. Louis *Dispatch,* March 25, 1938, quoted in Monty Noam Penkower, *The Federal Writers; Project: A Study in Government Patronage of the Arts* (Urbana: University of Illinois Press, 1977), p. 7.

43. Quoted in Hoffman, Allen, and Ulrich, *The Little Magazine,* p. 295.

44. It should not be concluded that *Prairie Schooner* was the first academically sponsored literary journal, though it was the earliest founded of those that have survived. Preceding *Prairie Schooner* were *The Midland* (edited at the University of Iowa, though not, strictly speaking, university-supported, 1915–33); *The Frontier* (University of Montana, 1920–39); *Laughing Horse* (University of California, 1922–23); *Casements* (Brown University, 1923–24); and *The Tanager* (Grinnell College, 1925–42). There may have been a few others. However, these remained isolated cases until the 1930s.

45. Ezra Pound, "This Subsidy Business," *Poetry* 35 (January 1930): 212–14.

46. Williams, *I Wanted to Write a Poem,* pp. 51–52.

47. George Oppen, in Charles Amirkhanian and David Gitin, "A Conversation with George Oppen," *Ironwood* 5 (1975): 23.

48. Quoted in Joel Roache, *Richard Eberhart: The Progress of an American Poet* (New York: Oxford University Press, 1971), p. 164.

49. Quoted in ibid., pp. 150–51.

50. Eileen Simpson, *Poets in Their Youth* (New York: Random House, 1982), p. 5.

51. Daniel Curley, George Scouffas, and Charles Shattuck, eds., *"Accent": An Anthology, 1940–60* (Urbana: University of Illinois Press, 1973), pp. xxi–xv.

52. [Sydney King Russell et al.], [Editorial], *Poetry Chap-Book* 1 (October–December 1942): [3].

53. These are my calculations, based on the Hoffman, Allen, and Ulrich bibliography, *The Little Magazine,* pp. 294–372.

54. Alan Swallow, in Hayden Carruth, ed., "A Symposium: Poet, Publisher, and Tribal Chant," *Poetry* 75 (October 1949): 54–55.

55. Dennis Barone, "Daisy Aldan: An Interview on *Folder,*" in Elliott Anderson and Mary Kinzie, eds., *The Little Magazine in America: A Modern Documentary History* (Yonkers, N.Y.: Pushcart Press, 1978), pp. 263–64.

CHAPTER 2

1. Daisy Aldan, in Dennis Barone, "Daisy Aldan: An Interview on *Folder,*" in *The Little Magazine in America: A Modern Documentary History,* ed. Elliott Anderson and Mary Kinzie (Yonkers, N.Y.: Pushcart Press, 1978), p. 269.

2. Elly Bulkin, "An Interview with Adrienne Rich, Part II," *Conditions,* no. 2 (1977): 59–60.

3. Quoted in Louise Bernikow, "Out of the Bell Jar," *New Times* 7 (October 29, 1976): 53.

4. In "Craft Interview with May Swenson," *New York Quarterly* 19 (Autumn 1977): 27.

5. For complete data supporting this conclusion, see: Mary Biggs, "The Publishing of American Poetry, 1950–1980" (Ph.D. dissertation, University of Chicago, 1986), Chapter 3.

6. The exact journals, dates, volumes examined, and figures derived are shown in ibid.

7. In Karla Hammond, "Interview with Jane Shore," *Choomia,* nos. 7/8 (December 1978-January 1979): 6.

8. In "Craft Interview with Erica Jong," in William Packard, ed., *The Craft of Poetry: Interviews from "The New York Quarterly"* (Garden City, N.Y.: Doubleday, 1974), p. 301.

9. In Elaine Showalter and Carol Smith, "A Nurturing Relationship: A Conversation with Anne Sexton and Maxine Kumin, April 15, 1974," *Women's Studies* 4 (1976): 135.

10. In Elly Bulkin, "An Interview with Adrienne Rich," *Conditions,* no. 1 [1977]: 51.

11. Jan Clausen, *A Movement of Poets: Thoughts on Poetry and Feminism* (Brooklyn, N.Y.: Long Haul Press, 1982). This essay sheds light on the feminism-poetry link and assesses the contributions and costs of politics to creative literature.

12. See, for example, a symposium edited by Jan Clausen: "The Politics of Publishing and the Lesbian Community," *Sinister Wisdom* 1 (Fall 1976): 95–115.

13. Ellen Marie Bissert. [Contributor's note] *Beyond Baroque* 11 (Summer 1980): 17.

14. Obviously, these categories overlap, and minority women may have been doubly disadvantaged—and occasionally, when an editor wished to balance a publication (or deflect criticism) by presenting alternative viewpoints, doubly distinguished. The minority woman poet is an exotic to many women editors, most of whom are white and of middle-class background. The black poet toi derricotte described experiences of being singled out because of her sex-race combination.

15. In Leonard Kniffel, "Broadside Press, Then and Now: An Interview with Dudley Randall," *Small Press* 1 (May–June 1984): 30.

16. Richard Kostelanetz, "The New Class," in Kostelanetz, *The Old Poetries and the New* (Ann Arbor: University of Michigan Press, 1981), p. 64. (This review was published originally in *Margins,* no. 28–30 [1976]: 26–28.)

17. Richard Kostelanetz, "Reactions and Alternatives: Post-World War II American Poetry," in Kostelanetz, *The Old Poetries and the New,* p. 45. Ginsberg's response was to this survey query: "As far as you *know* or *believe,* has being gay ever affected—positively or negatively, directly or indirectly—your ability to publish your work?" This should rule out the possibility that the major works in question were unacceptable because of their language or some other factor not related to sex.

18. Income data were gathered for 136 poets. Mean percentage of their income *not* generated by writing was 77 percent; the median was 88 percent. (These figures exclude royalties and fees not only for published poems but for all other writing as well, and also payments for poetry readings, workshops, contest judgeships, etc.) Means ranged from 86 percent for Older Nonprizewinners to 38 percent for Older Prizewinners, medians from 98 percent to 27.5 percent for the same two groups, respectively. For 16 percent of all poets, no income at all was generated by writing. While none of the Older Prizewinners and only two (7 percent) of the Newer Prizewinners made no money at all from writing, 19 percent of Older Nonprizewinners and 21 percent of Newer Nonprizewinners made nothing from it. More information about income is presented in chapter 7.

19. "Made Things: An Interview with Richard Howard," *Ohio Review* 16 (Fall 1974): 48.

20. In Kip Stratton, "An Interview with William Stafford," *Greenfield Review* 7 (Spring–Summer 1979): 86.

21. In William Childress, "William Stafford," *Poetry Now*, no. 8 (1975): 2.

22. It must be kept in mind that respondents categorized income from regular teaching appointments as "not dependent on writing," although many of these appointments were made because of their reputations as poets. Still, this income was essentially payment for another job—that is, teaching—and was not as *directly* dependent on writing as were royalties, reading fees, and so forth.

23. Margery Mansfield, "Comment: Wasting the Poets' Time," *Poetry* 31 (October 1927): 40.

24. In Karla Hammond, "An Interview with Maxine Kumin," *Western Humanities Review* 33 (Winter 1979): 14.

25. That is, average proportion of all time devoted to work, which was not necessarily forty hours per week.

26. In this study, such work was labelled "poetry-*related* activities" and expressly differentiated from "poetry-*writing*." For complete data on poets' use of working time, see Biggs, "The Publishing of American Poetry," pp. 570–71.

27. James Dickey, *Self-Interviews* (Garden City, N.Y.: Doubleday, 1970): pp. 43–46.

28. In Stratton, "An Interview with William Stafford," p. 94.

29. Gerald Clarke, "Checking in with Allen Ginsberg," *Esquire* 79 (April 1973): 92.

30. In "Andrei Vosnesensky and Allen Ginsberg: A Conversation," *Paris Review* 22 (Summer 1980): 157.

31. Questionnaire response.

32. Philip Levine, in "And See if the Voice Will Enter You: An Interview with Philip Levine," *Ohio Review* 16 (Winter 1975): 63.

33. Dickey, *Self-Interviews*, p. 63.

34. In Packard, ed., *The Craft of Poetry*, p. 139. The full quotation is: "I've given my life to poetry—I wrote it on troopships and in airplanes. I wrote it going on business trips. I wrote it in American business offices. I wrote it on weekends and vacations—simply for one reason: I love it. It's been the central concern of my being and my character all my life."

35. William Stafford, "Writing: The Discovery of Daily Experience," in Stafford, *Writing the Australian Crawl: Views on the Writer's Vocation* (Ann Arbor: University of Michigan Press, 1978), p. 48.

36. Diana Ó Hehir, "Making Us Speak," in *Nine New American Poets of the Golden Gate*, ed. Philip Dow (San Diego, Cal.: Harcourt Brace Jovanovich, 1984), p. 27.

37. In *Focus/Midwest* 2 (May 1963): 21.

38. In Albert Goldbarth, "An Interview with Galway Kinnell," *Crazy Horse*, no. 6 (1971): 37.

39. In Franklin Ashley, "James Dickey: The Art of Poetry XX," *Paris Review* 17 (Spring 1976): 55.

40. It is important to remember the exclusion in this study of periodicals devoted to one institution's student work or of strictly local distribution (e.g., student literary magazines, church newsletters, and local papers of all but the largest cities).

CHAPTER 3

1. Peter Davison, "My Say," *Publishers Weekly* 223 (March 18, 1983): 64. Davison was a poet, senior editor at Atlantic Monthly Press, and poetry editor of *The Atlantic.*

2. These percentages are based on 1,275 bibliographic citations to earliest periodical publications—the five earliest for newer poets, the ten earliest for older poets.

3. Dozens of citations could be given. On the blockbuster emphasis, see, for example: Thomas Whiteside, *The Blockbuster Complex* (Middletown, Conn.: Wesleyan University Press, 1982); Leonard Shatzkin, *In Cold Type: Overcoming the Book Crisis* (Boston: Houghton Mifflin, 1982); Ted Solotaroff, "The Publishing Culture and the Literary Culture," in *Publishers and Librarians: A Foundation for Dialogue*, ed. Mary Biggs (Chicago: University of Chicago Press, 1984); and remarks throughout *The Publication of Poetry and Fiction: A Conference held at the Library of Congress, October 21 and 22, 1975* (Washington, D.C.: Library of Congress, 1977).

4. *The Publication of Poetry and Fiction*, pp. 17, 21.

5. The proportions published by each sector of these selected Newer Prizewinners' first books were: commercial = 21 pecent (N = 5); academic = 58 percent (N = 14); independent = 21 percent (N = 5); organization not primarily a publisher = 3.5 percent (N = 1); and vanity = 3.5 percent (N = 1).

6. Robert Creeley, "Black Mountain Review," in *Was That a Real Poem, and Other Essays*, ed. Donald Allen (Bolinas, Cal.: Four Seasons Foundation, 1979), pp. 16–17. Creeley was a student at the college and later editor of the *Review.*

7. Phillip Lopate, "The Little Magazines Keep Coming," *Little Magazine* 7 (Fall 1973): 15.

8. On the first point, see: Frederick J. Hoffman, Charles Allen, and Carolyn F. Ulrich, *The Little Magazine: A History and a Bibliography* (Princeton, N.J.: Princeton University Press, 1946); James Boyer May, *Twigs as Varied Bent: The Recent Part of Little Magazines in Literature* (Corona, N.Y.: Sparrow Magazine, 1954). On the recent proliferation, see: Len Fulton, "Anima Rising: Little Magazines in the Sixties," in *Print, Image, and Sound: Essays on Media*, ed. John Gordon Burke (Chicago: American Library Association, 1972); Michael Anania, "Of Living Belfry and Rampart: On American Literary Magazines Since 1950," in *The Little Magazine in America: A Modern Documentary History*, ed. Elliott Anderson and Mary Kinzie (Yonkers, N.Y.: Pushcart Press, 1978); James Healey, ed., "Little Magazines: Too Much With Us?: A Symposium," *Prairie Schooner* 48 (Winter 1974/75): 317–26; James Boyer May, quoted in Morris Edelson, "Six Little Magazines" (Ph.D. dissertation, University of Wisconsin, 1973), p. 87.

9. Edward Dahlberg. [Letter to Richard Johns, dated February 8, 1931.] In Stephen Halpert with Richard Johns, *A Return to "Pagany": The History, Correspondence, and Selections from a Little Magazine, 1929–1932* (Boston: Beacon Press, 1969), p. 256.

10. Charles Haseloff, "Feminine, Marvelous and Tough: Letter from a '12-Year-Old' Fan to the Poetry Project (By Way of a Contribution to its *History*)," unpublished paper, 1979. Haseloff's paper is a memoir of the famous 1960s

Poetry Project at St. Mark's Church in the Bowery section of New York City. This quotation refers to the many magazines begun by the people involved in that project. Haseloff's own magazine was *Penumbra*.

11. See also: Wayne Dodd, "Robert Bly: An Interview," *Ohio Review* 19 (Fall 1978): 35–36. In this 1978 interview, Bly declared it "a responsibility of publishers not to publish so many books of poetry." Earlier, he had written that literary magazine editors should reduce voluntarily the number of issues published annually (in "Concerning the Little Magazines: Something Like a Symposium," *Carleton Miscellany* [Spring 1966]: 21–22).

12. Glenna Luschei, in Healey ed., "Little Magazines," p. 325.

13. James Boatwright, in Healey, ed., "Little Magazines," pp. 318–19.

14. Allen Ginsberg, quoted in "What is Literary Pollution?" [Advertisement for *Camels Coming Newsletter*.] In *The Whole COSMEP Catalog*, ed. Dick Higgins (San Francisco: Committee of Small Magazine Editors & Publishers, Inc., 1973), unpaginated.

15. [Barbara Holland], Biographical note, *Beyond Baroque* 10 (Summer 1979): 32.

16. Alan Brilliant, "Poetry and the Small Press," *Works* (Spring 1969): 66. ("Little magazines . . . have become the television sets of poetry readers"); William V. Davis, "Incest Among Editors," in "Editors (and Others) Write." *Trace* 71 (mid–1970): 228; Charles Bukowski, "Charles Bukowski Answers 10 Easy Questions," *Throb*, no. 2 (Summer-Fall 1971): 57. Here Bukowski wrote, "[The small press is] a crutch for 9th rate talents." In a 1972 letter to poet Harold Norse, reprinted by Norse in his magazine *Bastard Angel*, Bukowski fretted, "I'm afraid that the small press, the mimeo presses, have kept alive too many talentless darlings." (*Bastard Angel*, no. 2 [Spring 1974]: 61); Hayden Carruth, "Some Personal Notations," in *The Art of Literary Publishing: Editors on Their Craft*, ed. Bill Henderson (Yonkers, N.Y.: Pushcart Press, 1980), p. 52.

17. *Little Review* 12, no. 7; j[ane] h[eap], "Lost: A Renaissance," *Little Review* 12 (May 1929): 5. The masterpiece was James Joyce's *Ulysses*.

18. Ira Sadoff, in Healey ed., "Little Magazines," p. 322.

19. For complete dispersion information, see Biggs, "The Publishing of American Poetry," pp. 217–24, 582–83.

20. For complete lists of the periodicals, publishers, and poets cited, see Biggs, "The Publishing of American Poetry," pp. 585–618.

21. Rounded percentages of each group cited by at least one survey respondent as being among the "best" living American poets are: OPs, 100 percent; NPs, 53.3 percent (N=24); ONs, 12.5 percent (N=3); NNs, 7.6 percent (N=8).

CHAPTER 4

1. For complete data on poets' degree-granting institutions, see Mary Biggs, "The Publishing of American Poetry, 1950–1980," (Ph.D. dissertation, University of Chicago, 1986), pp. 565–66.

2. Hugh Kenner, "Manuscript to be Placed in a Bottle," *Spectrum* 1 (Winter 1957): 4.

3. Richard Kostelanetz, "The New Class," in Kostelanetz, *The Old Poetries and the New* (Ann Arbor: University of Michigan Press, 1981), p. 27; Kirby Congdon, "Editors (and Others) Write: Ideas 'Sold' for Commercial Prestige?," *Trace* 51 (Winter 1963): 288.

4. Charles Bukowski, "He Beats His Women," *Second Coming* 2, no. 3 (1977): unpaginated.

5. Robert Bly, in Wayne Dodd, "Robert Bly: An Interview," *Ohio Review* 19 (Fall 1978): 42; 38.

6. William Harmon, "The Even More Lost Generation," *American Book Review* 6 (May–June 1984): 3. Harmon, a university professor and distinguished younger poet (included in this study's NP group), had the "aging Beatniks" in mind specifically.

7. H[ayden] C[arruth], "The University and the Poet: An Editorial," *Poetry* 75 (November 1949): 89–93; and Yvor Winters, "The Poet and the University: A Reply," *Poetry* 75 (December 1949): 170–72, 174, 176–78.

8. William Joyce, "The Oink from the Literary Barn," *American Book Review* 6 (May–June 1984): 5.

9. Roger Mitchell, "On Being Large and Containing Multitudes," *American Book Review* 6 (May–June 1984): 10.

10. Peter Davison, "One of the Dangerous Trades," in "The Place of Poetry: Symposium Responses," *Georgia Review* 35 (Winter 1981): 728.

11. Winters, "The Poet and the University," p. 176.

12. Daryln Brewer, "Writers and Teaching," *Coda* 11 (February–March 1984): 17–18.

13. Winters, "The Poet and the University," p. 174; Mitchell, "On Being Large," p. 10.

14. Robert Frost, in Daniel Smythe, *Robert Frost Speaks* (New York: Twayne, 1964), p. 123.

15. "Craft Interview with W. D. Snodgrass," *New York Quarterly* 18 (Spring 1976): 38.

16. See "Interview with Jan Garrett," pp. 108–37, and "Interview with Tad Prozewicz," pp. 153–74," in Philip Levine, *Don't Ask* (Ann Arbor: University of Michigan Press, 1981).

17. James J. McKenzie, "To the Roots: An Interview with Galway Kinnell," *Salmagundi*, no. 22–23 (Spring–Summer 1973): 219.

18. "Craft Interview with Galway Kinnell," in *The Craft of Poetry: Interviews from "The New York Quarterly,"* ed. William Packard (Garden City, N.Y.: Doubleday, 1974), p. 102.

19. Leonard Randolph, "The Economics of Little Magazines: A Report from Leonard Randolph and the Literature Program of the National Endowment for the Arts," *Margins*, no. 17 (1975): 7.

20. Paul R. Stewart, *The "Prairie Schooner" Story: A Little Magazine's First Twenty-Five Years* (Lincoln: University of Nebraska Press, 1953), pp. 89–90.

21. Randolph, "The Economics of Little Magazines," p. 7.

22. Editorial, *Poet and Critic* 1 (Fall 1964): unpaginated.

23. William Knief, "An Introduction," *Cottonwood Review* 1 (Spring 1966): unpaginated.

24. L[loyd] K[ropp], "Editor's Notes," *Sou'wester* 8 (Summer 1980): unpaginated.

25. This number was arrived at by counting poetry titles on the lists of academic publishers of poetry whose catalogs were included in the 1984 edition of *Publishers Trade List Annual* (New York: R. R. Bowker, 1984).

26. For a complete list of outlets named by poets, see Biggs, "The Publishing of American Poetry," pp. 585–96 and 620–21.

CHAPTER 5

1. Founding dates and circulation figures are taken from Len Fulton and Ellen Ferber, eds., *International Directory of Little Magazines and Small Presses,* 21st ed. (Paradise, Cal.: Dustbooks, 1985).
2. In 1984, *kayak* was terminated by its founding editor, George Hitchcock.
3. In "Concerning the Little Magazines: Something Like a Symposium," *Carleton Miscellany* 7 (Spring 1966): 10.
4. Felix Pollak, "Elitism and the Littleness of Little Magazines," *Southwest Review* (Summer 1976): 297.
5. Peter Michelson, "On *Big Table, Chicago Review,* and *The Purple Sage,*" in *The Little Magazine in America: A Modern Documentary History,* ed. Elliott Anderson and Mary Kinzie (Yonkers, N.Y.: Pushcart Press, 1978), p. 375.
6. *Wormwood Review* 10 (or issue no. 39) (1970): [120]; *Wormwood Review* 9 (or issue no. 36) (1969): [40].
7. Quincy Troupe, "Editor's Statement," *American Rag* 1, no. 1 (1978): [1].
8. Charles L. P. Silet, "The Basilisk Press," *Poet and Critic* 8, no. 3 (1975): 32, 35.
9. C. W. Truesdale, "New Rivers Press," *Works* 2 (Spring 1969): 91.
10. Margaret C. Anderson, "Our First Year," *Little Review* 1 (February 1915): 3.
11. Stephen Halpert and Richard Johns, eds., *A Return to "Pagany": the History, Correspondence, and Selections from a Little Magazine, 1929–1932* (Boston: Beacon Press, 1969), p. 41; Ibid., p. 95.
12. Quoted in Felix Pollak, "The World of Little Magazines," *Arts in Society* 2 (Spring/Summer 1962): 65.
13. [Clarence Major], *The Coercion Review of Contemporary Power in Literature,* no. 1 (Summer 1958): 1.
14. R[ichard] R[ubenstein], "Foreword," *Gryphon,* no. 1 (Spring 1950): [5].
15. [Wallace Depew and Linda Bandt], "Our Statement," *Poetry Newsletter,* no. 1 (December 1964): 2.
16. *Proteus: A Literary Quarterly* [advertisement]," in *The Whole COSMEP Catalog,* ed. Dick Higgins (San Francisco and New York: Committee of Small Magazine Editors and Publishers, 1973), unpaginated.
17. [Donald Factor, Anthony Linick, and John Daly], "Path of the Nomad," *Nomad,* no. 1 (Winter 1979): 3–4.
18. Quoted in James W. Healey, "Little Magazines: 'A Little Madness Helps'," *Prairie Schooner* 47 (Winter 1973/74): 340.
19. Pollak, "Elitism and the Littleness of Little Magazines," p. 297.
20. [D.r. Wagner], "Editorial No. 1," *Moonstones* 1, no. 1 (1966): 3; Quoted in Daryln Brewer, "Starting Your Own Small Press," *Coda* (September–October 1982): 13.
21. Richard Kostelanetz, "Why Assembling?" *Assembling,* no. 1 (1970): unpaginated.

22. Pollak, "Elitism and the Littleness of Little Magazines."

23. Alan Swallow, "The Little Magazines," *Prairie Schooner* 16 (Winter 1942): 239.

24. Pollak, "Elitism and the Littleness of Little Magazines," p. 301.

25. "Foreword," *Umbra* 1, no. 1 (Winter 1963): 3; "Editorial: Introduction," *Premiere*, no. 1 [1965]: 2; Quoted in Beverly Gross, "Culture and Anarchy: Whatever Happened to Lit Magazines?" *Antioch Review* 29 (Spring 1969): 47.

26. Kirby Congdon, "Interim Books," *Works* (Spring 1969): 88; David C. Yates, "From . . . the Cedar Post," *Cedar Rock* (Winter 1978): 2.

27. David Moberg, in "Concerning the Little Magazines," p. 59.

28. Len Fulton, "Peopleship," in Higgins, ed., *The Whole COSMEP Catalog*, unpaginated.

29. See Len Fulton, "Anima Rising: Little Magazines in the Sixties," in *Print, Image, and Sound: Essays on Media*, ed. John Gordon Burke (Chicago: American Library Association, 1972), pp. 137–38; and Len Fulton, "See Bukowski Run," *Small Press Review* 4 (May 1973): inside front cover, 27–31 (published originally in *Quixote* 7 [April 1972]).

30. Paul Foreman, " 'Struggle Begets All'—Heraclitus," in Higgins, ed., *The Whole COSMEP Catalog*, unpaginated.

31. e. e. cummings, "let's start a magazine," in *No Thanks* (New York: Golden Eagle Press, 1932), p. 24.

32. Pollak, "The World of Little Magazines," p. 55.

33. Irv Broughton, "An Interview with Philip Levine," *Western Humanities Review* 32 (Spring 1978): 158.

34. Peter Martin, "An Annotated Bibliography of Selected Little Magazines," in Anderson and Kinzie, eds., *The Little Magazine in America*, pp. 666–750.

35. Leonard Randolph, "The Economics of Little Magazines: A Report from Leonard Randolph and the Literature Program of the National Endowment for the Arts," *Margins*, no. 17 (1975): 6–7.

36. D[avid] G[reisman], "The Abbey Interview—Merritt Clifton." *Abbey*, no. 20 (1976): unpaginated.

37. [Editorial statement]. *City Lights Journal*, no. 4 (1978): [2].

38. Felix Stefanile, "The Little Magazine Today," in Anderson and Kinzie, eds., *The Little Magazine in America*, pp. 651–52.

39. Merritt Clifton, *On Small Press as Class Struggle*, 4th ed. (High Ridge, Mo.: Blue Pentacle Press, 1976).

40. Merritt Clifton, "The Shovel-Man." *Northwoods Journal* 7 (Spring 1979): 39.

41. Merritt Clifton, "The Shovel-Man: A Call to Arms." *Northwoods Journal* 10 (Winter 1982): 1–3.

42. Phillip Lopate, "The Little Magazines Keep Coming," *Little Magazine* 7 (Fall 1973): 26.

43. Morty Sklar, letter to author, October 17, 1981.

44. Ellen Ferber, "Still Running," in Fulton and Ferber, eds., *International Directory of Little Magazines and Small Presses*, 19th ed., unnumbered front page. Fulton was quoted in Judith Appelbaum, "Small Publisher Power: New Perspectives on the Big Publishing Picture," *Publishers Weekly* 222 (September 10, 1982): 26.

45. Ibid.

46. In a symposium published as "Appendix A" in *How to Start and Sustain a Literary Magazine,* ed. Joseph Bruchac (Austin, Tex.: Provision House, 1980), p. 96.

47. William Carlos Williams, prefatory statement, *I Wanted to Write a Poem: The Autobiography of the Works of a Poet,* edited by Edith Heal (Boston: Beacon Press, 1958), p. vi.

CHAPTER 6

1. Quoted in Peter Davison, "One of the Dangerous Trades," in "The Place of Poetry: Symposium Responses," *Georgia Review* 35 (Winter 1981): 7–27. Banks, a well-known fiction writer, was founding co-editor of the defunct literary journal *Lillabulero.*

2. Letter to Grace Hart Crane, dated September 28, 1917, in *The Letters of Hart Crane, 1916–1932,* ed. Brom Weber (Berkeley: University of California Press, 1952), p. 9.

3. John Unterecker, *Voyager: A Life of Hart Crane* (New York: Farrar, Straus & Giroux, 1969), pp. 129–31.

4. Letter to Gorham Munson, March 6, 1920, in Weber, ed., *The Letters of Hart Crane,* p. 35.

5. James Atlas, *Delmore Schwartz: The Life of an American Poet* (New York: Farrar, Straus & Giroux, 1977); Allan Seager, *The Glass House: The Life of Theodore Roethke* (New York: McGraw-Hill, 1968).

6. This information was obtained from Linda Gregg's questionnaire.

7. Linda Gregg, *Too Bright to See* (Port Townsend, Wash.: Graywolf Press, 1981): back cover.

8. Gerald Stern, *The Red Coal* (Boston: Houghton Mifflin, 1981).

9. Mark Hillringhouse, "Gerald Stern: An Interview," *Americn Poetry Review* 13 (March–April 1984): 26–30.

10. Jack Gilbert, *Monolithos: Poems, 1962 and 1982* (Port Townsend, Wash.: Graywolf Press, 1982).

11. Donald Allen, ed., *Off the Wall: Interviews with Philip Walen* (Bolinas, Cal.: Four Seasons Foundation, 1978); Ekbert Faas, *Towards a New American Poetics: Essays and Interviews* (Santa Barbara, Cal.: Black Sparrow Press, 1979); Robert Creeley, *Was That a Real Poem, and Other Essays,* ed. Donald Allen (Bolinas, Cal.: Four Seasons Foundation, 1979); Gary Snyder, *The Real Work: Interviews and Talks, 1964–1979,* ed. William Scott McLean (New York: New Directions, 1980); Ted Morgan, *Literary Outlaw: The Life and Times of William Burroughs* (New York: Henry Holt, 1988).

12. "Black Sparrow Press." *Coda* 4 (September–October 1976): 25.

13. In *The Publication of Poetry and Fiction: A Conference Held at the Library of Congress, October 20 and 21, 1975* (Washington, D.C.: Library of Congress, 1977), p. 86.

14. Clayton Eshleman, "On Caterpillar," in *The Little Magazine in America: A Modern Documentary History,* ed. Elliott Anderson and Mary Kinzie (Yonkers, N.Y.: Pushcart Press, 1978), p. 457.

15. Robert Phillips, "The Art of Poetry XXXVI: Karl Shapiro" [interview], *Paris Review,* no. 99 (1986): 185.

16. Entitled *The Language Student*, it was published by the Louisiana State University Press in 1986.

17. In Sue Gangel, "John Ashbery," in *Americn Poetry Observed: Poets on Their Work*, ed. Joe David Bellamy (Urbana: University of Illinois Press, 1984), pp. 11–12.

18. For an elaboration of these responses, see Mary Biggs, "The Publishing of American Poetry, 1950–1980" (Ph.D. dissertation, University of Chicago, 1986), pp. 627–29, 630–31. Some explanation of the rankings is required. Most poets listed either two or three factors that determine where they send poetry and ranked them in importance. Some indicated that only one factor was taken into consideration, while others listed two or (very rarely) three and insisted that all were of primary importance. A few respondents gave several factors and explained that while not all carried equal weight, ranking them was impossible. Ranks were determined by assigning four points to a first-ranked factor, to any sole factor, and to two or three factors when this many were listed and all said to be of first importance; three points to a second-ranked factor; two points to a third-ranked factor; one point to any factor ranked lower than third, and to every factor when several were listed and the respondent refused to rank them. An overall score was compiled for each factor as well as separate scores by poet group. Ranks were drawn from these scores, the factor with the most points being ranked first, and so on. Also shown for each group are lists of factors most often ranked first and most often mentioned at all.

19. He later moved on to the University of Colorado.

20. "Interview with Jan Garrett," in Philip Levine, *Don't Ask* (Ann Arbor: University of Michigan Press, 1981), p. 124.

21. William Stafford, "Whose Tradition?," in Stafford, *Writing the Australian Crawl: Views on the Writer's Vocation* (Ann Arbor: University of Michigan Press, 1978), p. 78.

CHAPTER 7

1. Eileen Simpson, *Poets in Their Youth* (New York: Random House, 1982), p. 32.

2. Thomas Parkinson, "On Getting Published," *Beyond Baroque* 3, no. 1 (1973): 14.

3. Noel Stock, *The Life of Ezra Pound* (New York: Pantheon, 1970), p. 29.

4. Malcolm Cowley, *Exile's Return: A Literary Odyssey of the 1920s* (New York: Penguin, 1982), p. 120.

5. Lowell said this in a speech to the Authors' League Banquet, New York, April 11, 1917; quoted in S. Foster Damon, *Amy Lowell: A Chronicle* (Boston: Houghton Mifflin, 1935), p. 349.

6. H[arriet] M[onroe], "Editorial Comment: Hard Times Indeed," *Poetry* 9 (March 1917): 308–12.

7. John Unterecker, *Voyager: A Life of Hart Crane* (New York: Farrar, Straus & Giroux, 1969), p. 404. The original version of "The Wine Menagerie" was restored and included in Crane's first collection, *White Buildings* (New York: Horace Liveright, 1926).

8. Joel Roache, *Richard Eberhart: The Progress of an American Poet* (New York: Oxford University Press, 1971).

9. James Atlas, *Delmore Schwartz: The Life of an American Poet* (New York: Farrar, Straus & Giroux, 1977); Allan Seager, *The Glass House: The Life of Theodore Roethke* (New York: McGraw-Hill, 1968).

10. David Brooks and Don Bredes, "An Interview with Galway Kinnell," *Colorado State Review* 5 (Fall 1977): 6.

11. Gregory Corso, "Some of My Beginning . . . and What I Feel Right Now," in *Poets on Poetry*, ed. Howard Nemerov (New York: Basic Books, 1966), p. 178.

12. [Harriet Monroe], "Announcement of Awards," *Poetry* 13 (November 1918): 108.

13. Robert Creeley, "Preface," in *Was That a Real Poem, and Other Essays*, ed. Donald Allen (Bolinas, Cal.: Four Seasons Foundation, 1979), p. 9.

14. Maxine Kumin, "An Interview at Interlochen," in *To Make a Prairie: Essays on Poets, Poetry, and Country Living* (Ann Arbor: University of Michigan Press, 1979), p. 44.

15. "Craft Interview with Gary Snyder," in *The Real Work: Interviews and Talks 1964–1979: Gary Snyder*, ed. William Scott McLean (New York: New Directions, 1980), pp. 37, 41.

16. Karla Hammond, "An Interview with Maxine Kumin," *Western Humanities Review* 33 (Winter 1979): 15.

17. Robert Bly, "In Search of An American Muse," *New York Times Book Review* (January 22, 1984): 29.

18. Brooks and Bredes, "An Interview with Galway Kinnell," pp. 5–6.

19. Jeanie Thompson, "A Concert of Tenses: An Interview with Tess Gallagher," *Ironwood* 14 (1979): 47.

20. Donald Allen, ed., *On Bread and Poetry: A Panel Discussion with Gary Snyder, Lew Welch, and Philip Whalen* (Bolinas, Cal.: Gray Fox Press, 1977), pp. 5–6.

21. "Craft Interview with Gary Snyder," *New York Quarterly* 22 (1978): 23.

22. Jan Clausen, *A Movement of Poets: Thoughts on Poetry and Feminism* (Brooklyn, N.Y.: Long Haul Press, 1982), p. 42.

23. Christopher Clausen, *The Place of Poetry: Two Centuries of an Art in Crisis* (Lexington: University Press of Kentucky, 1981); and Christopher Clausen, "Poetry in a Discouraging Time," *Georgia Review* 35 (Winter 1981): 703–15; In Peter Barry Chowka, "The East West Interview," in Snyder, *The Real Work*, p. 121.

24. Robert Frost, *The Letters of Robert Frost*, ed. Louis Untermeyer (New York: Holt, Rinehart & Winston, 1963), pp. 8–9.

25. Jan Clausen, *A Movement of Poets*, p. 42.

26. James Dickey, *Self-Interviews*, ed. Barbara Reiss and James Reiss (Garden City, N.Y.: Doubleday, 1970), p. 63.

27. For a discussion of the problem, as well as a reprinting of P.E.N.'s standards, see "More on Manuscripts and Manners," *Coda* 6 (June–July 1979): 19–20.

28. Stephen Minot, "Hey, Is Anyone Listening?" *North American Review* 262 (Spring 1977): 10.

29. Curtis Zahn, "Towards Print: (Anti-Social) Protest Literature," *Trace* 40 (January–March 1961): 5.

30. Linda Pastan, in "The Place of Poetry: Symposium Responses," *Georgia Review* 35 (Winter 1981): 734.

31. Robert Creeley and Emily Keller, "An Interview by Emily Keller," *American Poetry Review* (May–June 1983): 25.

32. Letter to Mary Biggs, October 17, 1981.

33. Mary Oliver, "For the Man Cutting the Grass," in "The Place of Poetry: Symposium Responses," *Georgia Review* 35 (Winter 1981): 730, 733.

34. Gary Snyder, "Poetry, Community and Climax," in Snyder, *The Real Work*, p. 169.

35. Cynthia Haythe, "An Interview with A. R. Ammons," *Contemporary Literature* 21 (Spring 1980): 181–182.

36. Quoted in *Mountain Summer*, vol. 2 (1975): back cover.

37. Quoted in Richard Kostelanetz, "John Ashbery," in Kostelanetz, *The Old Poetries and the New* (Ann Arbor: University of Michigan Press, 1981), p. 104.

38. The book was published in 1984 by Alfred A. Knopf.

39. Quoted in Donald Hall, "Poetry Food," in *Solitude and Silence: Writings on Robert Bly*, ed. Richard Jones and Kate Daniels (Boston: Beacon Press, 1981), p. 32.

40. The NBA was replaced in 1980 by The American Book Awards (TABA); the original name was restored in 1987. In 1984 the twenty-seven categories of these awards, which had been criticized as overly commercial, were streamlined to three: "Fiction," "Nonfiction," and "Best New Writer." Thus a new poet could, in theory, win a TABA, but not an experienced one. A few months later, novelist-critic Doris Grumbach, head judge of the "First Work" (i.e., best new writer) panel, and her two fellow judges, announced their intention to limit consideration to first works of fiction, because "a work culminating 30 years of scientific research cannot fairly be judged against a first work of fiction." They were permitted to do this, denying poets and playwrights any possibility of winning a TABA.

41. Richard Eberhart, *Of Poetry and Poets* (Urbana: University of Illinois Press, 1979), p. 289.

42. Michael Ryan, "An Interview with Alan Dugan," *Iowa Review* 4 (Summer 1973): 90–97; and Edward Nobles, "Alan Dugan: An Interview," *American Poetry Review* 12 (May–June 1983): 4–15.

43. Ryan, "An Interview with Alan Dugan," pp. 92–93.

44. In *Poetspeak: In Their Work, About Their Work*, ed. Paul B. Janeczko (Scarsdale, N.Y.: Bradbury Press, 1983), p. 217.

45. Ginsberg was the only Older Prizewinner to have the same publisher for his first and, as of the end of 1981, most recent full-length book.

46. Genevieve Stuttaford, "PW Interviews: Allen Ginsberg," *Publishers Weekly* (November 14, 1977): 6.

47. In Hammond, "An Interview with Maxine Kumin," p. 15.

48. "Interview with Calvin Bedient," in Philip Levine, *Don't Ask* (Ann Arbor: University of Michigan Press, 1981), p. 106.

49. Quoted in Langston Hughes, *The Big Sea: An Autobiography* (New York: Alfred A. Knopf, 1940), p. 213.

50. Robinson Jeffers, "Let Them Alone," in *"The Beginnning & the End" and Other Poems* (New York: Random House, 1963), p. 35.

51. Simpson, *Poets in Their Youth*, p. 87.

52. Andrei Vosnesensky and Allen Ginsberg, "Andrei Vosnesensky and Allen Ginsberg: A Conversation," *Paris Review* 22 (Summer 1980): 157. The "conversation," which also included Peter Orlovsky, occurred on December 28, 1979.

53. Len Fulton and Bob Fay, "An Interview with Louis Simpson [Part 1]," *Dust* 1 (Fall 1964): 4.

54. Helena Minton et al., "James Tate," in *American Poetry Observed: Poets on Their Work*, ed. Joe David Bellamy (Urbana: University of Illinois Press, 1984), p. 249.

55. Joan Norris, "An Interview with Maxine Kumin," *Crazy Horse*, no. 16 (Summer 1975): 21.

56. David Dillon, "Toward Passionate Utterance: An Interview with W. D. Snodgrass," *Southwest Review* (Summer 1975): 284.

57. William Heyen and Gregory Fitz Gerald, " 'No Voices Talk to Me': A Conversation with W. D. Snodgrass," *Western Humanities Review* 24 (Winter 1970): 65.

58. Ron McFarland, "An Interview with James Dickey," *Slackwater Review* 3 (Winter 1979/80): 21.

59. Arthur Smith and Philip Levine, "Poetry and Politics [interview]," *Stand* 17, no. 4 (1976): 40, in Levine, *Don't Ask*.

60. Quoted in Damon, *Amy Lowell*, p. 349.

61. Kathleen Norris, "400 Miles to the Nearest Poetry Reading," *Coda* (March 1984): 14–15.

62. William Childress, "Mona Van Duyn," *Poetry Now*, no. 17 (1975): 37.

63. Quoted in T. S. Matthews, *Great Tom: Notes Toward the Definition of T. S. Eliot* (New York: Harper & Row, 1974), p. 174.

64. In William Packard, ed., *The Craft of Poetry: Interviews from "The New York Quarterly"* (Garden City, N.Y.: Doubleday, 1974), pp. 139, 151. (Dickey's sole novel had been *Deliverance*, which had become a bestseller and the basis of a hit movie. In 1987 Doubleday published his second novel, an experimental work entitled *Alnilam*. It did not seem to aim for, and did not achieve, the popular success enjoyed by *Deliverance*.)

65. Oliver, "For the Man Cutting the Grass," p. 733.

66. Marvin Bell, "The Impure Every Time," in Donald Allen, ed., *Claims for Poetry* (Ann Arbor: University of Michigan Press, 1982), p. 11.

CHAPTER 8

1. Telephone interview with Marion Stocking, February 2, 1989. (Interviews conducted for this chapter are noted only the first time that they are cited.)

2. Joseph Barbato, " 'Going Through Life with a Pencil': Carolyn Kizer," *Small Press* (November–December 1985): 54–48.

3. Interview with Marilyn Hacker, February 10, 1989.

4. Telephone interview with Diana Ó Hehir, February 10, 1989.

5. Telephone interview with Gerald Stern, February 13, 1989.

6. In some cases, interviewees are not identified in order to protect their privacy. Twenty-three interviews were conducted, all in February 1989, all with

poetry editors, poetry publishers, or with poets who participated in the original study. Interviews ranged in length from thirty minutes to two hours.

7. Len Fulton, ed., *International Directory of Little Magazines and Small Presses*, 23rd ed. (Paradise, Cal.: Dustbooks, 1987).

8. Coordinating Council of Literary Magazines, *1988–89 Directory of Literary Magazines* (Mt. Kisco, N.Y.: Moyer Bell Limited, 1988).

9. Fulton, ed., *International Directory of Little Magazines and Small Presses*, p. 177.

10. Telephone interview with John Gill, February 10, 1989.

11. Telephone interview with Ed Ochester, February 14, 1989.

12. Telephone interview with Robert Hass, February 15, 1989.

13. Telephone interview with Theodore Enslin, February 10, 1989.

14. Roya Camp, "Sun & Moon in Los Angeles," *Small Press* 5 (June 1988): 19.

15. In *Against the Grain: Interviews with Maverick American Publishers*, ed. Robert Dana (Iowa City: University of Iowa Press, 1986), p. 36.

16. Telephone interview with Gerald Stern, February 13, 1989. See also Gerald Stern, "What is this Poet?" in *What is a Poet?: Essays from the Eleventh Alabama Symposium on English and American Literature*, ed. Hank Lazer (Tuscaloosa: University of Alabama Press, 1987), pp. 145–56.

17. Fielding Dawson, in "Ten Years: Where From, Where To?" *American Book Review* 10 (March–April 1988): A–2.

18. Telephone interview with Philip Levine, February 3, 1989.

19. Telephone interview with Roger Aplon, February 6, 1989.

20. For example, see Donald Hall, "Poetry and Ambition," in *What is a Poet?* pp. 229–46; For example, telephone interview with Kenneth Rosen, February 7, 1989.

21. Letter from James Grabill to Mary Biggs, February 6, 1989.

22. Telephone interview with Bin Ramke, February 6, 1989.

23. Telephone interview with toi derricotte, February 15, 1989.

24. For example, see, Hall, "Poetry and Ambition," p. 241; and Liam Rector, "Donald Hall: An Interview," *American Poetry Review* 18 (January–February 1989): 42.

25. Jed Rasula, "To Moisten the Atmosphere: Notes on Clayton Eshleman," *Temblor*, no. 6 (1987): 105.

26. For example, Hacker interview; Enslin interview; Hall, "Poetry and Ambition"; Nathaniel Tarn, in Lee Bartlett, *Talking Poetry: Conversations in the Workshop with Contemporary Poets* (Albuquerque: University of New Mexico Press, 1987), p. 226.

27. In *Against the Grain*, p. 138.

28. Telephone interview with Scott Walker, February 17, 1989.

29. Thom Gunn in Bartlett, *Talking Poetry*, p. 90; William Everson in Bartlett, *Talking Poetry*, pp. 75–76; Allen Ginsberg in Linda Hamalian, "Allen Ginsberg in the Eighties," *Literary Review* 29 (Spring 1986): 296; Michael Palmer in Bartlett, *Talking Poetry*, p. 128; Hass interview; telephone interview with Linda Pastan, February 4, 1989; Ochester interview; Paul Zimmer in *What is the Future of Poetry?* (Sheboygan, Wis.: Seems Magazine, no. 14, 1983), p. 39; Robert von Hallberg, *American Poetry and Culture* (Cambridge, Mass.: Harvard University Press, 1985), pp. 10–17.

30. Gill interview; Walker interview; Jack Shoemaker quoted in Christopher Lehmann-Haupt, "Critic's Notebook: Are Books Becoming Relics?" *New York Times* (January 2, 1989): 15; Jonathan Williams in *Against the Grain*, p. 225; Diane Wakoski in Bartlett, *Talking Poetry*, p. 240; Brad Leithauser, "Hard Times in the Mail Order Poetry Business," *New York Times Book Review* (August 18, 1985): 27; Joseph Epstein, "Who Killed Poetry?" *Commentary* 86 (August 1988): 13–20.

31. Telephone interview with Joseph Parisi, February 8, 1989.

32. "Stephen Goodwin of the NEA: A Talk with the New Director of the Literature Program," *Small Press* (April 1988): 44–47. For example, with regard to *Beloit Poetry Journal*, interview with Stocking; and with regard to *Slow Motion*, telephone interview with Zack Rogow, February 11, 1989.

33. Telephone interview with Beth O'Rourke, March 16, 1989.

34. Joseph Bruchac, "The Decline and Fall of Prison Literature," *Small Press* 4 (January–February 1987): 28–32.

APPENDIX

1. Prizes were chosen for use as poet-selection criteria based on information in Olga Weber and Stephen J. Calvert, *Literary and Library Prizes* (New York: R. R. Bowker, 1980). The following award lists were also consulted and winners tabulated; originally, these prizes were to be used as criteria. They were eliminated because (through 1979) they were redundant—that is, using them would not have added any poets to the prizewinning groups: Academy of American Poets Fellowship, Award of Merit Medal, Harriet Monroe Poetry Award, and National Book Critics' Circle Award.

2. Laura Gilpin, who won the Walt Whitman Award in 1976, was deleted from the study because too little information could be obtained about her publication history, and she did not respond when contacted.

3. Hacker's first poetry book, published in 1967, was privately printed and very narrowly distributed.

4. Klappert's first published work was a short pamphlet of poems not uncovered by my bibliographic search, but called to my attention by the poet. Evidently, it was not considered a "book" by the Yale Younger Poets Series, which would have disqualified him from competing for the series' distinction if it had been.

5. In a few cases, a pre–1970 poetry book publication was discovered after much bibliographical investigation of a poet's career history had already been completed. In most cases, the poet drew this publication to my attention when returning a completed questionnaire. If the book in question was the only pre–1970 book publication, preceded that date by no more than three years, and was not widely distributed, the poet was retained as part of the NN-group.

6. In a few cases, a poet with a long history of publishing poetry in literary journals turned out not to have authored a first poetry book until after 1965, but before 1970. Partly because these poets' careers seemed rather comparable, in broad outline, to those of the Older Prizewinners, and partly because of the ON-group's relatively small size, some of these poets were retained in that group.

Bibliography

My most important sources of information were the poets themselves, who gave generously of their time, completing questionnaires, verifying data, and, in some cases, writing letters and giving interviews. Several publishers and editors also kindly submitted to interviews. By using indexes, card catalogs, computer databases, and personally examining thousands of issues of hundreds of literary magazines, I compiled the bibliographic information that allowed me to analyze the poets' publication patterns. Complete lists of these magazines and of the libraries and reference works consulted are appended to my Ph.D. dissertation: "The Publishing of American Poetry, 1950–1980" (University of Chicago, 1986).

Below is a selective list of books, articles, and poems that informed my research.

POEMS

cummings, e. e. " 'let's start a magazine.' " In *No Thanks*, p. 24. New York: Golden Eagle Press, 1935.

Dacey, Philip. "Form Rejection Letter." In *The Poet's Choice: 100 American Poets' Favorite Poems*, edited by George E. Murphy, Jr., pp. 45–46. Green Harbor, MA: Tendril, Inc., 1980.

Dobyns, Stephen. "Katia Reading." In *The Balthus Poems*, pp. 36–37. New York: Atheneum, 1982.

Gilbert, Jack. "In Dispraise of Poetry." In *Monolithos: Poems, 1962 and 1982*, p. 19. Port Townsend, WA: Graywolf Press, 1982.

Jeffers, Robinson. "Let Them Alone." In *"The Beginning and the End" and Other Poems*, p. 35. New York: Random House, 1963.

Kizer, Gary Allan. "To Poets." *Gravida* 16 (1979): 29.

Lifshin, Lyn. "You Understand the Requirements." In *Black Apples*, 2d ed., pp. 36–37.

Lopate, Phillip. "The Little Magazines Keep Coming." *Little Magazine* 7 (Fall 1973): 26–28.

Piercy, Marge. "The Poet Dreams of a Nice Warm Motel," pp. 24–26, and "Sacramento, Colorado Springs, Geneva, Middlebury," pp. 39–40. In *Twelve-Spoked Wheel Flashing*. New York: Alfred A. Knopf, 1978.

———. "Three Weeks in a State of Loneliness." In *Living in the Open*, pp. 56–57. New York: Alfred A. Knopf, 1976.

Stafford, William. "After Arguing Against the Contention that Art Must Come From Discontent," p. 64, and "A Course in Creative Writing," p. 65. In *A Glass Face in the Rain*. New York: Harper & Row, 1982.

Books, Pamphlets, and Dissertations

Ackroyd, Peter. *Ezra Pound and His World*. New York: Scribner's, 1980.

Allen, Donald, ed. *Claims for Poetry*. Ann Arbor: University of Michigan Press, 1982.

———. *Contexts of Poetry: Interviews 1961–1971*. Bolinas, CA: Four Seasons Foundation, 1973.

———. *On Bread and Poetry: A Panel Discussion with Gary Snyder, Lew Welch, and Philip Whalen*. Bolinas, CA: Grey Fox Press, 1977.

Anderson, Elliott, and Kinzie, Mary, eds. *The Little Magazine in America: A Modern Documentary History*. Yonkers, NY: Pushcart Press, 1978.

Anderson, Margaret. *My Thirty Years' War*. New York: Covici Friede, 1930.

———, ed. *The Little Review Anthology*. New York: Horizon Press, 1953.

Armstrong, David. *A Trumpet to Arms: Alternative Media in America*. Los Angeles: J. P. Tarcher, 1981.

Atlas, James. *Delmore Schwartz: The Life of an American Poet*. New York: Farrar, Straus & Giroux, 1977.

Baker, Denys Val. *Little Reviews, 1914–1943*. London: George Allen & Unwin, 1943.

Bartlett, Lee. *Talking Poetry: Conversations in the Workshop with Contemporary Poets*. Albuquerque: University of New Mexico Press, 1987.

Bellamy, Joe David, ed. *American Poetry Observed: Poets on Their Work*. Urbana: University of Illinois Press, 1984.

Bennett, Melba Berry. *The Stone Mason of Tor House: The Life and Work of Robinson Jeffers*. Pasadena, CA: Ward Ritchie Press, 1966.

Biggs, Mary. "The Publishing of American Poetry, 1950–1980." Ph.D. diss., University of Chicago, 1986.

Bogan, Louise. *What the Woman Lived: Selected Letters of Louise Bogan, 1920–1970*. Edited by Ruth Limmer. New York: Harcourt Brace Jovanovich, 1973.

Boyers, Robert, ed. *Contemporary Poetry in America: Essays and Interviews*. New York: Schocken Books, 1974.

Bruchac, Joseph. *How to Start and Sustain a Literary Magazine: Practical Strategies for Publications of Lasting Value*. Austin, TX: Provision House, 1980.

Cahill, Daniel J. *Harriet Monroe*. New York: Twayne Publishers, 1973.

Callaghan, Morley. *That Summer in Paris: Memories of Tangled Friendships with Hemingway, Fitzgerald, and Some Others*. New York: Coward, McCann, 1963.

Charters, Ann, ed. *Dictionary of Literary Biography*. Volume 16: *The Beats: Literary Bohemians in Postwar America*. Detroit: Gale Research Co., 1983.

Charvat, William. *Literary Publishing in America, 1790–1850*. Philadelphia: University of Pennsylvania Press, 1959.

Cheney, Anne. *Millay in Greenwich Village*. University: University of Alabama Press, 1975.

Clark, Tom. *The Great Naropa Poetry Wars*. Santa Barbara, CA: Cadmus Editions, 1980.

Clausen, Christopher. *The Place of Poetry: Two Centuries of an Art in Crisis*. Lexington: University Press of Kentucky, 1981.

Clausen, Jan. *A Movement of Poets: Thoughts of Poetry and Feminism*. Brooklyn, NY: Long Haul Press, 1982.

Clifton, Merritt. *On Small Press as Class Struggle*, 4th ed. High Ridge, MO: Blue Pentacle Press, 1976.

Clifton, Robin Michelle. *The Pillory Poetics*, 3d ed. Richford, VT: Samisdat, [n.d.].

Cowley, Malcolm. *Exile's Return: A Literary Odyssey of the 1920s*. New York: Penguin, 1982.

________. *A Second Flowering: Works and Days of the Lost Generation*. New York: Viking Press, 1973.

Crane, Hart. *The Letters of Hart Crane, 1916–1932*, edited by Brom Weber. Berkeley: University of California Press, 1952.

Creeley, Robert. *Was That a Real Poem, and Other Essays*. Edited by Donald Allen. Bolinas, CA: Four Seasons Foundation, 1979.

cummings, e. e. *Selected Letters of e. e. cummings*. Edited by F. W. Dupee and George Stode. New York: Harcourt Brace & World, 1969.

Curley, Daniel; Scouffas, George; and Shattuck, Charles, eds. *Accent: An Anthology, 1940–1960*. Urbana: University of Illinois Press, 1973.

Damon, S. Foster. *Amy Lowell: A Chronicle*. Boston: Houghton Mifflin, 1935.

Dana, Robert, ed. *Against the Grain: Interviews with Maverick American Publishers*. Iowa City: University of Iowa Press, 1986.

Davis, Thadious M., and Harris, Trudier, eds. *Dictionary of American Literary Biography*. Volume 41: *Afro–American Poets Since 1955*. Detroit: Gale Research Co., 1985.

Dickey, James. *Babel to Byzantium: Poets and Poetry Now*. New York: Ecco Press, 1981.

________. *Self–Interviews*. Edited by Barbara Reiss and James Reiss. Garden City, NY: Doubleday, 1970.

Dickinson, Donald C. *A Bio–Bibliography of Langston Hughes, 1902–1967*. New York: Archon Books, 1967.

Dowden, George, comp. *A Bibliography of Works by Allen Ginsberg, October, 1943 to July 1, 1967*. San Francisco: City Lights Books, 1971.

Dzwonkoski, Peter, ed. *Dictionary of Literary Biography*. Volume 46: *American Literary Publishing Houses, 1900–1980: Trade and Paperback*. Detroit: Gale Research, 1986.

Eberhart, Richard. *Of Poetry and Poets*. Urbana: University of Illinois Press, 1979.

Edelson, Morris. "Six Little Magazines." Ph.D. diss., University of Wisconsin, 1973.

Elledge, Jim. *James Dickey: A Bibliography, 1947–1974*. Metuchen, NJ: Scarecrow Press, 1979.

Faas, Ekbert. *Towards an American Poetics: Essays and Interviews*. Santa Barbara, CA: Black Sparrow Press, 1979.

Farley, Kathleen. *Poetry Magazine: A Gallery of Voices: An Exhibition from the Harriet Monroe Modern Poetry Collection, The Joseph Regenstein Library, The University of Chicago, May–October 1980*. Chicago: University of Chicago Library, 1980.

Fitch, Noel Riley. *Sylvia Beach and the Lost Generation*. New York: W. W. Norton, 1983.

Foley, Martha. *The Story of "Story" Magazine*. New York: W. W. Norton, 1980.

Ford, Hugh. *Published in Paris: American and British Writers, Printers, and Publishers in Paris, 1920–1939*. Yonkers, NY: Pushcart Press, 1975.

Francis, Robert. *Pot Shots at Poetry*. Ann Arbor: University of Michigan Press, 1980.

Frost, Robert. *The Letters of Robert Frost to Louis Untermeyer*. Edited by Louis Untermeyer. New York: Holt, Rinehart & Winston, 1963.

Galway Kinnell: A Bibliography and Index of His Published Works and Criticism of Them. Potsdam, NY: Frederick W. Crumb Memorial Library, State University College, 1968.

Gilmer, Walker. *Horace Liveright: Publisher of the Twenties*. New York: David Lewis, 1970.

Ginsberg, Allen. *Allen Verbatim: Lectures on Poetry, Politics, Consciousness*. Edited by Gordon Ball. New York: McGraw-Hill, 1974.

Glancy, Eileen. *James Dickey, the Critic as Poet: An Annotated Bibliography with an Introductory Essay*. Troy, NY: Whitston Publishing Co., 1971.

Glessing, Ronald J. *The Underground Press in America*. Bloomington: Indiana University Press, 1970.

Goodman, Michael Barry. *Contemporary Literary Censorship: The Case History of Burroughs' "The Naked Lunch."* Metuchen, NJ: Scarecrow Press, 1981.

Gould, Jean. *Amy: The World of Amy Lowell and the Imagist Movement*. New York: Dodd, Mead, 1975.

———. *The Poet and Her Book: A Biography of Edna St. Vincent Millay*. New York: Dodd, Mead, 1969.

Grant, Joy. *Harold Monro and the Poetry Bookshop*. Berkeley: University of California Press, 1967.

Greiner, Donald J., ed. *Dictionary of Literary Biography*. Volume 5: *American Poets Since World War II*. Detroit: Gale Research, 1980.

Halpert, Stephen, with Johns, Richard. *A Return to "Pagany": The History, Correspondence, and Selections from a Little Magazine, 1929–1932*. Boston: Beacon Press, 1969.

Hart, James D. *The Popular Book: A History of America's Literary Taste*. Berkeley: University of California Press, 1950.

Hemingway, Ernest. *A Moveable Feast*. New York: Scribner's, 1964.

Henderson, Bill, ed. *The Art of Literary Publishing: Editors on Their Craft*. Yonkers, NY: Pushcart Press, 1980.

Hoffman, Frederick J.; Allen, Charles; and Ulrich, Carolyn F. *The Little Magazine: A History and a Bibliography*. Princeton, NJ: Princeton University Press, 1946.

Howard, Richard. *Alone with America: Essays on the Art of Poetry in the United States Since 1950*. New York: Atheneum, 1969.

Hubbell, Jay B. *Who Are the Major American Writers?* Durham, NC: Duke University Press, 1972.

Hughes, Langston. *The Big Sea: An Autobiography*. New York: Alfred A. Knopf, 1940.

Jackson, Richard. *Acts of Mind: Conversations with Contemporary Poets*. University: University of Alabama Press, 1983.

Janeczko, Paul B., ed. *Poetspeak: In Their Work, About Their Work*. Scarsdale, NY: Bradbury Press, 1983.

Jones, Richard, and Daniels, Kate, eds. *Of Solitude and Silence: Writings on Robert Bly*. Boston: Beacon Press, 1981.

Joost, Nicholas. *Years of Transition: The Dial, 1912–1920*. Barre, MA: Barre Publishers, 1967.

Kennedy, Richard S. *Dreams in the Mirror: A Biography of e. e. cummings*. New York: Liveright, 1980.

Kermani, David K. *John Ashbery: A Comprehensive Bibliography Including His Art Criticism and with Selected Notes from Unpublished Material*. New York: Garland, 1976.

Kherdian, David. *A Biographical Sketch and Descriptive Checklist of Gary Snyder*. Berkeley, CA: Oyez, 1965.

Kinnell, Galway. *Walking Down the Stairs: Selections from Interviews*. Ann Arbor: University of Michigan, 1978.

Kirk, Russell. *Eliot and His Age: T. S. Eliot's Moral Imagination in the Twentieth Century*. New York: Random House, 1971.

Kostelanetz, Richard. *"The End" Essentials; "Intelligent Writing" Epitomized; "The End" Appendix; "Intelligent Writing" Reconsidered*. Brooklyn, NY: Assembling, 1978.

————. *The End of Intelligent Writing: Literary Politics in America*. New York: Sheed & Ward, 1974.

————. *The Old Poetries and the New*. Ann Arbor: University of Michigan Press, 1981.

Kramer, Jane. *Allen Ginsberg in America*. New York: Random House, 1969.

Kraus, Michelle P. *Allen Ginsberg: An Annotated Bibliography, 1969–1977*. Metuchen, NJ: Scarecrow Press, 1980.

Kruchkow, Diane, and Johnson, Curt, eds. *Green Isle in the Sea: An Informal History of the Alternative Press, 1960–1985*. Highland Park, IL: December Press, 1986.

Kumin, Maxine. *To Make a Prairie: Essays on Poets, Poetry, and Country Living*. Ann Arbor: University of Michigan Press, 1979.

Lathem, Edward Connery, ed. *Interviews with Robert Frost*. New York: Holt, Rinehart & Winston, 1966.

Lazer, Hank, ed. *What is a Poet?: Essays from the Eleventh Alabama Symposium on English and American Literature*. University: University of Alabama Press, 1987.

Levine, Philip. *Don't Ask*. Ann Arbor: University of Michigan Press, 1981.

Lewis, Thomas S. W., ed. *Letters of Hart Crane and His Family*. New York: Columbia University Press, 1974.

Macy, John, ed. *American Writers on American Literature: By Thirty–Seven Contemporary Writers*. New York: Horace Liveright, 1931.

Mangelsdorff, Rich. *Selected Essays of Rich Mangelsdorff*. Paradise, CA: Dustbooks, 1977.

Mariani, Paul. *William Carlos Williams: A New World Naked*. New York: McGraw–Hill, 1981.

Matthews, T. S. *Great Tom: Notes Toward the Definition of T. S. Eliot*. New York: Harper & Row, 1974.

May, James Boyer. *Twigs as Varied Bent: The Recent Part of Little Magazines in Literature*. Corona, NY: Sparrow Magazine, 1954.

McAlmon, Robert, and Boyle, Kay. *Being Geniuses Together, 1920–1930*. Garden City, NY: Doubleday, 1968.

Mikolyzk, Thomas A. "*The Beloit Poetry Journal*, 1949–1986." Master's thesis, University of Chicago, 1986.

Molesworth, Charles. *The Fierce Embrace: A Study of Contemporary American Poetry*. Columbia: University of Missouri Press, 1979.

Monroe, Harriet. *A Poet's Life: Seventy Years in a Changing World*. New York: Macmillan, 1938.

Morgan, Ted. *Literary Outlaw: The Life and Times of William Burroughs*. New York: Henry Holt, 1988.

Nemerov, Howard, ed. *Poets on Poetry*. New York: Basic Books, 1966.

Norman, Charles. *The Magic-Maker: e. e. cummings*. New York: Macmillan, 1958.

Novik, Mary. *Robert Creeley: An Inventory, 1945–1970*. Kent, OH: Kent State University Press, 1973.

Nye, Russel. *The Unembarrassed Muse: The Popular Arts in America*. New York: Dial Press, 1970.

Packard, William, ed. *The Craft of Poetry: Interviews from "The New York Quarterly."* Garden City, NY: Doubleday, 1974.

Peabody, Richard, ed. *Mavericks: Nine Independent Publishers*. Washington, DC: Paycock Press, 1983.

Peck, Abe. *Uncovering the Sixties: The Life and Times of the Underground Press*. New York: Pantheon, 1985.

Penkower, Monty Noam. *The Federal Writers' Project: A Study in Government Patronage of the Arts*. Urbana: University of Illinois Press, 1977.

Perry, Margaret. *A Bio–Bibliography of Countee Cullen, 1903–1946*. Westport, CT: Greenwood Press, 1971.

Poli, Bernard J. *Ford Madox Ford and the "Transatlantic Review."* Syracuse, NY: Syracuse University Press, 1967.

The Publication of Poetry and Fiction: A Conference Held at the Library of Congress, October 20 and 21, 1975. Washington, DC: Library of Congress, 1977.

Putnam, Samuel. *Paris Was Our Mistress: Memoirs of a Lost and Found Generation.* New York: Viking Press, 1947.

Quartermain, Peter, ed. *Dictionary of Literary Biography.* Volume 45: *American Poets, 1880–1945.* Detroit: Gale Research Co., 1986.

Reck, Michael. *Ezra Pound: A Close–Up.* New York: McGraw-Hill, 1967.

Rich, Adrienne. *On Lies, Secrets, and Silence: Selected Prose, 1966–1978.* New York: W. W. Norton, 1979.

Roache, Joel. *Richard Eberhart: The Progress of an American Poet.* New York: Oxford University Press, 1971.

Roethke, Theodore. *Selected Letters of Theodore Roethke.* Edited by Ralph J. Mills, Jr. Seattle: University of Washington Press, 1968.

Rood, Karen Lane, ed. *Dictionary of Literary Biography.* Volume 4: *American Writers in Paris, 1920–1939.* Detroit: Gale Research Co., 1980.

Ruggles, Eleanor. *The West–Going Heart: A Life of Vachel Lindsay.* New York: W. W. Norton, 1959.

Seager, Allan. *The Glass House: The Life of Theodore Roethke.* New York: McGraw-Hill, 1968.

Shatzkin, Leonard. *In Cold Type: Overcoming the Book Crisis.* Boston: Houghton Mifflin, 1982.

Simpson, Eileen. *Poets in Their Youth.* New York: Random House, 1982.

Smythe, Daniel. *Robert Frost Speaks.* New York: Twayne Publishers, 1964.

Snyder, Gary. *The Real Work: Interviews and Talks 1964–1979: Gary Snyder.* Edited by William Scott McLean. New York: New Directions, 1980.

Stafford, William. *Writing the Australian Crawl: Views on the Writer's Vocation.* Ann Arbor: University of Michigan Press, 1978.

Steuding, Bob. *Gary Snyder.* Boston: Twayne Publishers, 1976.

Stewart, Paul R. *The "Prairie Schooner" Story: A Little Magazine's First Twenty–Five Years.* Lincoln: University of Nebraska Press, 1953.

Stock, Noel. *The Life of Ezra Pound.* New York: Pantheon, 1970.

Strand, Mark; Armand, Octavio; and Brooks, David. *Mark Strand: A Profile.* Iowa City: Grilled Flowers Press, 1979.

Swallow, Alan. *An Editor's Essays of Two Decades.* Seattle: Experiment Press, 1962.

Tebbel, John. *A History of Book Publishing in the United States.* Volume 4: *The Great Change, 1940–1980.* New York: R. R. Bowker, 1981.

Thompson, Lawrance. *Robert Frost: The Early Years, 1874–1915,* and *Robert Frost: The Years of Triumph, 1915–1938.* New York: Holt, Rinehart & Winston, 1966 and 1970.

Unterecker, John. *Voyager: A Life of Hart Crane.* New York: Farrar, Straus & Giroux, 1969.

Vinson, James, ed. *Contemporary Poets.* 3d ed. New York: St. Martin's Press, 1980.

von Hallberg, Robert. *American Poetry and Culture, 1945–1980.* Cambridge, MA: Harvard University Press, 1985.

What is the Future of Poetry? Sheboygan, WI: Seems Magazine, 1983.

Whiteside, Thomas. *The Blockbuster Complex.* Middletown, CT: Wesleyan University Press, 1982.

Whittemore, Reed. *William Carlos Williams: Poet from Jersey.* Boston: Houghton Mifflin, 1975.

Wilbers, Stephen. *The Iowa Writers' Workshop: Origins, Emergence, Growth*. Iowa City: University of Iowa Press, 1980.

Williams, Ellen. *Harriet Monroe and the Poetry Renaissance: The First Ten Years of "Poetry," 1912–22*. Urbana: University of Illinois Press, 1977.

Williams, William Carlos. *I Wanted to Write a Poem: The Autobiography of the Works of a Poet*. Edited by Edith Heal. Boston: Beacon Press, 1958.

Wilson, Robert, comp. *A Bibliography of Works by Gregory Corso, 1954–1965*. New York: Phoenix Book Shop, 1966.

Wolff, Geoffrey. *Black Sun: The Brief Transit and Violent Eclipse of Harry Crosby*. New York: Random House, 1976.

Wright, Stuart. *A. R. Ammons: A Bibliography, 1954–1979*. Winston–Salem, NC: Wake Forest University Press, 1980.

Articles

"Aid to Writers and Publishers with Dependent Publications (A Tale)." *Contraband*, no. 12 (February 1976): front cover, inside front cover, inside back cover.

Aldridge, John W. "The Writer's Demotion to Solid-Citizen Status." *Saturday Review* 54 (September 18, 1971): 35–36, 39–40, 81–82.

"Alice James Books Now in Tenth Year." *News from Alice James Books* (Spring 1983): 1–2.

"All Quiet on the Mimeograph Front." *Snowy Egret* 21 (Spring 1956): 1.

Allen, Charles. "The Little Magazine in America: 1945–70." *American Libraries* 3 (October 1972): 964–71.

Amirkhanian, Charles, and Gitin, David. "A Conversation with George Oppen." *Ironwood* 5 (1975): 21–24.

Anania, Michael. "Of Living Belfry and Rampart: On American Literary Magazines Since 1950." In *The Little Magazine in America: A Modern Documentary History*, edited by Elliott Anderson and Mary Kinzie, pp. 6–23. Yonkers, NY: Pushcart Press, 1978.

"And See if the Voice Will Enter You: An Interview with Philip Levine." *Ohio Review* 16 (Winter 1975): 45–63.

[Anderson, Margaret]. "Announcement." *Little Review* 1 (March 1914): [1]–2.

________. "Editorial." *Little Review* 12 (May 1929): 3–4.

________. "Editorials and Announcements: Our Credo." *Little Review* 2 (June–July 1915): 36.

________. "Our First Year." *Little Review* 1 (February 1915): [1]–6.

________. "A Real Magazine." *Little Review* 3 (August 1916): [1]–2.

Appelbaum, Judith. "Small Publisher Power: New Perspectives on the Big Publishing Picture." *Publishers Weekly* 222 (September 10, 1982): 23–26, 28–30, 32–34, 36–38, 40–41, 44–46, 48–51.

________, ed. "The Question of Size in the Book Industry Today." *Publishers Weekly* 214 (July 31, 1978): 25–50.

"Are There 1,000 People in America Who Will Give $5 Apiece to Our Fund?" *Little Review* 7 (May–June 1920): 76–77.

Arnold, June. "Feminist Presses and Feminist Politics." *Quest: A Feminist Quarterly* 3 (Summer 1976): 18–26.

Ashley, Franklin. "James Dickey: The Art of Poetry XX." *Paris Review* 17 (Spring 1976): 52–88.

Balakian, Nona. "Poets, Printers, and Pamphleteers." In *Critical Encounters: Literary Views and Reviews, 1953–1977*, pp. 239–42. Indianapolis: Bobbs-Merrill, 1978

Baldwin, Neil. "Full Court Press." *Small Press* 1 (September–October 1983): 58–62.

————. "Poets & Writers and Galen Williams." *Small Press* 3 (May–June 1986): 42–45.

Banks, Russell. "Some Thoughts on Being a 'Small Press' Publisher." *Works* 2 (Spring 1969): 72–73.

————and M[atthews], W[illiam]. "From the Editors." *Lillabulero* 9 (Summer–Fall 1970): unnumbered front page.

Barbato, Joseph. "Black Sparrow: The House a Poet [Charles Bukowski] Helped to Build." *Publishers Weekly* 232 (October 23, 1987): 26–27.

————. " 'Going Through Life with a Pencil': Carolyn Kizer." *Small Press* 2 (November–December 1985): 54–58.

————. "The Small Press Promotion Project." *Small Press* 2 (September–October 1984): 74–77.

Barnett, Allen. "The Chapbook: A Slender Volume of Poems." *Coda* 10 (June–July 1983): 1, 8–10.

Barth, John. "Writing: Can It Be Taught?" *New York Times Book Review* (June 16, 1985): 1, 36–37.

Beacham, Walton. "Finding Poets Publishers." *Scholarly Publishing* 9 (January 1978): 159–66.

Bedient, Calvin. "An Interview with Philip Levine." *Parnassus* 6 (Spring–Summer 1978): 40–51.

[Bennett, John.] "The Lay of the Land (Or: Every Farmer Needs a Good Piece of Earth)." *Vagabond*, no. 27 (Spring 1978): [2–3].

————. "Letter of Resignation – COSMEP." *Margins*, nos. 24–26 (1975): 4–5.

————. "Why Poetry is Dangerous." *North Country Anvil*, no. 15 (August–September 1975): 69–70.

Bernikow, Louise. "Out of the Bell Jar." *New Times* 7 (October 29, 1976): 46–47, 49–54.

Biggs, Mary. "Academic Publishing and Poetry." *Scholarly Publishing* 17 (October 1985): 3–23.

————. "From Harriet Monroe to *AQ*: Selected Women's Literary Journals, 1912–1972." *13th Moon: A Feminist Literary Journal* 8 (1984): 183–216.

————. "Small Press: A Bibliographic Essay, Part 1" and "Part 2." *Choice* 23 (September 1985 and October 1985): 55–70 and 253–65.

————. "Trade Publishing and Poetry." *Book Research Quarterly* 1 (February 1985): 162–74.

————. "Women's Literary Journals." *Library Quarterly* 53 (January 1983): 1–25.

Blooston, George. "A Firm Where Fine Taste in Literature Transcends All Else [Ecco Press]." *Publishers Weekly* 222 (July 30, 1982): 45–46.

________. "Honor Without Profit." *Publishers Weekly* 224 (August 12, 1983): 48–52.

________. "The Odds Against Poets." *Publishers Weekly* 224 (August 12, 1983): 50.

Bly, Robert. "In Search of an American Muse." *New York Times Book Review* (January 22, 1984): 1, 29.

________. "Robert Bly on the Obsession with Early Publishing." *Coda* 8 (June–July 1981): 25.

________. "The Sixties Press." *Works* 2 (Spring 1969): 74–75.

________. and Duffy, William. [Editorial Statement.] *The Fifties* 1, no. 1 (1958): inside front cover.

________, *et al.* "Discussions During the Spring Poetry Festival, Martin, April 16–17, 1971." *Tennessee Poetry Journal* 4 (Spring 1971): 11–35.

Bodenheim, Maxwell. "American Menagerie." *Little Review* 12 (May 1929): 99–106.

________. "Correspondence: Words from a Departing Poet." *Poetry* 16 (July 1920): 227–29.

Bourjaily, Vance. "Notes on the Starting of Magazines." *December* 1 (1958): 4–6.

Bradley, Sam. "Reciprocity vs. Suicide: An Interview with William Stafford." *Trace* 46 (Summer 1962): 223–26.

Brewer, Daryln. "Poetry Readings: Why go to Them, Why Give Them?" *Coda* 11 (November–December 1983): 1, 8–11.

________. "Starting Your Own Small Press." *Coda* 10 (September–October 1982): 12–15.

________. "Writers and Teaching." *Coda* 11 (February–March 1984): 16–18.

Brilliant, Alan. "Poetry and the Small Press." *Works* 2 (Spring 1969): 64–71.

Brooks, David, and Bredes, Don. "An Interview with Galway Kinnell." *Colorado State Review* 5 (Fall 1977): 4–12.

Broughton, Irv. "An Interview with Philip Levine." *Western Humanities Review* 32 (Spring 1978): 139–63.

Bruchac, Joseph. "The Decline and Fall of Prison Literature." *Small Press* 4 (January–February 1987): 28–32.

Bukowski, Charles. "Charles Bukowski Answers Ten Easy Questions." *Throb*, no. 2 (Summer–Fall 1971): 56–59.

________. "He Beats His Women." *Second Coming* 2, no. 3 (1974): unpaginated.

________. "Manifesto: A Call for Our Own Critics." *Nomad*, nos. 5–6 (Winter–Spring 1960): 6.

________. "Who's Big in the 'Littles'?" *Literary Times* 4 (February–March 1966): 9.

Bulkin, Elly. "An Interview with Adrienne Rich, Part I" and "Part II." *Conditions*, nos. 1 and 2 (1977): 50–65 and 53–66.

Camp, Roya. "Sun & Moon in Los Angeles." *Small Press* 5 (June 1988): 18–20.

C[arruth], H[ayden]. "The University and the Poet: an Editorial."*Poetry* 75 (November 1949): 89–93.

________, ed. "Poet, Publisher, and Tribal Chant: A Symposium." *Poetry* 75 (November 1949): 22–61.

Castro, Michael, and Castro, Jan. "Gary Snyder [interview]." *River Styx*, no. 4 (1979): 35–39.

"*Chicago Review* Little Magazine Symposium." *Chicago Review* 24 (Spring 1973): 36–48.
Childress, William. "Mona Van Duyn." *Poetry Now*, no. 7 (1975): 1–2, 37.
———. "William Stafford." *Poetry Now*, no. 8 (1975): 1–2, 37.
Clarke, Gerald. "Checking in with Allen Ginsberg." *Esquire* 79 (April 1973): 92–95, 168, 170.
Clausen, Christopher. "Poetry in a Discouraging Time." *Georgia Review* 35 (Winter 1981): 703–15.
Clausen, Jan, ed. "The Politics of Publishing and the Lesbian Community." *Sinister Wisdom* 1 (Fall 1976): 95–115.
Clifton, Merritt. "Helping Themselves." *Northwoods Journal* 5 (November 20, 1977): 10–11.
———. "On a Shifting Axis: Small Press Politics in the Eighties." *New Northwoods Journal* 9 (Fall 1981): 8–9, 13.
———. "The Shovel–Man." *Northwoods Journal* 7 (Spring 1979): 37–40.
———. "The Shovel–Man: A Call to Arms." *Northwoods Journal* 8 (Fall 1979): 48–51.
———. "What Happened to the Small Press Movement?" *Northwoods Journal* 10 (Winter 1982): 1–3.
Clifton, Michael. "W. S. Merwin: An Interview." *American Poetry Review* 12 (July–August 1983): 17–22.
Coblentz, Stanton A. "Consider the Little Magazines." *Wings* 14 (Winter 1960): 3–5.
Committee of Small Magazine Editors and Publishers. "COSMEP Position Paper: The Fiscal Health of Intellectual Freedom in the United States, Small Business Loans for Independent Presses?" *Beyond Baroque* 9 (July 1978): 55–56.
"Concerning the Little Magazines: Something Like a Symposium." *Carleton Miscellany* 7 (Spring 1966): 3–79.
Congdon, Kirby. "Grant Experience: Magazine." *Margins*, no. 14 (October–November 1974): 6–7.
———. "Ideas 'Sold' for Commercial Prestige?" *Trace* 51 (Winter 1963): 288–89.
———. "Interim Books." *Works* 2 (Spring 1969): 88–90.
Connolly, Cyril. "Little Magazines." In *The Evening Colonnade*, pp. 375–86. New York: Harcourt Brace Jovanovich, 1975.
"A Conversation with Mark Strand." *Ohio Review* 13 (Fall 1971): 54–71.
"A Conversation with W. S. Merwin." *Audience* 4, nos. 3–4 (1956): 4–6.
Cook, Carole. "PW Interviews Alice Quinn." *Publishers Weekly* 223 (April 15, 1983): 52–53.
Cook, Geoffrey. "Tabloid Literary Magazines: A Survey." *Margins*, no. 19 (1975): 14–19, 68–70.
———, ed. "Grants: A Flurry of Opinions." *Margins*, no. 14 (October–November 1974): 3–17, 66–68.
C[uscaden], R. R. "Editorial: Responsibilities of Editorship." *Odyssey* 1, no. 3 (1959): 3–5.
Daunt, Jon. "In the Guise of a Voice." *Small Press Review* 20 (September 1988): 3.

Davison, Peter. "My Say." *Publishers Weekly* 223 (March 18, 1983): 64.
Dillon, David. "Toward Passionate Utterance: An Interview with W. D. Snodgrass." *Southwest Review* 60 (Summer 1975): 278–90.
D[illon], G[eorge] H. "Spring Cleaning." *Poetry* 30 (April 27, 1927): 36–41.
"Discussion: 'The Public Taste.' " *Little Review* 7 (July–August 1920): 32–33.
Dodd, Wayne. "Robert Bly: An Interview." *Ohio Review* 19 (Fall 1978): 29–48.
———; Plumly, Stanley; and Tevis, Walter. "Talking with Adrienne Rich." *Ohio Review* 13 (Fall 1971): 29–46.
"Does Public Funding Buy Writing Time?" *Coda* 8 (November–December 1980): 6.
[Drake, Albert]. "How Little Mags Fail—The Problem and a Possible Solution." *Happiness Holding Tank*, no. 10 (1973): unpaginated.
Dvosin, Andrew. "Faggot Culture Quarterlies." *Margins*, no. 20 (1975): 21–23.
[Editorial.] *Poet and Critic* 1, no. 1 (Fall 1964): unpaginated.
"Editorial: Introduction." *Premiere*, no. 1 [1965]: 2.
[Editorial statement.] *City Lights Journal*, no. 4 (1978): [2].
Edwards, Debra L. "An Interview with Amiri Baraka." *Unspeakable Visions of the Individual* 10 (1980): 129–44.
Elledge, Jim. "James Dickey: A Supplementary Bibliography, 1975–1980: Part 1." *Bulletin of Bibliography* 38 (April–June 1981): 92–100.
Ellsworth, Peter. "A Conversation with William Stafford." *Chicago Review* 30 (Summer 1978): 94–100.
Epstein, Joseph. "Who Killed Poetry?" *Commentary* 86 (August 1988): 13–20.
Eshleman, Clayton. "A Note on the N.E.A. Poetry Fellowships." Text 1 (Winter 1976–77): 79–83.
Esty, Jane, and Lett, Paul. "Why 'Mutiny'?" *Mutiny* 1 (Autumn 1960): 1–3.
"An Exchange Regarding COSMEP." *Happiness Holding Tank*, no. 1 (1970): unpaginated.
Faas, Ekbert. "An Interview with Robert Bly." *Boundary 2* 4 (Spring 1976): 677–700.
Fields, Howard. "Giving Money Away." *Small Press* 1 (September–October 1983): 42–44.
Finney, Kathe Davis, and Finney, Michael. "An Interview with Peter Klappert." *Falcon* 8 (Spring 1977): 3–27.
"First-Book Publishing." *Coda* 6 (February–March 1979): 22–23.
Fleischer, Leonore. "Talk of the Trade: Merchandising Poetry." *Publishers Weekly* 224 (November 4, 1983): 63.
Foreman, Paul. "What Price CCLM: A Report on the Coordinating Council of Literary Magazines." *Margins*, no. 14 (November–December 1974): 10–11, 76.
"Foreword." *Umbra* 1 (Winter 1963): 3–4.
Fried, Philip. " 'A Place You Can Live': An Interview with A. R. Ammons." *Manhattan Review* 1 (Fall 1980): 1–28.
Friedman, Sanford. "An Interview with Richard Howard." *Shenandoah* 24 (Fall 1972): 5–31.
"Friend of the Poet and Fiction Writer: University Presses."*Coda* 7 (February–March 1980): 22–23.
"From Us: Thoughts on the Feminist Media." *Second Wave* (Spring 1974): 2–4.
Fulton, Len. "Anima Rising: Little Magazines in the Sixties." In *Print, Image,*

and Sound: Essays on Media, edited by John Gordon Burke. Chicago: American Library Association, 1972.

———. "See Bukowski Run." *Small Press Review* 4 (May 1973): inside front cover, pp. 27–31. (Reprinted from *Quixote* 7 [April 1972].)

———. "Touching the Biosphere." *American Libraries* 5 (February 1974): 73–75.

———, and Fay, Bob. "An Interview with Louis Simpson, Part II." *Dust* 1 (Winter 1965): 9–24.

Furnas, J. C. "The Amateur Profession: Career Counseling for Writers." *American Scholar* 57 (Autumn 1988): 608–16.

Gerber, Philip L., and Fitz Gerald, Gregory. "The Individual Voice: A Conversation with William Heyen." *Western Humanities Review* 23 (Summer 1969): 223–33.

Gioia, Dana. "Poetry and the Fine Presses." *Hudson Review* 35 (Autumn 1982): 483–98.

———. "The Successful Career of Robert Bly." *Hudson Review* 40 (Summer 1987): 207–23.

Goff, Ted. "Interview with Lyn Lifshin." *Mikrokosmos*, no. 19 (1974): 20–23.

Goldbarth, Albert. "An Interview with Galway Kinnell." *Crazy Horse*, no. 6 (1971): 30–38.

Gordon, Jaimy. "The Undeciphered Audience: An Inquiry into Small Presses and Related Matters." *Open Places*, nos. 31–32 (Fall 1981): 184–91.

"Granite Magazine Case Lost." *Coda* 3 (October–November 1975): 7–8.

Gregory, Horace. "Prologue as Epilogue." *Poetry* 48 (May 1936): 92–98.

G[reisman], D[avid]. "The *Abbey* Interview—Merritt Clifton." *Abbey*, no. 20 (1976): unpaginated.

Gross, Beverly. "Culture and Anarchy: What Ever Happened to Lit Magazines?" *Antioch Review* 29 (Spring 1969): 43–56.

Grossvogel, D. I. "Interview: A. R. Ammons." *Diacritics* 3 (Winter 1973): 47–53.

Hall, Donald. "Poetry and Ambition." In *What is a Poet?: Essays from the Eleventh Alabama Symposium on English and American Literature*, edited by Hank Lazer, pp. 229–46. University: University of Alabama Press, 1987.

Hamalian, Linda. "Allen Ginsberg in the Eighties." *Literary Review* 29 (Spring 1986): 293–300.

Hammond, Karla. "An Interview with Jane Shore." *Choomia*, nos. 7–8 (December 1978–January 1979): 5–17.

———. "An Interview with Maura Stanton." *Paintbrush* 6 (Autumn 1979): 34–40.

———. "An Interview with Maxine Kumin." *Western Humanities Review* 33 (Winter 1979): 1–15.

Hampl, Patricia. "A Letter to Our Readers." *Lamp in the Spine* (Summer–Fall 1974): 9–10.

Hargitai, Peter. "CO–rrespondence." *Hiram Poetry Review*, no. 32 (Spring–Summer 1982): 3–5.

[Hartwell, David G., and Kirkpatrick, Carolyn]. "Frontmatter." *Little Magazine* 13, nos. 1–2 [1981?]: inside front cover.

Haseloff, Charles. "Feminine, Marvelous, and Tough: Letter from a '12-Year-

Old' Fan to the Poetry Project (By Way of a Contribution to its History)." Unpublished paper, 1979.

Haythe, Cynthia. "An Interview with A. R. Ammons." *Contemporary Literature* 21 (Spring 1980): 173–90.

Hazo, Samuel. "Poetry and the American Public." *American Scholar* 45 (Spring 1976): 278–90.

Healey, James W. "Little Magazines: 'A Little Madness Helps." ' *Prairie Schooner* 48 (Winter 1973–74): 335–42.

———, ed. "Little Magazines: Too Much With Us?: A Symposium." *Prairie Schooner* 48 (Winter 1974–75): 317–26.

h[eap], j[ane]. "Lost: A Renaissance." *Little Review* 12 (May 1929): 5–6.

Heller, Scott. "Creative Writing Teachers Scramble to Fill Scarce Teaching Jobs at Colleges." *Chronicle of Higher Education* 32 (July 9, 1986): 17.

———. "For a Poet with Two Books, the Job Market Takes Notice." *Chronicle of Higher Education* 32 (July 9, 1986): 17.

———. " 'In My Generation the Role Models Were Young Bohemians, Not Endowed Chairs.' " *Chronicle of Higher Education* 32 (July 9, 1986): 17.

H[enderson], A[lice] C[orbin]. "The Rejection Slip." *Poetry* 8 (July 1916): 197–99.

Hershon, Robert. "The Crossing Press." *Small Press* 1 (May–June 1984): 49–54.

Heyen, William, and Fitz Gerald, Gregory. " 'No Voices Talk to Me': A Conversation with W. D. Snodgrass." *Western Humanities Review* 24 (Winter 1970): 61–71.

———. " 'Tireless Quest': An Interview with W. S. Merwin." *English Record* 29 (February 1969): 9–18.

Hillringhouse, Mark. "Gerald Stern: An Interview." *American Poetry Review* 13 (March–April 1984): 26–30.

Hills, Rust. "The Big Trend in Little Magazines." *Saturday Review* 42 (May 9, 1959): 10–12, 50.

Holley, Anne. "Struggling in Poetry." *Massachusetts Review* 14 (Autumn 1973): 847–64.

"Interview with George Hitchcock." *Durak*, no. 1 (1978): 23–40.

Jacob, John. "The Friendly Cunundrum [sic]: An Interview with Wine Press." *Margins*, no. 17 (1975): 30–36, 69.

———. "Playing the Writing Workshop Game." *Margins*, no. 12 (June–July 1974): 44–45, 80.

Johnson, Maurice. "The *Prairie Schooner*: Ten Years." *Prairie Schooner* 11 (Spring 1937): 71–82.

Jones, Roger. "A Conversation with Galway Kinnell." *New Orleans Review* 7 (Summer 1980): 193–95.

Joyce, William. "The Oink from the Literary Barn." *American Book Review* 6 (May–June 1984): 5–6.

Juhasz, Suzanne. "Feminist Presses, Feminist Poetry in 1980." *Open Places*, nos. 31–32 (Fall 1981): 177–83.

J[unker], H[oward]. "Editor's (and Publisher's) Note." *Zyzzyva* 4 (Spring 1988): [3].

———. "Editor's Note." *Zyzzyva* 2 (Spring 1986): [3].

———. "Editor's Note." *Zyzzyva* 2 (Fall 1986): [3].

Kalstone, David. "Talking with Adrienne Rich." *Saturday Review* 55 (April 22, 1972): 56–59.

Kearney, Lawrence, and Cuddihy, Michael. "Ai: An Interview." *Ironwood*, no. 12 (1978): 27–34.

Keller, Emily. "An Interview [with Robert Creeley] by Emily Keller." *American Poetry Review* 12 (May–June 1983): 24–28.

Kenner, Hugh. "Manuscript to be Placed in a Bottle." *Spectrum* 1 (Winter 1957): 3–10.

Kenny, Maurice. "Thank You for Coming: A Poet on Tour Reading." *Margins*, nos. 28–30 (1976): 54–56, 215.

King, Martha. "Is Academia the Writer's Best Friend?" *Coda* 8 (June–July 1981): 10–14.

———. "On the Distribution Front: Making Literary Publications Public." *Coda* 7 (June–July 1980): 18–22.

———. "Poets in Other Countries—Is the Grass Greener?" *Coda* 7 (November–December 1979): 3–9.

———"Who Reads in the United States?" *Coda* 7 (September–October 1979): 3–6.

———. "Women's Publishing." *Coda* 8 (September–October 1980): 5.

Kingston, Paul W.; Cole, Jonathan R.; and Merton, Robert K. "The Columbia Economic Survey of American Authors: A Summary of Findings." New York: Authors' Guild Foundation/Center for the Social Sciences, Columbia University, February 1981.

Kizer, Carolyn, and Boatwright, James. "A Conversation with James Dickey." *Shenandoah* 18 (Autumn 1966): 3–28.

Knief, William. "Ginsberg." *Cottonwood Review* 1 (Spring 1966): unpaginated.

———. "Robert Creeley Interview." *Cottonwood Review* (1968): unpaginated.

Kniffel, Leonard. "Broadside Press, Then and Now." *Small Press* 1 (May–June 1984): 27–31.

Knight, Etheridge. "Prison and the Creative Artist." *Indiana Writes* 3 (Spring 1979): 68–71.

Kostelanetz, Richard. [Letter to Galen Williams.] *Margins*, no. 17 (1975): 57–58.

———. "The Literature Program at the National Endowment for the Arts: A Critique." *Northwoods Journal* 5 (November 20, 1977): 5–8, 11.

———. "Why *Assembling*?" *Assembling*, no. 1 (1970): unpaginated.

———. "Why Fifth *Assembling*?" *Assembling*, no. 5 (1974): unpaginated.

———. "Why Fourth *Assembling*?" *Assembling*, no. 4 [1973]: unpaginated.

———. "Why Seventh *Assembling*?" *Assembling*, no. 7 (1977): unpaginated.

K[ropp], L[loyd]. "Editor's Notes." *Sou'wester* 8 (Summer 1980): unpaginated.

Laurans, Penelope. "News, the Scores—and a Poem." *New York Times* (September 3, 1988): 23.

Lawson, Todd. "Poets' Coalition—Organized Poetry: Will it Work?" *Margins*, no. 15 (December 1974): 31–33, 48, 68.

Leed, Jacob. "Robert Creeley and *The Lititz Review*: A Recollection with Letters." *Journal of Modern Literature* 5 (April 1976): 243–59.

Lehmann-Haupt, Christopher. "Critic's Notebook: Are Books Becoming Obsolete?" *New York Times* (January 2, 1989): 15.

Leithauser, Brad. "Hard Times in the Mail Order Poetry Business." *New York Times Book Review* (August 18, 1985): 1, 26–28.

Locklin, Gerald, and Stetler, Charles. "The Locklin–Stetler (or Vice-Versa) Interview." *Big Boulevard* 2, no. 1 (1974): 2–13.

Lockwood, Willard A. "Publishing Poetry." *Panache*, no. 2 (1968): 34–39.

Lofsness, Cynthia. "An Interview with William Stafford." *Iowa Review* 3 (Summer 1972): 92–106.

MacArthur, Mary. "Where to Look for Funding." *Small Press* 2 (March–April 1985): 74–76.

"Made Things: an Interview with Richard Howard." *Ohio Review* 16 (Fall 1974): 43–58.

Major, Clarence. [Letter.] *Trace* 36 (March–April 1960): 16–18

________. "Statement." *The Coercion Review of Contemporary Power in Literature*, no. 1 (Summer 1958): 1.

Maloff, Saul. "Writers at Work in Iowa." *Publishers Weekly* 230 (July 4, 1986): 22–24.

"Manifesto: No More Cattlemen or Sheepmen—We Want Outlaws!" *Crazy Horse*, no. 2 ([1967?]): verso of front cover.

Mansfield, Margery. "Comment: Wasting the Poets' Time." *Poetry* 31 (October 1927): 37–40.

"The Market for Poetry." *The Writer* 95 (December 1982): 23–27.

Martin, John. "Black Sparrow Press." *Works* 2 (Spring 1969): 76–79.

Martin, Peter. "An Annotated Bibliography of Selected Little Magazines." In *The Little Magazine in America: A Modern Documentary History*, edited by Elliott Anderson and Mary Kinzie, pp. 666–750. Yonkers, NY: Pushcart Press, 1978.

Masters, Hilary. "Go Down Dignified: The NEA Writing Fellowships." *Georgia Review* 35 (Summer 1981): 233–45.

Mayer, Debby. "Is There a Poetry Mafia?" *Coda* 9 (April–May 1981): 10–14.

________. "The Poet as Business Person." *Coda* 7 (June–July 1980): 3–7.

________. "Poetry Anthologies: Boon or Bane?" *Coda* 7 (February–March 1980): 3–7.

________. "Radical New Way to Help Little Magazines: Ask the Writer to Buy an Issue." *Coda* 6 (November–December 1978): 3–7.

McFarland, Ron. "An Interview with James Dickey." *Slackwater Review* 3 (Winter 1979–80): 17–33.

McFee, Michael. " 'Reckless and Doomed': Jonathan Williams and Jargon." *Small Press* 3 (September–October 1985): 101–6.

McKenzie, James J. "To the Roots: An Interview with Galway Kinnell." *Salmagundi*, nos. 22–23 (Spring–Summer 1973): 206–21.

Meek, Martha George. "An Interview with Maxine Kumin." *Massachusetts Review* 16 (Spring 1975): 317–27.

Michelson, Peter. "On *Big Table, Chicago Review*, and *The Purple Sage*." In *The Little Magazine in America: A Modern Documentary History*, edited by Elliott Anderson and Mary Kinzie, pp. 340–75. Yonkers, NY: Pushcart Press, 1978.

Milofsky, David. "Writers as Teachers: A Survey." *AWP Newsletter* (November 1983): 2–3.

[Milton, John R.], ed. "A Small Symposium on a Few (Alas, Defunct) Magazines." *South Dakota Review* 6 (Autumn 1968): 3–46.

Minot, Stephen. "Hey, Is Anyone Listening?" *North American Review* 262 (Spring 1977): 9–12.

Mirsky, Mark Jay. "Writing Programs: A Defense." *American Book Review* 6 (May–June 1984): 9.

Mitchell, Roger. "On Being Large and Containing Multitudes." *American Book Review* 6 (May–June 1984): 10.

Moberg, Verne. "The New World of Feminist Publishing." *Booklegger* 1 (July–August 1974): 14–18.

[Monroe, Harriet]. "Announcement of Awards." *Poetry* 13 (November 1918): 108–11.

———. "Comment: Another Chance." *Poetry* 40 (August 1932): 270–72.

———. "Comment: Art and Propaganda." *Poetry* 44 (July 1934): 210–15.

———. "Comment: Birthday Reflections." *Poetry* 39 (October 1931): 32–39.

———. "Comment: A Century in Illinois." *Poetry* 13 (November 1918): 90–94.

———. "Comment: Coming of Age." *Poetry* 37 (October 1930): 34–37.

———. "Comment: Fifteen Years." *Poetry* 31 (October 1927): 32–37.

———. "Comment: Frugality and Deprecation." *Poetry* 17 (October 1920): 30–35.

———. "Comment: Give Him a Nobel Prize." *Poetry* 39 (November 1931): 88–93.

———. "Comment: In These Days." *Poetry* 43 (March 1934): 328–33.

———. "Comment: Mea Culpa." *Poetry* 20 (September 1922): 323–37.

———. "Comment: A Poet's Contract." *Poetry* 40 (September 1932): 330–35.

———. "Comment: These Five Years." *Poetry* 11 (October 1917): 33–41.

———. "Comment: Twenty Years." *Poetry* 41 (October 1932): 30–40.

———. "Comment: Twenty–One." *Poetry* 43 (October 1933): 32–37.

———. "Editorial Comment: Hard Times Indeed." *Poetry* 9 (March 1917): 308–12.

———. "The Motive of the Magazine." *Poetry* 1 (October 1912): 26–28.

———. "The Open Door." *Poetry* 1 (November 1912): 62–64.

———. "Our Contemporaries: I." *Poetry* 6 (September 1915): 315–17.

———. "Poetry of the Left." *Poetry* 48 (June 1936): 212–21.

———. "The Poet's Bread and Butter." *Poetry* 4 (August 1914): 195–98.

———. "Review [of *My Thirty Years' War*, by Margaret Anderson]: Personality Rampant." *Poetry* 37 (October 1930): 95–100.

———. " 'That Mass of Dolts'." *Poetry* 1 (February 1913): 168–70.

Montag, Tom. "An Interview with Len Randolph." *Margins*, nos. 24–26 (1975): 30–41, 196–97.

———. [Letter to Nancy Hanks, National Endowment for the Arts.] *Margins*, no. 17 (1975): 1.

———. "Notes on Women's Publications and Other Things."*Margins*, no. 7 (August–September 1973): 21–25, [37].

———. "Some Polemics, Practical Considerations, or a Modest Proposal." *Margins*, no. 14 (October–November 1974): 14–15, 80–81.

Montenegro, David. "Carolyn Forché: An Interview." *American Poetry Review* 17 (November–December 1988): 35–40.

Moore, James. "Why I'm Quitting *The Lamp in the Spine* and Why Poetry is Essential to the Revolution." *The Lamp in the Spine* (Summer–Fall 1974): 1–8.

"More on Manuscripts and Manners." *Coda* 6 (June–July 1979): 19–20.

Morris, Richard. "How to Get a Grant from CCLM." *Margins*, no. 14 (October–November 1974): 5.

Nobles, Edward. "Alan Dugan: An Interview." *American Poetry Review* 12 (May–June 1983): 4–15.

Norris, Joan. "An Interview with Maxine Kumin." *Crazy Horse*, no. 16 (Summer 1975): 20–25.

Norris, Kathleen. "400 Miles to the Nearest Poetry Reading." *Coda* 11 (February–March 1984): 14–15.

Ó Hehir, Diana. "Making Us Speak." In *Nineteen New American Poets of the Golden Gate*, edited by Philip Dow, pp. 25–28. San Diego, CA: Harcourt Brace Jovanovich, 1984.

[Oandasan, William]. [Editorial.] *A: A Journal of Contemporary Literature* 1 (Fall 1976): inside front cover, [1].

"Once is Not Enough: Finding the Repeat Book Buyer." *Coda* 4 (June–July 1977): 3–7.

"Only Three Living Poets on Booksellers' Recommended List." *Coda* 3 (October–November 1975): 8.

Otto, Kathy, and Lofsness, Cynthia. "An Interview with Robert Bly." *Tennessee Poetry Journal* 2 (Winter 1969): 29–48.

Parkinson, Thomas. "On Getting Published." *Beyond Baroque* 3, no. 2 (1973): 13–14.

Peters, Robert. "Energy: The Crossing Press." *Margins*, no. 9 (December 1973–January 1974): 37–38, 64.

Peterson, Theodore. "The Role of the Minority Magazine." *Antioch Review* 23 (Spring 1963): 57–72.

Phillabaum, L. E., and Jarrett, Beverly. [Comments on Louisiana State University Press.] *Chowder Review*, nos. 16–17 (Spring–Winter 1981): 104–5.

Phillips, William, and Rahv, Philip. "Private Experience and Public Philosophy." *Poetry* 48 (May 1936): 98–105.

"Place of Poetry: Symposium Responses." *Georgia Review* 35 (Winter 1981): 716–56.

"Poet Queries Forty-One Publishers—Finds Three Possibilities." *Coda* 6 (February–March 1979): 24–25.

"Poetry Readers in America: The Tip of the Iceberg." *Coda* 3 (April–May 1976): 1, 3–6.

Pollak, Felix. "Elitism and the Littleness of Little Magazines." *Southwest Review* 61 (Summer 1976): 297–303.

________. "To Hold with the Hares and Run with the Hounds: The Littlemagger as Librarian." In *Editor's Choice*, edited by Morty Sklar and Jim Mulac, pp. 413–18. Iowa City: The Spirit That Moves Us Press, 1980.

________. "The World of Little Magazines." *Arts in Society* 2 (Spring–Summer 1962): 50–66.

Pound, Ezra. "Editorial." *Little Review* 4 (May 1917): [3]–6.

________. "Mr. Pound on Prizes." *Poetry* 2-31 (December 1927): 157–59.

________. "The Renaissance: II." *Poetry* 5 (March 1915): 287.

________. "The Renaissance: III." *Poetry* 6 (May 1915): 91.

________. "Small Magazines." *English Journal* 19 (November 1930): 689–704.

________. "This Constant Preaching to the Mob." *Poetry* 8 (June 1916): 144–45.

________. "This Subsidy Business." *Poetry* 35 (January 1930): 212–14.

________, and M[onroe], H[arriet]. "The Audience." *Poetry* 5 (October 1914): 29–32.

Ranbom, Sheppard. "New Poetry from the University Presses: More than 'Syntax, Language, Science.' " *Chronicle of Higher Education* 26 (March 23, 1983): 25–26.

Randolph, Leonard. "The Economics of Little Magazines: A Report from Leonard Randolph and the Literature Program of the National Endowment for the Arts." *Margins*, no. 17 (1975): 4–11.

Rector, Liam. "Donald Hall: An Interview." *American Poetry Review* 18 (January–February 1989): 39–46.

Roberts, Francis. "James Dickey: An Interview." *Per/Se* 3 (Spring 1968): 8–12.

Roberts, T. J. "True Story of a Little Magazine's Birth, Life and Death." *Trace* 41 (1961): 89–96.

Robinson, Charles. "Academia and the Little Magazine." *Trace* 64 (Spring 1967): 1–6.

R[obinson], J[ay] T. "Authors and Editors: Allen Ginsberg." *Publishers Weekly* 195 (June 23, 1969): 18.

[Russell, Sydney King, et al.]. [Editorial.] *Poetry Chap-Book* 1 (October–December 1942): [3].

Ryan, Michael. "An Interview with Alan Dugan." *Iowa Review* 4 (Summer 1973): 90–97.

Sankey, John. "A Survey of Little Magazine Publishing." *Trace*, no. 5 (October 1953): 1–7.

Schumacher, Mike. "Ginsberg." *Oui* 11 (June 1982): 82–83, 113–15.

Settle, Mary Lee. "Works of Art or Power Tools?" *Virginia Quarterly Review* 57 (Winter 1981): 1–14.

Sholl, Betsy. "alice james books: A Report on a New Cooperative Press." *Margins*, no. 11 (April–May 1974): 35–36.

Showalter, Elaine, and Smith, Carol. "A Nurturing Relationship: A Conversation with Anne Sexton and Maxine Kumin, April 15, 1974." *Women's Studies* 4 (1976): 115–35.

Silet, Charles L. P. "The Basilisk Press." *Poet and Critic* 8 (1975): 32–36.

________. "The Best Cellar Press: An Interview with Greg Kuzma." *Poet and Critic* 9 (1976): 33–39.

________. "David Kherdian and the Giligia Press." *Poet and Critic* 9 (1975): 39–46.

Solotaroff, Ted. "The Publishing Culture and the Literary Culture." In *Publishers and Librarians: A Foundation for Dialogue*, edited by Mary Biggs, pp. 72–80. Chicago: University of Chicago Press, 1984.

Spencer, Brett. "Inside the Programs: Iowa." *AWP Newsletter* (November 1983): 4, 13.

Spurr, David. "An Interview with Kenneth Koch." *Contemporary Poetry* 3 (Winter 1978): 1–12.

Stahl, Jim. "Interview with A. R. Ammons: 'The Unassimilable Fact Leads Us On . . .' " *Pembroke Magazine*, no. 18 (1986): 77–85.

"Stephen Goodwin of the NEA: A Talk with the New Director of the Literature Program." *Small Press* 5 (April 1988): 44–47.

Stern, Gerald. "What is This Poet?" In *What is a Poet?: Essays from the Eleventh Alabama Symposium on English and American Literature*, edited by Hank Lazer, pp. 145–56. University: University of Alabama Press, 1987.

Stitt, Peter. "The Art of Poetry XXXIII: John Ashbery." *Paris Review*, no. 90 (1983): 30–59.

Stratton, Kip. "An Interview with William Stafford." *Greenfield Review* 7 (Spring–Summer 1979): 85–97.

Stuttaford, Genevieve. "PW Interviews: Allen Ginsberg." *Publishers Weekly* 212 (November 14, 1977): 6–7.

Swallow, Alan. "The Little Magazines." *Prairie Schooner* 16 (Winter 1942): 238–43.

———. "Postwar Little Magazines." *Prairie Schooner* 23 (Spring 1949): 152–57.

"Symposium on the Relationship of Government to the Arts." *Arts in Society* 2 ([late] 1963): 24–39.

"TABA Cuts Categories to Three with $10,000 Prize." *Publishers Weekly* 225 (January 27, 1984): 27.

Taylor, Charles. "Those Nasty Rejection Slips." *Northwoods Journal* 5 (Gemini 1977): 10–12.

Taylor, Phil. "Charles Bukowski Interview." *Stone Cloud*, no. 1 (1972): 33–41.

Teasdale, Trish Ann. "The First Word" [editorial]. *UNM Honors Review: Southwestern Forum for the Arts and Sciences* 2 (Spring 1988): 1–2.

Thompson, Jeanie. "A Concert of Tenses: An Interview with Tess Gallagher." *Ironwood*, no. 14 (1979): 37–52.

"Tidal Waves: Editors Deluged by Submissions." *Coda* 5 (September–October 1977): 24–25.

Troupe, Quincy. "Editor's Statement." *American Rag* 1 (1978): [1].

Truesdale, C. W. "New Rivers Press." *Works* 2 (Spring 1969): 91.

[Tullos, Will]. "In This Richest Land of All Time, Why Should Poetry Be the Neglected Art?" *New Athenaeum* (Summer 1956): [1].

———. "Poetry, Our Cause." *New Athenaeum* (Winter 1957): inside front cover.

Turco, Lewis. "On The Profession of Poetry." *Arts in Society* 3 (1963): 298–300.

"Unprecedented Decision from CCLM Panel: Grants Divided Equally Among 129 Magazines." *Coda* 5 (April–May 1979): 14–16.

"Vale." *Poetry* 49 (December 1936): 137–65.

"Vanity Press: Stigma or Sesame?" *Coda* 4 (November–December 1976): 3–8.

Veeder, William, and von Hallberg, Robert. "A Conversation with James McMichael." *Chicago Review* 26, no. 1 (1975): 154–64.

Vosnesensky, Andrei, and Ginsberg, Allen. "Andrei Vosnesensky and Allen Ginsberg: A Conversation." *Paris Review* 22 (Summer 1980): 149–77.

[Wagner, D.r.] "Editorial No. 1." *Moonstones* 1, no. 1 (1966): 2–3.

Wagner, Linda W., and MacAdams, Lewis, Jr. "Robert Creeley: The Art of Poetry X." *Paris Review*, no. 44 (Fall 1968): 154–87.

Wagner, Susan. "How Effective is the National Endowment for the Arts?" *Publishers Weekly* 212 (July 25, 1977): 45–48.

Wallenstein, Barry. "Academic Poetry: The Term Itself." *American Book Review* 6 (May–June 1984): 4.

Warsh, Lewis. "Angel Hair Press." *Works* 2 (Spring 1969): 86–87.

[Weichel, Ken]. "Some Notes: Small Presses, Surrealism, and Everyday." *Androgyne*, no. 7 (1982): 48–53.

Weil, James L. "An Un–Swan Song." *Elizabeth* 18 (December 1971): inside back cover.

Weil, Lise. [Editorial.] *Trivia: A Journal of Ideas*, no. 10 (Spring 1987): [4].

Wendroff, Michael. "Should We Do the Book?" *Publishers Weekly* 218 (August 15, 1980): 24–30.

Williams, William Carlos. "The Advance Guard Magazine." *Contact: An American Quarterly Review* 1 (February 1932): 86–90.

———. "Comment." *Contact: An American Quarterly Review* 1 (February 1932): 7–9.

Winant, Fran. "Lesbians Publish Lesbians: My Life and Times with Violet Press." *Margins*, no. 23 (1975): 62, 64, 66.

Winters, Yvor. "The Poet and the University: A Reply." *Poetry* 75 (December 1949): 170–72, 174, 176–78.

"The Writer's Situation: Symposium." *New American Review*, no. 9 (1970): 61–99.

Yates, David C. "From ... the Cedar Post." *Cedar Rock* (Winter 1978): 2, 23.

Young, Karl. "*Assembling*." *Margins*, nos. 21–22 (1975): 32–36.

Z[abel], M[orton] D[auwen]. "Comment: The Way of Periodicals." *Poetry* 34 (September 1929): 330–34.

———. "Harriet Monroe: December 23, 1860–September 26, 1936." *Poetry* 49 (October 1936): 85–93.

———. "Recent Magazines." *Poetry* 39 (December 1931): 166–70.

———. "Recent Magazines." *Poetry* 48 (April 1936): 51–56.

Zahn, Curtis. "Towards Print: (Anti–Social) Protest Literature." *Trace* 40 (January–March 1961): 5–9.

———. "Towards Print (Are Littlemags Our Final Voice?)." *Trace* 44 (Winter 1962): 8–10.

Index

About the Author

MARY BIGGS is Director of Libraries at Mercy College in Westchester County, New York and an adjunct professor at the Columbia University School of Library Service. Dr. Biggs has served as an Editor or Co-editor for a number of titles, including *Editor's Choice II: Poetry, Fiction, and Art from the U.S. Small Press, 1978–1983; Men & Women: Together & Alone;* and *Publishers and Librarians: A Foundation for Dialogue.*

About the Author

[illegible]